COMING OF AGE

Protestantism in Contemporary Latin America

Edited by
Daniel R. Miller

Lanham • New York • London

Calvin Center Series

University Press of America®, Inc.
4720 Boston Way
Lanham, Maryland 20706

3 Henrietta Street
London WC2E 8LU England

Printed in the United States of America
British Cataloging in Publication Information Available

Copublished by arrangement with the
Calvin Center for Christian Scholarship

Library of Congress Cataloging-in-Publication Data

Coming of age : Protestantism in contemporary Latin America / Daniel R. Miller, editor.
p. cm. — (Calvin Center series ; 1)
Includes bibliographical references.
1. Protestant churches—Latin America—History—20th century.
2. Evangelicalism—Latin America—History—20th century.
3. Pentecostal churches—Latin America—History.
4. Latin America—Church history—20th century.
I. Miller, Daniel R., 1950- .
BR600.C56 1994 280'.4'098—dc20 94-998 CIP

ISBN 0–8191–9406-9 (cloth : alk. paper)
ISBN 0-8191-9407-7 (pbk. : alk. paper)

The paper used in this publication meets the minimum requirements of American National Standard for Information Sciences—Permanence of Paper for Printed Library Materials, ANSI Z39.48–1984.

DEDICATION

Gordon Spykman 1926-1993

To his friends and to those with whom he disagreed, he was open and ready to listen. Not all shared his convictions, he recognized that and sometimes debated with tenacity, but he was always a Christian gentleman and scholar. How much a divided church needs his catholic spirit; how much the world needs his apostolic fervor; how much the poor and oppressed need his keen sense of justice! We his loved ones and friends hear in the heat of the struggle and at the close of the day, the gentle promise, "He that believes in me shall never die." And then we know it is true; his spirit still walks with us.

Sidney H. Rooy
October 1993

Contents

Social and Political Implications of Protestant Growth in Latin America

Protestant and Catholic Viewpoints

List of Tables

Acknowledgments

This book exists due to the generous financial support of the Calvin Center for Christian Scholarship. A grant from the Center permitted Arie Leder and me to call together a group of scholars to examine the topic of Protestantism in Latin America; and afterward, enabled me to prepare the conference papers for publication in this volume. Thanks are also due to the contributors whose first hand experience and wide knowledge are on display in these pages. Their willingness to put time and energy into these essays and to accept the somewhat arbitrary editorial constraints that a collected volume imposes was essential to the success of the project. The Center's Director, Ronald Wells, gave valuable advice at crucial times and welcome support at all times. I am especially grateful to him for his enthusiastic support of the idea for the book when I first broached it; he gave me the courage of my convictions. The Center's administrative assistants -- Kate Miller and Donna Romanowski -- went far beyond the call of duty to guarantee a smoothly run conference and a manuscript ready for publication. Their good-spirited collaboration made the enterprise remarkably pleasant. Finally, I would like to thank my colleague Arie Leder of Calvin Seminary for his help in bringing together a group of scholars whose work is well worth studying. I will be happy to work with him again anytime.

Sadly, one of the invited contributors, Gordon Spykman of the Calvin College Religion and Theology Department, died before he was able to complete his essay and so his work is not presented here. We have inserted instead a brief tribute to him by Sydney Rooy, a long-time friend and collaborator of Gordon's who lives in Costa Rica. In recognition of his life of dedication to the Christian cause and of his special interest in the Biblical call for justice for the poor and oppressed, this book is dedicated to Gordon Spykman.

DRM

Foreword

This book is a product of the Calvin Center for Christian Scholarship (CCCS) which was established at Calvin College in 1976. The purpose of the CCCS is to promote creative, articulate and rigorous scholarship that addresses important, theoretical, and practical issues. Such scholarship would focus on areas of life in which it may be expected that a Christian position could be worked out and for which previous Christian scholarship has been too parochially expressed, too superficially developed, or too little in accord with Christianity itself.

The present volume is the result of the efforts of Daniel R. Miller. While he was aided by many others in bringing this volume into being, the responsibility was his. Professor Miller was awarded a grant from the CCCS to host a conference that would produce this book. The conference was held at Calvin College in May 1993.

The question on which the concerns of the conference turned was first asked by David Stoll in his book, *Is Latin America Turning Protestant*? (1990). Most of the contributors in this book make reference to that work. Until recently, most Christians in North America had not been aware of the religious change going on in Latin America. However, the change is so striking and thorough-going that no one can now ignore this remarkable phenomenon.

The book is a scholarly book. It issues no calls for action nor strident pleas for one or another form of old-time religion, whether Catholic or Protestant. The world has changed forever in the southern hemisphere. The scholars writing in this book present timely and lively essays that, taken together, illumine fascinating aspects of religious change in the region of the world arguably most Christian.

Grand Rapids
December 1993

Ronald A. Wells
Director, CCCS

Introduction

Daniel R. Miller

Until just a few decades ago, a conservative and hierarchical Catholicism was one of four or five institutions that defined Latin America. As much as haciendas, machismo, military dictatorships, and the glaring contrast between rich and poor, traditional Catholicism seemed inseparable from Latin American-ness. Of course, Latin America was never as simple as that, but the last thirty years have witnessed such profound changes in the region that we can no longer repeat the facile generalizations with even a modicum of conviction.

In no area has change been more dramatic than in the area of religion. First came the surprising appearance of Liberation Theology and the development of a politically progressive "popular church" within the Catholic Church. Simultaneous in occurrence but much slower to attract the interest of academic observers was the swelling tide of Protestant, more precisely Pentecostal, religion.

This second phenomenon gained renewed attention with the publication of Sheldon Annis' slender volume, *God and Production in a Guatemalan Town* in 1987. Annis went to Guatemala to study the influence of the tourist industry on the Indians of the highlands but soon found that religious questions were far more urgent to the people he was trying to understand than were the secular matters he was interested in. So he turned his project into an exploration of the reasons why thousands of Guatemalan Indians were converting to Protestantism in the midst of violence and the stresses of modernization.

Two books that appeared in 1990, *Is Latin America Turning Protestant? The Politics of Evangelical Growth* by David Stoll, and *Tongues of Fire: The Explosion of Protestantism in Latin America* by David Martin, offered assessments of Protestantism that were region-wide in scope in contrast to Annis' village-level analysis. Both concluded that Protestantism has the potential to reshape Latin American society in ways that will make it less Ibero-Catholic and more like Protestant Europe and North America.

The presence of Jean-Pierre Bastian's chapter, "Protestantism in Latin America," in Enrique Dussel's edited volume on *The Church in Latin America* (1992), published by the Catholic Church's Commission for the Study of Church History in Latin America, indicates that the story of Protestantism in Latin America can no longer be ignored or treated as an aberration but is an integral part of the region's religious history. In contrast to Stoll and Martin, Bastian does not regard Pentecostalism as a movement with great potential to reshape Latin America, rather he believes it has itself been "Latin Americanized;" it has abandoned the liberal and reformist tendencies of classic Protestantism in favor of authoritarian and corporatist patterns more familiar to Latin America's marginalized classes and more congenial to the region's paternalistic elites.

The issues raised by the four authors cited above as well as by others have excited great interest in North American Protestants. Hence in the spring of 1992, the Calvin Center for Christian Scholarship offered a generous grant to Arie Leder of Calvin Seminary and myself to host a conference of leading scholars on the topic of the current state of Protestantism in Latin America. The conference which met over three days in May of 1993 brought together scholars from a variety of ecclesial traditions and academic disciplines. The essays presented at that conference comprise the chapters in this volume.

Seven Layers of Explanation for the Growth of the Protestant Church

The second day of the conference opened with a lively and informal address by Annis on "Seven Layers of Explanation for the Growth of Protestantism." Since writing his pathbreaking study of religious conversion among the indigenous people of Guatemala, Annis has continued to reflect on the phenomenon. His address to the Calvin Center considered seven possible explanations for the growth of Protestantism in Guatemala, ranking them in order of increasing plausibility. While Annis' explanations relate specifically to the Indian population of a single Latin American country, they are also relevant to the growth of Protestantism in the region as a whole. Taken together, they comprise a synopsis of contemporary views on the subject and as such provide a convenient point of entry into the book.

1. The Political Explanation: Cultural Manipulation by Foreign Missionaries and the U.S. Religious Right

Protestant missionaries from the U.S. are an "invasive force" in the lives of indigenous Guatemalans, according to Annis. He noted that missionaries often come with training in linguistics, with impressive technical skills and organizational ability, and with substantial financial backing from a host of donor churches in North America. Add to this the evident dedication of many missionaries who remain in-country far longer than the average secular development worker and one begins to see how missionaries can seem omnicompetent, especially in the wake of natural disasters or political crises which leave the indigenous Guatemalans feeling helpless. At the same time, the missionaries' conservative theology diverts the attention of believers away from social concerns and toward personal salvation, a development that served U.S. geopolitical interests and those of Guatemala's ruling elite so perfectly during the civil war of the 1970s and 80s that many observers concluded that Protestantism was part of a right-wing conspiracy to halt the spread of Third World liberation movements. While Annis ranked this explanation at the bottom in terms of its persuasiveness, he noted that it remains very appealing to people on the left end of the political spectrum.

2. The Practical Explanation: A Safe Conduct Pass

The counterpart to the identification of Protestantism with the right in Guatemala during the 1970s and 1980s was the identification of Catholicism with the left. The prominence of Liberation Theology and the presence of priests in the ranks of the guerrillas made that identification understandable if somewhat exaggerated, but perceptions counted for more than reality during the extremely violent campaign of repression which the Guatemalan military waged in the highlands. Annis recounted how whole categories of people -- village mayors, community organizers, co-op leaders -- were killed just because they were involved in efforts to improve society and thus seemed more likely to be "communist." In this atmosphere of pervasive terror, identification as a Catholic was a liability while identification as a Protestant tended to allay suspicion since no one believed that Protestants favored revolution. Particularly after the elevation of General Rios Montt to the Presidency, Protestants were viewed as natural allies of the military and were often spared during campaigns of repression. Hence, if someone were thinking about converting to Protestantism for any reason, the greater safety of Protestant identification would powerfully reinforce that inclination. Annis acknowledged that this explanation is very space- and time-specific -- it does little to explain Protestant growth in places and at times where there is no repression -- but he thought it might help to explain the dramatic growth of Guatemalan Protestantism during the Rios Montt administration. In any case, as with the first explanation, this one is very appealing to non-Protestants, especially those on the political left.

3. The Medical Explanation

When he asked Guatemalans to define a Protestant for him, Annis most frequently got a behavioral description rather than a theological one: Protestants are people who don't drink alcohol. Given the prevalence of alcoholism in Guatemala and the serious social problems associated with it, the abstemious character of Protestantism makes it very appealing. Annis likened this appeal to that which would be generated in the U.S. by a religion that promised to reduce one's weight. For Guatemalans who seek control over the personal vices of drinking, smoking, and the like, Protestantism seems a surer path to recovery than purely medical techniques which lack a spiritual dimension in their treatment of these problems.

4. The Economic Explanation: "He did it for the money"

While acknowledging that other researchers dispute his findings, Annis insisted that his data supports the notion that Protestants do better economically than Catholics. The typical Protestant testimony turns on the phrase "del suelo al cielo" (from the earth to the sky), which connotes both spiritual transformation and material improvement. One reason for the improvement is that Protestants embrace profit-maximizing behaviors that are often shunned by Catholics who cling to traditional communitarian ideals. Conversely, Protestants eschew traditional practices such as the celebration of saints days which impose an economic burden on their Catholic neighbors. Hence, Catholics are inclined to regard Protestant conversion as an expression of greedy self-interest, while Protestants regard it as an escape from economic as well as spiritual slavery.

5. The Sociological Explanation: An Improved Fit between Indian Identity and a Changing World

This explanation is the obverse of the previous one; it refers to the crumbling of indigenous communities in the face of modernization. The "traditional" Indian community was actually a creation of the Spanish conquest. Different groups of indigenous people were forced to live together in newly created towns under the spiritual tutelage of the Catholic Church and the economic control of the Spaniards. To preserve communal solidarity and to avoid having their surplus wealth extracted by outsiders, native Guatemalans developed a peculiar way of dealing with money -- they invested it in religious celebrations and in highly decorated textiles that had value only within the village. Looked at from one perspective, these practices encouraged the abuse of alcohol and retarded the accumulation of wealth; looked at another way, they guaranteed that no family would acquire enough money to buy another family's land and they provided everyone with an acknowledged place in the community. In recent decades, population growth, modernization, political violence, and other developments have left some too poor to participate in the traditional activities while others have profited from the changes, placing further strain on the communitarian ideal. Since the traditional system is closely identified with the Catholic Church, its erosion leaves many looking for a new way of understanding the world and their own place in it. Protestantism, with its emphasis on individual salvation and its expectation that one must break with the old way of life, provides a theology better fitted to the individualistic, self-improving world which the formerly isolated indigenous people increasingly must inhabit.

6. The Psychological Explanation: Controlling the Fear

Guatemala, said Annis, is a terrifying place for the indigenous people. It is a place where earthquakes and volcanoes level whole villages and where soldiers take people away in the middle of the night. The indigenous people face inner terrors as well, such as the temptations of alcohol and illicit sex. For Guatemalans, these terrors are personified by Satan, a terribly real being who lurks just outside the door waiting for a chance to get in and destroy their lives. Protestantism takes these fears seriously; its lively music and ecstatic worship provide viscerally satisfying ways of resisting temptation and defying Satan. The passionate intensity of Protestants is a measure of both the depth of their fears and the fierceness of their determination to control those fears.

7. The Spiritual Dimension of Protestantism

As a religious skeptic and an academic observer committed to rational explanations, Annis confessed that the most difficult explanation for him to accept is the one most often given by Protestants themselves: that Jesus loves them personally and that they have come to love Jesus personally in a way unlike what they experienced in Catholicism. He concluded that although he did not share the Protestants' faith, he ought not to trivialize it by reducing it to psychological or economic categories, but should simply acknowledge that the love which Protestants profess is as real and inexplicable as the love which Annis himself feels for the members of his family. In the end, he said, the growth of Protestantism among the highland Indians of Guatemala is a matter of faith and the satisfaction people derive from believing in God.

Latin American Protestantism: Facets of the Topic

The essays which follow this introduction take up important facets of the topic. Samuel Escobar examines how the phenomenon of Protestantism in Latin America has been interpreted in the past. He finds that most observers tended to fall into one of two camps: either they were apologists who focused on the movement's virtues and ignored its faults, or they were ecclesiastical or ideological adversaries who felt compelled to denigrate the movement. Escobar believes that a truer perspective recognizes Protestantism's great missiological accomplishments while acknowledging areas where it has not yet lived up to its potential, what he calls its "Promise and Precariousness."

Explanations for the remarkable growth of Protestantism are offered by the authors of the next three essays. David Smilde looks at changing gender relations in Latin America and sees an "elective affinity" for women in Protestantism. Quentin Schultze focuses on the role of orality in Pentecostalism to explain why that particular form of Protestantism continues to have such an enormous popular appeal to Latin America's marginalized groups. Everett Wilson offers an intimate view of Pentecostal conversion as a seven step process which incorporates new believers into evangelistically oriented, morally disciplined communities.

The implications of Protestant growth for the larger society of which Latin America's Protestants are a part is the subject of the next two essays. Guillermo Cook argues that it is simplistic to believe that Protestants are invariably right-wing or unconcerned about social issues. Timothy Steigenga offers a cautionary tale from Guatemala about how Protestants have been manipulated by both liberalizing and counterrevolutionary regimes, but he notes also that the "new wine" of Protestantism cannot always be contained in the old wineskins prepared for it by political elites.

The last two essays offer a glimpse of how Protestants and Catholics view each other in Latin America. In Roger Greenway's account of Protestantism's long struggle for acceptance in Latin America one can still hear echoes of Protestant frustration over the obstructionist role played by the Catholic Church in times past. Now however, his most urgent concern is not with external opposition from the Catholic Church but the internal challenge of defections from Protestant congregations. Edward Cleary ends the book with the fascinating but little known story of dialogue between Catholics and Pentecostals. Cleary hopes to see a Christian Church, united in purpose and spirit even if not in ecclesiastical structure, working together to evangelize the world.

Taken together, these observers point to several areas of scholarly consensus. First, they indicate that the Protestant movement is not only large, but is largely independent of North American missionary control, having long ago established an indigenous leadership and being well on the way to developing its own distinctive theological emphases. Second, they agree that Pentecostalism is the largest and fastest growing segment of the Protestant movement in Latin America; why this is so continues to be a source of lively debate however. Third, they offer a collective counterpoint to those who would stereotype the movement as invariably right-wing or uninterested in social concerns. A general tendency toward moralistic solutions to social and political problems may indeed be discernible among Latin American Protestants today, but Protestants have played many roles in the past and their view of the Church's place in society is constantly evolving. Indeed, one conclusion that comes through forcefully in these articles is that Latin American Protestants are a diverse lot and full of surprises.

What remains unclear, of course, is the future of the movement. The authors in this volume see many hopeful signs but they also have serious concerns. The ability of Protestantism to continue growing in numbers begins to seem problematic. Whether Protestants can develop authentically Christian ways to live and preach the gospel or whether they will succumb to political manipulation or narrowly personal matters is another concern. Finally, the relationship between Protestants and Catholics remains troubled by theological and historical differences despite recent efforts at cooperation in several places. In the end, these concerns do not negate Protestantism's already vast achievements, they merely whet our appetites to see what the coming years will bring.

CONTEXT

Chapter 1

The Promise and Precariousness of Latin American Protestantism

J. Samuel Escobar

Protestant Growth in Latin America

Catholic, Protestant, and non-committed observers agree that since the decade of the 1960s, the religious map of Latin America has been significantly transformed because of the rapid numerical growth of Protestantism, especially in its popular forms. In spite of the "lack of reliable quantification" (Stoll 1990, 6) of this process, scholars and journalists insist on the spectacular rate of growth. One Catholic observer even predicts that "If current growth rates continue Latin America will have an Evangelical majority in the early 21st century" (McCoy 1989, 2). Although this unexpected spiritual revolution has been taking place in Latin America for almost a century, only recently has it become the subject of continuous journalistic debate and scholarly research.

Is this Latin American spiritual revolution only the byproduct of social and political changes in the region? Is it just some kind of instinctive response of the uprooted poor to the hardships of their massive migration to the cities? Is it the escape valve of the impoverished masses from the intolerable conditions that have been the outcome of both failed socialism and the relentless aggression of market economies? Or is this revolution a quiet process of deep spiritual transformation destined to provide the inner dynamism and guiding motif of lasting structural changes in the economic and political arenas?

Interpretative approaches shaped by the perspective of the Enlightenment have not allowed scholars to see the deep spiritual nature of some of the movements that are emerging. They are inclined to see only their socio-political dimension. Thus far, the theological dimension has usually been presented as a reaction or an accommodation of religious institutions to the great historical events that have shaken the continent. Only recently have scholars begun to adopt a more nuanced view of the way in which spiritual experiences generate social and political movements.

The approach chosen for this introductory chapter will be to focus on key points of interpretation from a missiological perspective. Such an approach is interdisciplinary, looking at missionary acts from the perspectives of the biblical sciences, theology, history, and the social sciences. It aims to be systematic and critical, but it starts by affirming that the missionary task is part of the fundamental reason for being of the Church. In the case of Latin America there are two factors that add urgency to the need for a more accurate understanding of the way in which Christians have fulfilled their missionary obligation. On the one hand, despite the fact that Latin America is the region where the largest proportion of Roman Catholics (42%) now live, their church has to face the fact that currently "every hour in Latin America an average of 400 Catholics move to membership in Protestant sects" (Damen 1987, 45). On the other hand, because the background for this phenomenal change of religious affiliation is one in which the condition of the urban and rural poor has deteriorated to levels of bare subsistence, religious leaders as well as political analysts must constantly ask what effect Protestantism will have on efforts to transform Latin American societies into more viable forms of human coexistence.

Promise and Precariousness

The author shares a conviction that John A. Mackay expressed eloquently in 1950. Recalling the fact that of the great Christian traditions, Catholicism, Eastern Orthodoxy, and Protestantism, the last was the youngest in its institutional expression, Mackay went on to say:

> Protestantism, let it be emphasized, has not yet reached its religious majority, nor discharged its full historical mission. It is still in process of becoming; its heyday is not behind it but before it. The complete meaning of what happened at the Reformation four hundred years ago has still to be expressed in life and doctrine and ecclesiastical organization. Other things too must happen which did not enter into the thought of the Reformers (Mackay 1950, 124-125).

It is proposed here that in the growth of Latin American Protestantism there are enough signs to perceive it as a way through which "the complete meaning of what happened at the Reformation" will come to be expressed, together with "other things...which did not enter into the thought of the Reformers." This means that the significant numerical growth of Protestants in Latin America could contribute to the revitalization of church life, theology, and ecclesiastical organization in Protestantism at large, around the world. It would also mean that in the specific case of Latin America, Protestantism could make a distinctive contribution to the social transformation that is now taking place. This is the promise of Latin American Protestantism.

On the other hand, as a Latin American Protestant, the author is aware of a certain precariousness in the status of Protestantism in the region. The first meaning for the word "precarious" is "dangerously lacking in security or stability." It describes adequately the characteristics of Latin American Protestantism when it comes under close sociological scrutiny. The observer that goes beyond the triumphalistic literature of missionary promotion and analyzes the life of these churches and their role in society could well become skeptical about the true nature of their assumed "Protestantism." Large Pentecostal churches in some places reproduce the authoritarian patterns of leadership and association which are characteristic of the corporate tradition Latin American derived from Iberian Catholic culture. They also exhibit some liturgical forms more akin to native or African religiosity than to what is known as Protestant. Equally, some so-called "historic" Protestant churches tend to be as dependant on a professional clergy as the predominant Catholicism in the region. The spread and persistence of these patterns lead observers such as the author of the first global history of Protestantism in Latin America, Swiss historian Jean Pierre Bastian (1990) to rather negative conclusions: "In so far as Protestant principles no longer inhabit these popular forms of Protestantism, we have to deal not so much with a Protestant religious phenomenon as with a collection of new non-Roman Catholic religious movements" (Dussel 1992, 346). These patterns indicate some of the perils which continue to threaten Protestantism in Latin America.

A missiological approach enables the observer to see both the promise and the precariousness that mark Latin American Protestantism in a wider frame of reference that lends a certain perspective to both. At this end of the second great century of Protestant global missionary advance, it is evident that the vitality, relevance, and creativity of both Catholic and Protestant churches have shifted to the South. These qualities now mark the churches in Africa, Latin America, and parts of Asia, right when European Christianity seems paralyzed by fatigue and a sense of irrelevance. Missiologists keep reminding us that the southern forms of Christianity which developed out of the missionary thrust of Europeans and North Americans have now taken on a form of their own. Bühlman interprets this process as "the coming of the third church" and Walls states that "Indeed, most of the discernible changes in Christianity since 1945 come from this fundamental southward shift" (Bühlman 1986, 80-81). What seems at some points to be an unbearable tension between promise and precariousness may only be a critical new phase in the advance of Christianity from its Mediterranean and European enclave into a truly global existence.

A Basic Typology of the Protestant Movement

To speak of a "Latin American Protestantism" can be misleading. It is better to refer to a Protestant movement that has several distinct expressions. The most understandable typology uses historic origins, theological emphases, and global alliances as criteria to identify three main types of Protestant churches. The first general type, known as *Transplanted Protestantism*, refers to churches that came at various times with groups of European migrants, most of whom had no intention of propagating their faith among Latin Americans. Thus, for instance, in the early decades of the nineteenth century, Anglicans established chaplaincies in the seaports of Brazil, Argentina, and the Pacific coast for the growing number of British subjects that had come to the newly independent countries then opening up to British capital and commerce. Later on, as Brazil opened to massive German migration, the Lutheran church accompanied the Protestant colonists who established themselves in the southern states. The same happened in the case of Mennonites who migrated in large groups to Paraguay.

The second general type, *Missionary Protestantism*, resulted from two kinds of intentional evangelistic activity. One was the work of missions from mainline Protestant churches such as Methodists, Presbyterians, and Baptists, which developed during the second half of the nineteenth century and flourished before World War II. The other was the work of faith missions and new denominations from Great Britain and North America such as the Central America Mission, the Gospel Missionary Union, the Evangelical Union of South America, and the Christian and Missionary Alliance. Some of these came as early as the 1890s but most of them flourished after World War II.

The third general type is *Pentecostal Protestantism*. It also resulted from two movements. One was the missionary work of Pentecostal churches that, right from the beginning, demonstrated a great concern to send missionaries abroad. Such were the Assemblies of God from the USA and the Swedish Pentecostals. Besides them there were also revival movements that originated in Latin America itself, such as the Methodist Pentecostal Church in Chile and "Brasil para Cristo." It is this third type that has grown in the most spectacular way among the poor urban masses in the last three decades.

Of the three Protestant types, popular Pentecostal churches are generally the largest in size, and the most indigenous in ministry and lifestyle. They are inspired by a contagious apostolic and evangelistic spirit. They have some of the marks of the early Pentecostal movement in North America that were outlined by Walter Hollenweger in *The Pentecostals* (1972) and successive publications (1986). According to Hollenweger, Latin American Pentecostals have the same characteristics as indigenous, non-white churches in other parts of the world, namely: an oral liturgy, a narrative style in preaching and witness, maximum participation at the levels of prayer, reflection, and decision making, inclusion of dreams and visions in worship, and a unique understanding of the body-mind relationship applied in the ministry of healing by prayer. An appropriate name for these churches would be "Popular Protestantism," given the social strata from which their adherents come in their initial phase of development. More recently there are also a growing number of independent charismatic churches which are difficult to place in this typology because they cater to the middle and upper middle classes. In Guatemala, this is the type of church in which well known politicians Efraín Rios Montt and Jorge Serrano Elías are members. Rios Montt became president of his country after a military coup and Serrano Elías was elected to the same position. They are linked to charismatic groups in the United States, and in their style and ideology they reproduce patterns from the American television subculture.

Nature and Significance of Protestant Growth

Political significance is what has brought the most recent wave of Protestant growth to headlines in the mass media. However, Protestants were also in the headlines at the beginning of this century when they were still a very insignificant minority. Their presence and courageous disposition to stand up for their faith brought constitutional changes that provided for religious freedom and a more pluralistic society in several countries (Kuhl 1982). The participation of Protestants in politics goes back to the 1950s in countries such as Brazil and Perú. Recent studies have demonstrated the key role played by Protestants in the Mexican revolution, during the second decade of this century (Bastian 1989; and Ruiz Guerra 1992). Still, in the 1990s the trend has accelerated: Jorge Serrano Elías, an Evangelical charismatic, became president in Guatemala; Carlos García, a Baptist minister, was elected Vice-President of Perú; and Jaime Ortiz Hurtado, an Evangelical lawyer and theological educator, was elected to the Constitutional Assembly of Colombia (Padilla 1992). This level of participation as well as the influence of the Protestant vote in the general election process demonstrate the rise of a minority to a new status of visibility, at the very moment when the masses have lost confidence in the traditional parties. The Protestant presence could develop into an unexpected political alternative during the years of transition and ideological confusion that Latin American societies are experiencing.

The social impact of the Protestant presence was acknowledged long before they reached the current level of political visibility. It was especially visible in such areas as popular schools, rights of Indian communities, rural medicine, agrarian reform, bilingual education, sports, and literacy. In the early 1940s, when he was trying to gain support from the Latin American countries for the Allied cause in Second World War, President Franklin Roosevelt started a diplomatic effort known as the Good Neighbor policy. In reaction, the American Catholic hierarchy launched a media campaign to promote the idea that the presence of Protestant missionaries was resented by Latin American leaders, and represented an obstacle to closer inter-American relations. An immediate response was prepared by Jorge P. Howard, a well known evangelist from Argentina. He published an impressive collection of opinions favorable to Protestants, gathered from dozens of Latin American writers, politicians, and educators, many of them Catholics. The statements appeared in a book entitled *Religious Liberty in Latin America?* (Howard 1944). Most of them made reference to the significant social work that Protestants were doing, especially among the poorest and most oppressed sectors of society. However, the Protestantism that was praised by those observers in 1944 is not the same Protestantism that is reaching the headlines in 1993.

Until the 1940s, Missionary Protestantism was growing significantly and taking root in Latin America. From national churches came a generation of outstanding leaders who, together with missionary statesmen, gave shape to a strategy of Protestant advance that may be traced by a study of the continental Evangelical Congresses of Panamá (1916), Montevideo (1925), Havana (1929) and Buenos Aires (1949). Some of them became well known for their contribution to the Protestant ecumenical initiative that culminated with the formation of the World Council of Churches in 1948. Precisely in that year, writing in the *International Review of Missions*, Mexican Congregationalist Alberto Rembao offered figures and a narrative of a continental trip which brought him to the conclusion that "Today, the twenty Latin American nations may well be classified as Protestant, in the sense that in each of them the Evangelical community is already too numerous to be regarded as a minority and strong enough to cause the general public to stop and look and listen" (Rembao 1948, 57). Against the repeated argument that Protestantism was "foreign," the answer of Methodist Gonzalo Baez Camargo (1959) was that missions are always an importation, and that the Christian faith was strictly indigenous only to Palestine. He also pointed out that Evangelical churches were already self-supporting and self-propagating so that they could outlive without much difficulty the withdrawal of foreign missionaries. For him, this rootage of Evangelical communities in Latin American soil was evidence that the Evangelical experience was relevant to these societies and that a significant number of Latin Americans were receptive to the message of the Reformation.

The social crisis that preceded and followed the triumph of the Cuban revolution (1959) was the background of significant Protestant growth but it also produced divisions among Protestants. The dramatic theological confrontations between modernists and Fundamentalists in North America became influential on Latin American Protestantism only after World War II. While the missionary efforts of mainline denominations started to decline, the independent conservative missions intensified their activity (Carpenter and Shenk 1990). Mainline missionaries as well as Latin American leaders before the war had always seen Protestantism as a force for social progress, and they had also taken part in the developing ecumenical movement. Conservative missionaries in the 1950s brought to Latin America a strongly negative view of ecumenism and a Cold War mentality that made them hostile to the very idea that structural changes were necessary for social progress.

When it comes to inter-church cooperation for mission, global relations, and representation before civil authorities, Protestants of the different types have grouped around two movements. There is on the one hand an *Ecumenical* movement linked to the conciliar efforts of the Geneva based World Council of Churches (WCC), that carries on an active dialogue and joint programs of action with the Roman Catholic Church. Its most visible corporate expression of unity is the Latin American Council of Churches (CLAI). Several transplanted churches as well as those related to what Americans call mainline denominations, and a handful of Evangelical and Pentecostal churches, are members of CLAI and of the WCC. On the other hand, there is an *Evangelical* movement in which we can place most Evangelical and Pentecostal churches, by far the largest segment of the Protestant presence in Latin America today. Some of them are linked through a loosely connected fellowship called Confraternity of Evangelical Churches (CONELA), which is associated with the World Evangelical Fellowship. Some members of CONELA would call themselves "Fundamentalists" but the majority prefer the name "evangélico".[1]

[1] The distinction I am making between "Ecumenical" and "Evangelical" makes more sense in the English language. Traditionally all Protestants in Latin American have preferred the term "Evangélico" as a synonym for "Protestant". Another important distinction must be made at this point between the American and the European usage of the term "Evangelical." In the U.S.A. the term has come to identify a sector of American Protestantism characterized increasingly by a Fundamentalist ethos and close association with the Republican Party. This is the case for instance of the

Some historians and missiologists prefer to differentiate Pentecostalism from Evangelicalism because they think that a term like "Evangelical" could be misleading about the movement. Pentecostals define their faithfulness to God and the authenticity of their experience more by the signs of spiritual power in their ministry than by correctness of doctrine or ecclesiastical alliance (Newbigin 1953). It is also argued that because they do not have a written theology it is difficult to make assumptions about their beliefs. My own observation is that if attention is paid to the hymnbooks that these churches adopt or adapt, one can see that they reflect a basic Evangelical theology. The Latin American experience thus far demonstrates that a good number of Pentecostal churches and denominations consider themselves Evangelical, and associate with the Evangelical movement for cooperative ventures in mission.

The polarization between Ecumenicals and Evangelicals in Latin America increased in recent years due to a variety of reasons, including their different concepts about mission and divergent attitudes towards the Catholic Church. Political views have become another factor in the dispute. There has been an open identification of CLAI with Liberation Theologies and socialism, while many members of CONELA espouse conservative views and have supported military regimes.[2] This polarization explains, though it may not justify, why ecumenical Protestants have been predisposed to use negative sociological categories for popular Protestantism. There are a good number of Evangelicals in Latin America who regret this polarization because it frequently hurts the life of the churches at the grassroots. They also regret that in spite of its significant numerical growth, Protestantism finds itself today too polarized to offer spiritual guidance in the search for novel approaches to the region's social and political crises. Many Protestant individuals and churches have remained away from both CLAI and CONELA. They find fellowship and avenues of cooperation in movements open to all types of Protestants, regardless of their political views. Padilla (1985) and Escobar (1993) offer a clear expression of the theological stance behind this position, manifested by such organizations as the Latin American Theological Fraternity and the Lausanne movement.

National Association of Evangelicals. In Europe the term "Evangelical" is used more to describe a conservative theological position with less uniform or overt political implications. Here we prefer the European meaning of the term.

[2] Bastian (1990: 215-257) offers an application of Marxist analysis to the description and evaluation of these positions. While Kirkpatrick (1988) has edited a sample of writings by ecumenical Latin American Protestants, Núñez and Taylor (1989) offer an example of the more conservative Evangelical outlook.

Patterns of Interpretation of the Protestant Presence

I have proposed a view of the Protestant presence in Latin America that oscillates between the paradigms of promise and precariousness. The fact that the global history of the Protestant missionary efforts and their effects is still in the process of being written accounts in part for the markedly different interpretations provided by historians and social scientists up to this point. Historical work from the Protestant side has tended to fluctuate between an apologetic or a triumphalistic tone, which reflects the attitudes of a persecuted minority. On the Catholic side, hostility to what is seen as an imperfect form of Christianity, foreign to Latin American culture, is expressed even by academically respectable scholars. In recent decades, the traditional Catholic suspicion that Protestants are subverters of the established order has been augmented by progressive Catholic accusations that Protestants are part of a CIA-led right-wing conspiracy. The difficulty these conflicting theological and ideological commitments pose for those who seek to interpret the Protestant movement in an even-handed way has been well expressed by British sociologist of religion David Martin, who warns his readers that "the whole field is fraught with propaganda and the investigator is bound to be caught in a cross-fire whatever position he takes up" (Martin 1990, 292).

The impressive amount of literature accumulated in recent years, especially about popular Protestantism, evinces these contradictory patterns of interpretation.[3] There is an almost studied lack of clarity in the way such terms as "Fundamentalist" and "Sect" are used, and a lack of regard for the religious history of the continent. Pentecostals are singled out for harsh criticism while other forms of popular religiosity escape critical scrutiny. As pastor Juan Sepúlveda notes, "Social scientists' opinion of Pentecostalism is shown among others in the following expressions: opium, domination via religion, religious proclamation of social conformism, 'refuge of the masses'" (Sepúlveda 1989, 81). A careful scrutiny of hundreds of official documents from the Catholic hierarchies, ecumenical organizations, anthropological and sociological studies in academic publications, and popular reports in the mass media reveal an amazing inadequacy to deal with their subject.

Conspiracy Theories and Sociologism

Academic hostility to Protestantism comes from two main sources, the conspiracy theory and sociologism. There have always been those in the

[3] For an initial look at the numerous studies published during the more recent decades see the bibliographies of Bastian (1990), Martin (1990), Stoll (1990) and Westmeier (1986).

Catholic hierarchies who tried to explain the Protestant presence as part of a foreign plot against the Roman Catholic Church and the Hispanic identity. Until the 1950s in places like Colombia or Argentina, bishops warned against the "liberal-masonic-Protestant" conspiracy. During the years of violence in Colombia following 1948, hundreds of Protestants were killed. They were usually accused of being politically liberal and of opening the door to Communism. (For examples of these versions see Arévalo 1963, 148-149; Prien 1985, 800-801). After the 1960s, the conspiracy theory took a new turn. A Catholic journalist in *Latinamerica Press* summarizes recent reactions to Protestant growth in this way:

> So far, the typical reaction of the Catholic hierarchy to losing its flock has been to advance the "conspiracy theory." According to its most extreme version Protestant sects bankrolled by the CIA are sent to Latin America to destroy Liberation Theology and further U.S. imperialism (McCoy 1989, 2).

In 1987, Franz Damen, a Belgian Catholic missionary in Bolivia, called for a dismissal of the conspiracy theory in a Jesuit magazine published in Cochabamba. He quotes statements from leading bishops which warn about a Protestant conspiracy and refer to "the avalanche of the sects" (Damen 1987, 44-65). Damen does not rule out the possibility that there may be politicians in the United States who try to manipulate existing Latin American Pentecostal churches, but he notes that the Protestant groups that grow fastest are either indigenous to the continent or, if they had their origin in North America, they have quickly become latinoamericanized in both leadership and finance. Damen's conclusion is that "it is yet impossible to prove that a strategic connection exists between the expansionist North American policy towards Latin America and the proliferation of religious sects in the continent" (Damen 1987, 52). For him, the frequently used term "avalanche" is indicative of the frustration felt by the Catholic hierarchies over the loss of the Catholic Church's privileged status as the official religion of the region.

The other source of scholarly hostility to popular Protestantism is what may be called *sociologism*. I am not referring here to sociological study in general, but to the kind of approach that evaluates and analyzes a movement mainly from the perspective of a political project embraced by the researcher. If the social effect of a movement is not favorable to the researcher's political project, the analysis and the evaluation are negative in advance and produce biased selectivity of data in the research and semantic hostility in the presentation of the results. David Martin offers a warning against this academic bias in the introduction to his own study of popular Protestantism. He wants to avoid "framing" the religious experience of the poor people he is studying "in language of covert political hostility, or encasing them in grand notions of the right or main path of social evolution" (Martin 1990, 1).

He calls such use of political correctness "a strange perversion of our intellectual culture." This caveat is especially relevant to Latin America because of the collapse of Marxist "grand notions of the right or main path of social evolution" that have dominated the academic world of Latin American studies, as well as the vocabulary of politics. The uncritical use of Marxist categories for sociological analysis accounts for the extreme forms of sociologism that have been applied especially to the study of Latin American Protestantism. The sociologistic approach is reductionist; it does not do justice to the theological elements which must be taken into account as a frame of reference for a movement that claims to be Christian. Neither does it take adequate account of the self-understanding of the people that are being studied and the plausibility of their worldview and their interpretation of the Biblical text and of Christian history.

The Modernizing Promise of Protestantism

During the decade of the sixties, "modernization" became a predominant viewpoint for understanding the rapid social changes that the Latin American societies were experiencing. This notion served as a framework for explaining the role of religion in society. The way in which the Roman Catholic Church faced social change became one of the first subjects for research.[4] The classic study by Ivan Vallier, *Catholicism, Social Control and Modernization in Latin America* (1970) made use of the tools of institutional analysis to explore the internal structure of the Catholic Church and the interaction of the Church with the secular forces at work in society. Some studies of Protestantism that were carried on during that period also analyzed the internal life of the Protestant churches in order to formulate and interpret their social and political significance. This approach coincided with a distinctive view which Protestants had of themselves.

In the creed and self-understanding of missionary Protestantism there was a clear conviction about its modernizing potential, especially in the fostering of spiritual conditions that would be favorable to the spread of democracy. This is, for instance, the position of W. Stanley Rycroft, a British missionary who worked as an educator in Perú for eighteen years and later as a mission executive in the United States. Rycroft wrote two books (1942, 1958) which analyzed Latin American social problems from the perspective that there was

[4] Catholics in the United States and Europe fostered the understanding of this process through research and publications. See for instance the proceedings of a conference sponsored by the University of Notre Dame with a grant from the Rockefeller foundation (D'Antonio and Pike 1964), or the Feres-Friburgo program (Escobar 1987b, 45, n.10).

an intimate relationship between spiritual experience and social reality and that Protestantism was destined to play a key role in the transition from the old feudal order to a new one. Thus he wrote in the first that "In its historical perspective the growth of democracy in Latin America is vitally related to the spread of Evangelical Christianity" (Rycroft 1942, 186). In the later study, having outlined the main pillars of Protestant faith in contrast with the nominal and formal Catholicism of the region, he said:

> The four pillars of Protestantism, namely, the priesthood of all believers, justification by faith, the right of private interpretation and the authority of the Word of God, are also of fundamental importance in the development of a free democratic society (Rycroft 1958, 152).

Commenting from the perspective of a person who has lived as a member of a religious minority in Latin America, Cuban born historian Justo González describes a belief that he held in his early youth:

> In the midst of a society built on the general assumption of an agreement between Catholicism and culture, we found it comforting to be able to point to another society where there seemed to be a similar connection between Protestantism and culture. And we found it particularly comforting when we could point to the technological, political and economic triumphs of that society (González 1990, 23).

Though González states later on that he has "radically altered" his views, he also says that this is still a widespread attitude among Protestants in Latin America. It is a view that drew strength from a sociological interpretation that stressed the connection between certain traits of character that developed out of Protestantism and the kind of virtues which were necessary for survival in a society that was leaving its feudal past behind.

Understanding Protestantism as a contributor to modernization appealed especially to writers and analysts of mainline or historic denominations. However, it is important to keep in mind that the first type of Protestantism that was analyzed sociologically on the basis of a systematic collection of empirical data was the popular Pentecostal movement in those countries where its growth was most significant, Chile and Brazil. The key work about both countries in this area is the book *Followers of the New Faith*, by Emilio Willems (1967). In his interpretation, Pentecostal Protestantism emerged as a byproduct of changes such as foreign immigration and secularization that were affecting the social structures and values of Brazilian and Chilean societies. Once established, Protestantism became itself a factor contributing to social change because the value orientation that can be described as "the Protestant ethic" helped converts to function better in the new situation created by industrialization, urbanization, internal migration, and the opening of new frontiers (Willems 1967, 13).

In Willems' view, the fact that Pentecostalism was attracting the lower classes in these societies meant that the Pentecostal experience might be one of the options open to masses who were in a state of latent or overt rebellion. As a consequence, "...conversion to Protestantism, especially to its sectarian varieties, constitutes one of the many ways in which hostility and rebellion against a decaying social structure may be expressed" (Willems 1964, 103). Because of its alliance with the rich and powerful, the Roman Catholic Church was perceived by the people as a part of the decaying social structure. There may have been more than a coincidence in the fact that the Catholic clergy of Brazil and Chile, the Latin American nations where Pentecostal churches have grown most rapidly, were among the most enthusiastic exponents of the "preferential option for the poor" that the Bishops adopted at the Medellín conference in 1968.[5]

The method of institutional analysis applied by Willems to his study of Pentecostal congregations allowed for a better understanding of the link between liturgy, legitimation, and social change. At the time, Pentecostals were being criticized and even despised not only by Catholic and Marxist observers, but even by Latin American Protestants of transplanted or missionary churches for their personal, political, and social isolation. By contrast, Willems pointed to the participatory nature of Pentecostal liturgy and congregational life, a characteristic that was easy to miss because it did not depend on literacy or education but on a disposition to be touched by the power of the Holy Spirit.

In his analysis, Willems referred especially to the significance of the *tomada de Espíritu* or "seizure" by the Spirit that "puts a seal of divine approval on the individual who can now be elected or appointed to any office" (Willems 1964, 106-107). The seizure was a form of legitimation within the Pentecostal congregations that had to be validated by energetic and successful proselytism. The seizure had an integrative effect allowing thousands of persons from the lower social classes to become part of an organized group in which they could enter into community, contribute their gifts, and receive affirmation, comfort, and a sense of belonging. The seizure experience also had an egalitarian effect, because participation in the community did not require the symbols of status such as money, education, or even verbal articulateness. What started at the level of liturgical participation could be extended to the level of decision making in the community. Willems concluded that "The principle of unrestricted social mobility embodied by the

[5] For a recent Catholic evaluation of that significant moment of change in the life of the Roman Catholic Church see Edward L. Cleary, ed. (1990).

Pentecostal sects, is obviously at variance with the limited opportunities for upward mobility within the general society" (Willems 1964, 107). That in itself was an excellent training ground for participation in the secular society where a democratization process was taking place.

Another important component of the Pentecostal message is an emphasis on certain marks of character as indicators of the "changed life" which results from the redeeming power of Christ. As in the case of Evangelical Protestants, Pentecostals present the convert with specific prohibitions against the use of alcohol and tobacco. But what is especially significant in Pentecostal practice is that the prohibitions are accompanied by a strong emphasis on an emotional experience of conversion, a seizure by God's power, that in some cases is the key point of breaking away from old habits such as alcoholism which is prevalent among the popular classes of the urban world. In the Pentecostal experience, the ascetic lifestyle inaugurated by conversion is accompanied by a celebrative form of worship and communal life that greatly helps to promote endurance among the converted. This change of lifestyle also has economic and social consequences in the improvement of housing conditions and eating habits. Savings are generated and sometimes matched with a newly discovered ability for entrepreneurship that brings upward mobility: "The economic significance of Protestant asceticism lies in the fact that it frees part of one's income for the acquisition of things that symbolize a higher level of living" (Willems 1964, 251).

Positive evaluations of the Protestant experience which majored in the "promise" of Protestantism were usually connected with a tacit or explicit acceptance of the modernization process in which Latin American societies followed the pattern of the Western capitalist nations. In this interpretation, the modernization process was frequently contrasted with the feudal order of colonial days that had remained in spite of a century and a half of independence from Spain. This interpretation did not question the applicability to Latin America of patterns of modernization and democratization taken from the Anglo-Saxon and European experience. In fact, it adopted the "liberal project" that had been the ideological frame of reference for Western political and economic developments until the Second World War. This analysis stressed transformative processes at a micro level within the Protestant communities on the assumption that the general direction of historical development, the macro process of Latin American society as a whole, would follow almost naturally the western pattern of development which Protestants were already emulating.

The Precariousness of Protestant Modernization

Criticism of the Protestant presence did not come only from Catholic conservatives who defended the Hispanic tradition. The arrival of European

Marxism at the beginning of the 20th century and the rise of a labor union movement that followed the new waves of European immigration contributed to the development of a Latin American brand of Marxism. In the application of Marxism to the Latin American situation and its history, Marxists paid special attention to the theory of imperialism that Lenin had formulated. For many Latin Americans, the kind of North American imperialism that was experienced especially after the Spanish-American War of 1898 was as bad as the Spanish imperialism of the 16th century. Latin America would not become free, democratic, and developed, they reasoned, unless it broke away from all forms of imperial power. The political analysis that was a component of the liberal project had developed a critique of the Iberian colonial order. Now Marxism provided a new kind of analysis that centered on the economic factors and developed into an articulate criticism of the penetration of Latin America by British and American capitalism.[6] Suspicion became the key to a new understanding of the history of Latin America. Slowly but clearly, Protestantism of every kind came to be seen as an instrument of Anglo-Saxon penetration into Latin lands.[7] This idea was not new, and in fact a strong anti-AngloSaxon sentiment was part of the conservative tradition, especially of Catholic Fundamentalists in Spain and Argentina, the most vocal proponents of a conspiracy theory (Pike in Wiarda 1992, 158-159).

The anti-Protestant point of view was adopted by a growing number of political leaders and opinion makers. It was intensified by the growing volume of American investments in the region and changes in the foreign policies of the United States towards its Latin American neighbors. Some of the most alert Protestant missionaries and missiologists understood this issue and warned North American Protestants about it. An editorial in the *International Review of Missions* pointed out that there was a growing sense of solidarity among the Latin American republics and it went on to comment "today there is a growing fear of domination by foreign powers, a fear of military force behind the strong economic hold on the countries which loans and investments have given" (1932, 306). A footnote tells us that the previous year the same magazine had informed its readers that between 1913 and 1928, U.S. investments in Latin America had increased from about two

[6] There are two documentary collections that illustrate several aspects of the debates about Anglo-Saxon penetration in Latin America: Donald Marquand Dozer, ed. *The Monroe Doctrine: Its modern significance*, New York: Knopf, 1965; and Marvin D. Bernstein, ed. *Foreign investment in Latin America: Cases and attitudes*, New York: Knopf, 1966.

[7] As early as 1928, this was the view of Argentinean socialist Alfredo Palacios as quoted by José Carlos Mariátegui, a Peruvian Marxist (Valcárcel 1972, Prólogo).

hundred million to over two thousand million dollars. Already in 1935, in his book *That Other America*, Presbyterian missionary John A. Mackay provided a long list of military aggressions by the United States in Mexico, Central America, and the Caribbean, and reminded his readers that "United States marines have been landed in Caribbean countries in order to guarantee orderly government, or the kind of government that would be most advantageous to American financial interests in those countries" (Mackay 1935, 26). For Mackay, this kind of action "has done more to unite Latin American sentiment against the United States than any other happening in the history of the last hundred years" (Mackay 1935, 26). Reflecting the view of several other missionaries, he lamented the consequences and concluded that "any kind of inter-American relationship of a spiritual character which one may attempt to establish is subjected inevitably to close scrutiny, lest it should prove at bottom to be of this egotistical, acquisitive species" (Mackay 1935, 29).

Things worsened after World War II when American policy makers adopted the manichean vision of the Cold War and became obsessed with anti-Communism. Rycroft represented the view of many missionaries in the historic denominations when he analyzed the situation. He pointed out that the Latin American nations had joined the Allies in a war to defend those famous "four freedoms" that in fact few Latin Americans enjoyed. He then described the irony of what followed:

> Then came the end of the war and the beginning of the cold war. In the anti-Communist struggle the United States, home of rebellion against oppression and leader of political independence and freedom, has appeared to the Latin Americans to assume the role of the political conservative and the reactionary (Rycroft 1958, 35).

At a time of change and transition, civil and military dictators who represented traditional conservative ideologies could count on the cooperation and protection of the United States because they had learned how to wave the flag of anti-Communism. In many cases, Catholic priests or Protestant missionaries who were critical of dictatorships or advocated even moderate change were accused of being Communists, not only by repressive governments, but also by their own Protestant communities.[8] The precariousness of Protestantism became evident as this process developed.

Other reasons that help explain why the bright promise envisaged by the early missionaries did not come to fruition include: the loss of initial vigor in the case of some historic missions and churches, the inability of Evangelical

[8] Rubem Alves offers a devastating analysis of this kind of witch hunt in Brazil (1985).

and Pentecostal missionaries to overcome their North American cultural conditioning, and divisive policies that polarized all sectors of Protestantism. The older missionary movement which predated the Second World War declined because of the growth of autonomous national church bodies, the loss of missionary zeal, and the influence of theological liberalism. Meanwhile, a new movement of independent Fundamentalist, Evangelical, and Pentecostal missions flourished.[9] To avoid falling into what they considered the trap of the Social Gospel, they adopted a strong dualism that separated completely the spiritual realm from social and political realities. They also accepted the ideology of the cold war. It was at this point, in the decade of the 1960s, that all forms of Protestantism were placed under the magnifying glass of a new kind of interpretative analysis.

This new interpretation of Protestantism placed religious phenomenon within the global historical process of imperialism in a critical way. The Leninist elements of the theory of imperialism were used to forge a new interpretation of Latin American history, one which paid special attention to the economic factors that underlay the political and cultural ones. In that form, "dependency theory" came to be formulated. José Míguez Bonino says "The basic categories for understanding our history are not development and underdevelopment but domination and dependence. That is the crux of the matter" (Míguez Bonino 1975, 16). The oppressive domination of one social class inside Latin American societies was linked to the oppressive domination of the Latin American nations by powerful developed nations, especially the United States. What was even worse, according to Marxist theory, religion was an ideology developed to justify that domination.

Contemporary liberation movements and Liberation Theologies can only be understood within the frame of this kind of analysis. They propose a "historical project," a pattern of political action that will bring an end to all types of oppression. A Lutheran theologian from Argentina writing in 1970 described the many contradictions of Latin American societies. Then he expressed very clearly what became a party line in many ecumenical circles: "We Latin Americans know, however, that at this point of historical circumstances the fundamental contradiction which confronts us involves North American imperialism and its local accomplices" (Yutzis 1970, 19). The solution to the problem was expressed not so much in terms of a viable proposal for a different kind of society, but through the negation of the North American model:

> It is not possible for us to get rid of a wasting of our resources, infant mortality, unemployment and illiteracy without carrying out radical reforms in

[9] The best analysis of this movement is still Kenneth Strachan (1957).

> the economic, social, political and ideological structures. But this in turn will not be possible as long as the United States preserves its hegemony over Latin America. And the path toward the liberation of Latin America will not lead through the capitalistic system, but will be anti-capitalistic and anti-imperialistic (Yutzis 1970, 19).

At a time when Russia, China and Cuba were still being praised as alternative models for developing societies, the political program of "liberation" was usually described in terms of the search for some kind of "socialist" project.[10] Everything from Sunday School material to curriculum in theological schools, from liturgical practices to missionary methods came to be evaluated from this anti-capitalist, pro-socialist perspective.[11] The militant literature of those days seems devoid of logic now in light of the fall of the Berlin Wall, but at the time it conveyed a heady aura of irrefutable logic and historical inevitability.

The most consistent and clear expression of this kind of analysis applied to Latin American Protestantism was provided by Argentinine theologian José Míguez Bonino in many of his writings, but especially in his book *Towards a Christian Political Ethics* (1983). Míguez Bonino evaluated the role of mainline and Evangelical Protestantism in Latin America from the perspective of his critical appraisal of the liberal project. According to his reading of history, the introduction of Protestantism became possible thanks to a new colonial pact that, on the external front, favored relationships with Protestant countries and on the internal front allowed the triumph of modernizing elites over traditional ones. In Míguez Bonino's analysis, Protestantism comes to be seen less as a movement with a dynamism of its own, than as one which serves the purposes of the liberal political elites: "What is clear in relation to Latin America, is that Protestantism claimed and (within its limitations) assumed the role that the Latin American liberal elites had assigned it in the transition from a traditional society to the modern bourgeois world" (1983, 62). Awareness of this fact produced a "crisis of conscience," says Míguez Bonino. He applauds the fact that Protestantism played a significant role in breaking the power of the traditional colonial mentality, but reminds us of the Anglo Saxon missionary base from which Protestantism came; and he poses the burning question "Did we not in fact contribute to create the benevolent

[10] There has been a development beyond the simplistic categories of the 1970s. José Míguez Bonino offers a discussion of this socialist historical project using key ideas from Gustavo Gutiérrez as well as his own (1983: 77-78).

[11] I have analyzed the influence of the Marxist utopia on historical and theological discourse in my book *La fe evangélica y las teologías de la liberación* (1987a).

and idealized image of the colonial powers (mainly the U.S.) which has disguised the deadly character of their domination?" (Míguez Bonino 1975, 18).

To varying degrees, other interpreters of Protestantism took Míguez Bonino's critical and even condemnatory approach. The field of church history was overtaken by a revisionist attitude that in many cases offered a simplistic ideological selection and interpretation of facts.[12] This is the kind of reading that one finds in some sections of the brief history of Protestantism in Latin America by Swiss historian Jean Pierre Bastian (1990). His periodization and his presentation of the material follow closely Míguez Bonino's approach, especially in his treatment of the period from 1959 to 1983. The Protestant and Catholic theologians and leaders who adopted the "historical project" of liberation discourse are described as "ideological vanguards linked to revolutionary processes," while those who for any reason remained distant from it are described as "ideological vanguards that legitimated the established order" (Bastian 1990, 220-232). Bastian's ideological simplification does not allow him to give adequate consideration to the actual theological and ecclesiological convictions behind these differing Protestant positions.[13] An even more extreme case is the work of Rosa del Carmen Bruno-Jofré about Methodist educational work in Perú (1988). She places the dynamics of Protestant advance in the strategic design of North American imperialism.

Some Protestant theologians broke away from their churches at the time of crisis in the 1960s and 1970s because they saw no future for Protestantism. This was especially the case for theologians from the historical or mainline denominations. Among them, the most vocal was Brazilian Rubem Alves, formerly a Presbyterian minister, who published a book on Liberation Theology even before the classic work of Gustavo Gutiérrez was published in its Spanish original (Alves 1969). Reacting to the crisis that shook Protestant denominations in Brazil during the 1960s, Alves reflected on Paul Tillich's notion of "the end of the Protestant era" and the difficulties of applying his formulation to Latin America:

> It is not possible to speak of the end of the Protestant era in a continent that never experienced it. Here the same phenomenon adopts a different form, because Protestantism aged prematurely. Although still in infancy it became senile. All this took place before it made our continent fruitful with its more creative vitality (Alves 1970, 49).

[12] Though in many academic circles the simplistic phase of this ideological approach has been abandoned, publications such as NACLA Report have kept it.

[13] In a more recent essay Bastian has modified the simplistic ideological scheme of his previous work, incorporating new perceptions derived from more recent research (Dussel 1992, 313-350).

For Alves the promise of Protestantism had been its emphasis on "community" in contrast with the Catholic emphasis on "institution." However that promise had been betrayed because developments in the older denominations had frozen them "in structures which have been historically baptized as Protestant, but which in their essence are a resurrection of medieval Catholicism" (Alves 1970, 59).

Some of the elements of the critical approach described in the first part of this section have been applied by Methodist theologians José Míguez Bonino and Mortimer Arias to a new reading of the significance of Methodism in the English speaking countries (Kirkpatrick 1988). Míguez Bonino summarizes one of their conclusions in the statement: "Historically, Methodism seems to have been useful for the incorporation of significant sectors of the rising British proletariat to the liberal burgeois ideology that undergirded the consolidation of the capitalist system and reinforced its imperialist expansion" (Duque 1983, 72).

The analysis offered by Míguez Bonino and Arias helps to clarify the social and political significance of some basic doctrines in the Wesleyan heritage. Because theological doctrines are usually understood only in terms of their intellectual significance in relation to other doctrines and to the ideologies of a particular historical moment, this new understanding of social conditioning and its implication for doctrinal developments can contribute to the formulation of pastoral and missiological practices that will take more seriously the context of the church. On the other hand, uncritical application of this kind of analysis runs the risk of reductionism when it places the initiative for religious life and behavior only or mainly on the economic and political motivations of the imperial forces at work at a particular moment. For example, one of the weaknesses of the "Black Legend" about the missionary work of Spain and Portugal in Latin America during the 16th and 17th centuries is precisely that it did not take adequate account of missionary actions that were not motivated by imperial interests or were even in open conflict with them. The Black Legend ignored facts and its analysis was marred by the selective use of data. That is precisely what happens today when the reductionist approach is used in the formulation of a new "Black Legend" in Latin America, this time about Protestantism, especially in its popular forms.

New Approaches in the Interpretation of Popular Protestantism

A new stage in the process of interpretation of Latin American Protestantism was opened with the publication of the global studies by David Stoll and David Martin. Drawing on the vast body of data that has accumulated in recent years, Stoll and Martin provide clues for new interpretations of Protestantism in general, though they have focused specially on the rapid growth of Pentecostalism in recent decades.

David Martin places Latin American Protestantism in two broad contexts: "the four hundred year clash between the Hispanic imperium and the Anglo-Saxon imperium" (Martin 1990, 9), and "the dramatically different ways in which Catholic cultures and Protestant cultures have entered into what we call modernity" (26). As global frames of reference, these do more justice to the nature of the object being studied than does the reductionist approach of class analysis in neo-Marxian dependency theory.

As background, Martin provides a sociological interpretation of the evolution of Protestantism in Europe and in the English speaking world including the United States. He is aware that there is no historical continuity between some forms of popular Protestantism in Latin America and Protestantism in the English speaking world, but he thinks that the evolution of the Wesleyan movement offers parallels that may yield helpful sociological patterns of interpretation to Pentecostalism in Latin America. The Pentecostal experience is explained by Martin as a way in which "millions of people are absorbed within a protective social capsule where they acquire new concepts of self and new models of initiative and voluntary organization" (Martin 1990, 284). His analysis coincides at many points with the analysis of Willems considered above. Martin thinks that, like Methodism at the beginning of the industrial revolution in Britain, Pentecostalism thrives today in Latin America as a "temporary efflorescence of voluntary religiosity which accompanies a stage in industrialization and/or urbanization" (294). However he is careful to point out that the European experience may not necessarily provide a universal paradigm.

David Stoll is also an interpreter interested in the social and political effect of the presence and message of popular Protestantism. He uses a basically anthropological approach and a journalistic style, paying little attention to theological or historical factors. His earlier studies of Protestant missionary activity combined elements of the conspiracy theory with institutional analysis (Stoll 1982). In his more recent work his agenda has changed as he sees a need to correct inadequate explanations of the Protestant presence (Stoll 1990, xv). He wants to explore the reasons for the growth of a popular Protestantism that does not have a specific social agenda. Writing especially about Evangelicals he says "Despite their seeming indifference to oppression they succeed in attracting millions of poor people from a Catholic Church which seems far more socially conscious" (xiv). Also, he would like to warn Evangelicals about "the danger of allowing their missions to be harnessed to U.S. militarism by the religious right" (xv).

Stoll takes us back to the theme of the precariousness of Protestantism. He believes that "the history of social movements is replete with shifts from a redemptive (saving one's soul) to a transformative (changing the world) emphasis, or vice-versa, often after the first generation" (Stoll 1990, 329). As he speculates about the future social effect of Evangelicals and Pentecostals in Latin America, he envisions three possible scenarios: a confrontation with the state that would make them a redemptive force, social mobility that would create a dynamic rising middle sector to change society by negotiation and leadership ability, or failure to become a major force for social change because of sectarianism and a refusal to assume political responsibilities. Though he thinks that the third "is the most defensible scenario at present," he also believes that "Evangelical Protestants are giving Latin Americans a new form of social organization and a new way to express their hopes," thus acting as "survival vehicles" in a time of serious social crisis (331).

The relevance of the Evangelical experience for people who face social change is summarized by Stoll in the following way, "Where traditional social organization is breaking up, Evangelical churches constitute new, more flexible groups in which participation is voluntary, where leadership is charismatic, and which are therefore more adaptable to rapidly changing conditions" (Stoll 1990, 331). Stoll's observations can be compared to the reflections of Juan Sepúlveda, on the theological evolution of Pentecostals in Chile. Some researchers have stressed the "social strike" of Pentecostals in that country, referring to their abstention from political participation or social militancy (Lalive d'Epinay 1969) and others have analyzed their support for the military regime of Augusto Pinochet after the military coup that overthrew socialist president Salvador Allende (Lagos Schuffeneger 1988). However, Sepúlveda's recent experiences with Pentecostals at the grassroots level provides examples of a Pentecostal evolution away from the social conservatism that the movement adopted at a given point (Sepúlveda 1988).

On the basis of their conclusions about the social role of Evangelicals and Pentecostals, both Martin and Stoll develop a fascinating critique of Liberation Theologies. Martin reminds us that "Liberation Theology is a major rival to Pentecostalism," a reason that explains why the more cautious members of the Catholic hierarchy have accepted it in spite of its critical attitude to traditional Catholicism. But Martin goes on to point out that Liberation Theology has not been a successful competitor to the Pentecostal advance:

> The reason is that however much it represents "an option for the poor" taken up by hundreds of thousands of the poor themselves, that option is most eloquently formulated by radical intellectuals...not usually "of the people." Liberation Theology has a decidedly middle class and radical intellectual accent alien to the localized needs of peril the poor" (Martin 1990, 290).

Stoll concurs with Martin, pointing to the many risks involved in the task of consciousness-raising assumed by the propounders of Liberation Theologies.

He says that "To begin with there is the risk of failing to speak to the actual needs of the poor as opposed to idealized versions of those needs" (Stoll 1990, 312). Stoll comments that the defiance of the established order that Liberation Theologians encourage among the poor reflects the fact that "safely situated intellectuals have had an outsize role in its production" (313). Such actions in many cases have been suicidal for the poor.

There are important contributions to the understanding of Protestantism in the works of Martin and Stoll. Their approaches coincide with the development of new and more eclectic approaches in the interpretation of the history of Roman Catholicism in Latin America. Scott Mainwaring (1986, 1990) has provided methodological insights which are applicable not only to his study of Catholicism but also to the interpretation of Protestantism. He is aware of the limitations of a functionalist approach that centers on institutional analysis within the frame of modernization, but he thinks that it clarifies issues that otherwise would remain hidden. While Mainwaring benefits from insights coming from dependency theory and Liberation Theologies, he thinks that neo-Marxian analysts "tend to understate the autonomy of religion and the Church vis-a-vis class. Religion can be a powerful force in determining political orientation, frequently even more powerful than class" (Mainwaring 1990, 12).

Conclusion: The Possibilities of a Missiological Approach

The paradigm of promise and precariousness may be better understood from a missiological perspective that uses critically all previous efforts at interpretation. The development of Protestantism in Latin America, and especially the recent growth of its popular forms, raises the question of continuity. Will this new, popular Protestantism become the depository of the heritage of the Reformation that took place in Europe in the 16th century? The same question may be asked about popular forms of Protestantism in Asia and Africa now that mainline Protestantism is retreating in other parts of the world. What churches will supply the energies for Christian mission in the 21st century? What shape will that mission take in a global village which is coming to look like a large scale reproduction of Latin America with its extremes of immense wealth and insulting poverty?

As has already been observed, massive conversion of nominal Catholics to popular Protestantism brings back to the mind of Catholic hierarchies the social and religious movements of the 16th century. One of the reasons for this is that traditionally the Church of Rome saw her religious conquest of America as a compensation for the loss of Northern Europe to the Protestant Reformation. A most disturbing fact for Catholic missiologists at this juncture is that after five centuries of Catholic presence, in the region where

42% of the Catholics of the world are now living, a large foreign missionary force is still necessary to keep that church alive. The opposite should be the case they say: a Catholic missionary force should be going from Latin America to the unevangelized regions of the world. However, a writer in *COMLA 4*, the official report from their 4th Catholic Missionary Congress (Lima February 1991), laments the fact that "the proportion of Latin American missionaries does not even reach 2% of the total missionary force in the world" (*COMLA 4*, 267).

Protestant missiologists are also trying to derive some lessons from the Latin American case for the mission of the church at large. Probably the best known are those of the "Church Growth" school, also known as "Managerial Missiology" (Read, Monterroso, Johnson 1969; Wagner 1973). I think it is important to warn against an undue "appropriation" of the popular Protestant movement in Latin America by North American missiological schools and agencies that use statistics and studies about Pentecostals in order to sell their own sociological or spiritual techniques. Popular Protestant churches are not growing because they have applied some technique learned in a missiological school in North America. It is the other way round. Missiological schools are trying to detect in their growth some principles that might be helpful to other Christians concerned with the mission of the Church today.

Missiology can benefit from the new methodological convergence between the approaches of Martin, Stoll and Mainwaring and the insights that can be critically selected from previous approaches. What missiologists see in their study depends very much on their theological biases and their methodological presuppositions. For that reason I have found it valuable to compare previous studies with the observations about popular Protestantism coming from some Catholic missiologists who are missionaries in Latin America, and who, out of deep pastoral concern, have decided to go beyond simplistic conspiracy theories or sociologisms. This represents a new trend in the interpretation of popular Protestantism offered by observers that have followed closely its growth in recent years. We will be paying special attention to three Catholic missiologists, Franz Damen, Roger Aubry, and José Luis Idígoras[14]. Their conclusions may be summarized in four points.

[14] Franz Damen, a Passionist priest, is a Belgian missionary who has specialized in the study of sects and serves as Executive Secretary of the Department of Ecumenism of the Conference of Bishops in Bolivia. Mgr. Roger Aubry is a Swiss Redentorist priest, who was president of the Department of Missions of CELAM from 1974 to 1979, and has been a missionary in the jungle of Bolivia since 1970. José Luis Idígoras, was a Jesuit theologian who taught in several Catholic theological schools in Peru, died in 1992.

Popular Protestantism is a Religious Movement

The key to understanding popular Protestantism is to acknowledge that it has "its own religious dynamism and logic" says Damen (1987, 53). Roger Aubry (1990) observes that Pentecostal churches "respond in their own way to the religous demand of the popular masses" (Aubry 1990, 106-107) and he describes the tremendous spiritual vacuum felt by millions of poor people going through social transitions, unattended by the Catholic Church. Idígoras observes that through reading of the biblical text and explanations of pastors "the members of the sects search above all for the religious experience of God. An emotional experience that will communicate his spiritual riches to them" (Idígoras 1991, 242). He goes even further, contrasting mainline Protestantism with the popular vision. He says that secularism has diluted and weakened the faith of many mainline liberal Protestants and that "liberal faith has no energies to throw itself into the missionary task" (237). He also criticizes the elitist theological education of Catholic priests who have an initial philosophical formation "in an environment which is obsessed by rationality" (242).

Popular Protestantism is a Popular Movement

Aubry observes that popular Protestantism grows among the most destitute and marginal sectors of the population, the masses that are disarticulated socially and culturally. Idígoras says that "they are popular Christians, with a rudimentary theology, endowed with heavenly visions and itinerant preachers that move through streets and squares" (Idígoras 1991, 238). Both authors concur in the opinion that one of the secrets of the Protestant growth is the ability of their leadership to remain close to the people, speak their language, and develop patterns of ministry that avoid elitism. For Idígoras, although both Catholic priests and Protestant pastors come from the same popular sectors, the latter "live closer to the people, and their training is usually less philosophical and more theological" (245). Their preference for simple Bible reading and commentary without resource to exegetical methods allows them to remain closer to the religious feeling and the mind of the people. "Because of that there are not many theologians among the pastors of the sects, but there are charismatic preachers and speakers of theatrical television programs" (246).

Popular Protestantism Mobilizes People for Mission

Observers of popular Protestantism agree that it has a remarkable ability to mobilize all members of their churches for the missionary task. "All converts are active members that have to promote the life of the sect and work for the conversion of people who are not converted yet," says Aubry (1990, 111). He criticizes the fact that sometimes there is more of a proselytizing than an evangelistic spirit, and that some methods do not show respect for the freedom that is necessary in evangelization. And with reference to Catholics he adds, "we must confess that among us, in spite of the serious efforts that are being carried on, there are few lay people actively involved in the pastoral life of their parish or their Church" (111-112). Idígoras analyzes carefully the missionary methodology of popular Protestantism with its massive meetings in the open air "where faith is proclaimed and the multitudinous emotion is transmitted like fire" (Idígoras 1991, 243). He stresses the fact that the Evangelistic activity is not limited to the church building, but that groups invade streets and squares, "and audaciously they even go house by house and speak *opportune et importune*." He adds that "A Catholic priest, because of his training, would feel out of place in such situations" (244).

Popular Protestantism Creates Community

Missiologists do not spare criticism of these popular churches. They criticize "escapist eschatology" that makes them insensitive to social problems, "dualistic theology" that condemns the world as "completely lost," and their ostentatious display of healing and prophetic gifts. However, missiologists also acknowledge the positive social effect of popular Protestantism. Aubry points out the value of community life in these churches, in face of the uprooted experience of persons who have lost their previous points of reference:

> The atmosphere of a community of converted people which praise the Lord and find religious and human warmth in the midst of a faceless society and of almost anonymous parishes, is something essential for human life. Only within a community can the new convert persevere, experience the riches of faith and its implications for life (Aubry 1990, 112).

Idígoras carefully analyzes not only the popular nature of this Protestantism but also some characteristics that stamp it as an elitist antipopular movement. He refers, for instance, to the adoption of a more ascetic lifestyle, and a more literate spirituality. These new attitudes and habits, adopted consciously and in tension with their previous Catholic lifestyle, can be -- according to Idígoras -- the source of a certain arrogance through which a minority distances itself from the masses and finds a new self-identity and a new source strength to endure social ostracism. To this could be added the self-affirmation of the lay people in contrast with a more hierarchical Catholic church life centered in the person of the priest. Idígoras observes that during the 16th century Reformation, certain enlightened and progressive minorities adopted the same attitudes against the Catholic church. What is new in the case of Latin America is that "the elitism of the enlightened ones has been passed on to simple and ignorant people" (Idígoras 1991, 241).

With this observation, Idígoras takes us full circle back to what could be a clue to the future promise and precariousness of Protestantism in Latin America. As John A. Mackay, an interpreter of Latin American Protestantism said:

> The Protestant advent in Latin America gave expression to yearnings and experiences and ideas which were present centuries earlier in the Spanish reformers and mystics, and in missionary personalities such as Bartolomé de las Casas. Today this revolutionary fact is being recognized. There has began to emerge in Roman Catholic circles a new "Evangelicalism" and in Protestant circles a new "Catholicism", as members of both groups become dedicated to exploring in Biblical perspective the eternal dimension and the contemporary relevancy of Christ and the Church (Mackay 1967, 179).

The promise is still open in spite of the precariousness evident in some of its realizations.

Reference List

Alves, Rubem. 1969. *A theology of human hope.* Washington D.C.: Corpus Books.

________. 1970. Is there any future for Protestantism in Latin America? *Lutheran Quarterly* 22(1): 49-59.

________. 1985. *Protestantism and repression: A Brazilian case study.* Maryknoll: Orbis Books.

Arévalo, J. J. 1963. *Anti-Kommunism in Latin America.* New York: Lyle Stuart.

Aubry, Mgr. R. 1990. *La misión siguiendo a Jesús por los caminos de América Latina.* Buenos Aires; Ed. Guadalupe.

Báez Camargo, G. 1959. Evangelical faith and Latin American culture. In *The ecumenical era in church and society*, ed. E. J. Jurji, 126-147. New York: Macmillan.

Bastian, J. P. 1983. *Protestantismo y sociedad en México.* Mexico: CUPSA.

_______. 1985. Para una aproximación teórica del fenómeno religioso Protestante en América Central. *Cristianismo y Sociedad* n.s. 85: 61-68.

_______. 1989. *Los disidentes: Sociedades Protestantes y revolución en México, 1872-1911.* Mexico: Fondo de Cultura Econoómica.

_______. 1990. *Historia del Protestantismo en América Latina.* Mexico: CUPSA.

Bernstein, M. D., ed. 1966. *Foreign investment in Latin America: Cases and attitudes.* New York: Knopf.

Bruno-Jofré, Rosa del Carmen. 1988. *Methodist education in Peru. Social gospel, politics, and American ideological and economic penetration, 1888-1930.* Waterloo: Wilfrid Laurier University Press.

Bühlman, W. 1986. *The church of the future.* Maryknoll: Orbis.

Carpenter, J A. and W. R. Shenk, eds. 1990. *Earthen vessels, American Evangelicals and foreign missions, 1880-1980*. Grand Rapids: Eerdmans.

CELAM (Consejo Episcopal Latinoamericano). n.d. *Elementos de pastoral ecuménica*. no. 52 Bogotá.

Cleary, E. L., ed. 1990. *Born of the poor, the Latin American church since Medellin*. Notre Dame: University of Notre Dame Press.

COMLA 4 (IV Congreso misionero Latinoamericano). 1991. *Memorias del COMLA-4*. Lima, Perú: Ediciones Paulinas.

Costas, O. E. 1976. *Theology of the crossroads in contemporary Latin America*. Amsterdam: Rodopi.

Damen, F. 1987. Las sectas ¿avalancha o desafío? *Cuarto Intermedio* n.s. 3, Cochabamba (May): 44-65.

D'Antonio, W. B. and F. B. Pike, eds. 1964. *Religion, revolution and reform*. New York: Praeger.

Dozer, D. M., ed. 1965. *The Monroe Doctrine: Its modern significance*. New York: Knopf.

Duque, J., ed. 1983. *La tradición Protestante en la teologia Latinoamericana*. San José: DEI.

Dussel, E. D., ed. 1992. *The church in Latin America 1492-1992*. Turnbridge Wells, Kent England: Burnes and Oates and Maryknoll, NY: Orbis Books.

Escobar, S. 1987a. *La fe evangélica y las teologias de la liberación*. El Paso: Casa Bautista de Publicaciones.

________. 1987b. Missions and renewal in Latin American Catholicism. *Missiology* XV(2): 33-46.

________. 1991. *Los evangélicos: ¿Nueva leyenda negra en América Latina?* Mexico: Casa Unida de Publicaciones.

________. 1993. The whole gospel for the whole world from Latin America. *Transformation* 10(1): 30-32.

Gonzalez, J. L. 1990. *Mañana. Christian theology from a Hispanic perspective*. Nashville: Abingdon Press.

Gutiérrez, G. 1982. The irruption of the poor in Latin America. In *The challenge of basic Christian communities*, eds. S. Torres and J. Eagleson, 107-123. Maryknoll: Orbis.

Hollenweger, W. J. 1972. *The Pentecostals: The charismatic movement in the churches*. Minneapolis: Augsburg Publishing House.

________. 1986. After twenty years' research on Pentecostalism. *International Review of Mission* (IRM) 75(297): 3-12.

Howard, G. P. 1944. *Religious liberty in Latin America*. Phildadelphia: The Westminster Press.

Idígoras, J. L, SJ. 1991. *La religión fenómeno popular*. Lima, Perú: Ediciones Paulinas.

International Review of Missions. 1932. The missionary significance of the last ten years: A survey. 21: 305-320.

Kirkpatrick, D. ed. 1988. *Faith born in the struggle for life*. Grand Rapids: Eerdmans.

Kuhl, P. E. 1982. *Protestant missionary activity and freedom of religion in Ecuador, Perú and Bolivia*. Ph.D. diss., Southern Illinois University.

Lagos Schuffeneger, H. 1988. *Crisis de la esperanza, religión y autoritarismo en Chile*. Santiago: PRESOR-LAR.

Lalive d'Epinay, C. 1969. *Haven of the masses*. London: Lutterworth Press.

Mackay, J. A. 1935. *That other America*. New York: Macmillan.

________. 1950. *Christianity on the frontier*. New York: Macmillan.

________. 1967. Historical perspectives of Protestantism. In *Integration of man and society in Latin America*, ed. S. Shapiro, 170-190. Notre Dame: Univerity of Notre Dame Press.

Maduro, Otto. 1982. *Religion and social conflict*. Maryknoll: Orbis.

Mainwaring, S. 1986. *The Catholic church and politics in Brazil*. Stanford: Stanford University Press.

________. 1990. Democratization, socioeconomic disintegration, and the Latin American churches after Puebla. In *Born of the poor*, ed. E. Cleary, 143-167. Notre Dame: University of Notre Dame Press.

Martin, D. 1990. *Tongues of fire*. Oxford: Basil Blackwell.

Míguez Bonino, J. 1975. *Doing theology in a revolutionary situation*. Philadelphia: Fortress Press.

________. 1983. *Toward a Christian political ethics*. London: SCM Press.

McCoy, J. 1989. Robbing Peter to pay Paul. *Latinamerica Press* (29 June): 1-8.

Newbigin, L. 1953. *The household of God*. London: SCM.

Núñez, E. A. and W. D. Taylor. 1989. *Crisis in Latin America*. Chicago: Moody Press.

Padilla, R. 1985. *Mission between the times*. Grand Rapids: Eerdmans.

________. 1992. Latin American Evangelicals enter the public square. *Transformation* 9(3) Issue about "Evangelicals and Politics in Latin America." (July-Sept.): 2-7.

Prien, H. J. 1985. *La Historia del Cristianismo en América Latina*. Salamanca: Sígueme.

Read, W. R., V. M. Monterroso, and H. A. Johnson. 1969. *Latin America church growth*. Grand Rapids: Eerdmans.

Rembao, A. 1948. The presence of Protestantism in Latin America. *International Review of Mission* n.s. 37: 57-70.

Ruiz Guerra, R. 1992. *Hombres nuevos, metodismo y modernización en México*. Mexico: CUPSA.

Rycroft, W. S. 1942. *On this foundation. The Evangelical witness in Latin America.* New York: Friendship Press.

________. 1958. *Religion and faith in Latin America.* Philadelphia: The Westminster Press.

Sepúlveda, J. 1988. Pentecostal theology in the context of the struggle for life. In *Faith born in the struggle for life*, ed. D. Kirkpatrick, 298-318. Grand Rapids: Eerdmans.

________. 1989. Pentecostalism as popular religiosity. *International Review of Mission* 78(309): 80-88.

Stoll, D. 1982. *Fishers of men or founders of an empire? The Wycliffe Bible Translators in Latin America.* London: Zed Press.

________. 1990. *Is Latin America turning Protestant?* Berkeley: University of California Press.

Strachan, K. 1957. *The missionary movement of the non-historical groups in Latin America.* New York: Committee of Cooperation in Latin America.

Valcárcel, E. 1972. *Tempestad en los Andes*. 2nd ed. Lima: Ed. Universo.

Vallier, I. 1970. *Catholicism, social control and modernization in Latin America.* Englewood Cliffs: Prentice Hall.

Wagner, C. P. 1973. *Look out! The Pentecostals are coming.* Carol Stream, IL: Creation House.

Walls, A. 1985. Culture and coherence in Christian history. *Evangelical Review of Theology* 9(35): 214-225.

________. 1987. The Christian tradition in today's world. In *Religion in today's world*, ed. F. Whaling, 76-109. Edinburgh: T. and T. Clark.

Westmier, K-W. 1986. *Reconciling heaven and earth.* The Transcendental enthusiasm and growth of an urban Protestant community, Bogotá, Colombia. Berne: Verlag Perter Lang.

Wiarda, H. J., ed. 1992. *Politics and social change in Latin America. Still a distinct tradition?* Third ed. Boulder: Westview Press.

Willems, E. 1964. Protestantism and cultural change in Brazil and Chile. In *Religion, revolution and reform*, eds. W. V. D'Antonio and F. B. Pike, 93-108. New York: Praeger.

________. *Followers of the new faith: Culture change and the rise of Protestantism in Brazil and Chile.* Nashville: Vanderbilt University Press, 1967.

Yutzis, M. 1970. The Revolutionary process and Latin American Christianity. *Lutheran Quarterly* 22(1): 11-28.

EXPLANATIONS FOR PROTESTANT GROWTH

Chapter 2

Gender Relations and Social Change in Latin American Evangelicalism

David A. Smilde

Insofar as women participate in greater numbers than men in all forms of Latin American religion, from indigenous and African religions to traditional Catholic churches and Catholic base communities (see Drogus 1992), the numerical predominance of women in Evangelicalism is not unexpected. Nevertheless, this numerical predominance deserves attention for two reasons. First, in trying to understand Evangelical growth in Latin America, it makes sense to look at it from the experience of those who constitute a majority of the converts: women. Second, insofar as the conservative, often patriarchal character of Evangelical religion seems inimical to what we commonly think of as women's liberation, we need a more profound understanding of the experience of these women to understand this movement.

In this chapter, I do not aspire to explain the movement as such, nor do I examine a specific case study. Rather, I wish to provide a sociological framework through which we might better understand the "elective affinity" of Evangelicalism to Latin American women[1] in certain circumstances. I will use "Evangelicalism," interchangeably with "Pentecostalism," and "charismatic Christianity," and follow the definition of Evangelical beliefs given by Stoll: "(1) the complete reliability and final authority of the Bible, (2) the need to be saved through a personal relation with Jesus Christ, often experienced in terms of being 'born again,' and (3) the importance of spreading this message of salvation to every nation and person, a duty often referred to as the Great Commission" (Stoll 1990, 3). My analysis of the movement is divided into three parts. The first section looks at general treatments of authority and power in gender relations and applies them to Latin American societies past and present. The argument developed there is that despite the tendency for males and male activities to be the loci of status and power, within traditional Latin America peasant society there has been a relatively even balance of power between men and women; that these gender relations have been changing along with the social and economic transformations affecting the lower strata of Latin American society; and that these changes lead to several problems that particularly affect women. Theologian Ernst Troeltsch's classic treatment of the "dual ethic" of Christianity provides the framework for the second section which uses case studies to reveal the way Evangelicalism's ideology and forms of participation can ameliorate problems that result from changing gender relations. In the third section we compare the long-term impact of this process with the Second Great Awakening in nineteenth century United States.

The Gender Division of Labor, Authority, and Power in Processes of Economic Change

As a first step we need to try to understand the striking ubiquity of the fact that "male, as opposed to female, activities are always recognized as predominately important, and cultural systems give authority and value to the roles and activities of men" (Rosaldo 1974, 19). The root of this phenomenon, maintains anthropologist Michelle Rosaldo, lies in the form of social and cultural organization that tends to result from the biological differences of men and women.[2] The fact that a large part of a woman's

[1] As these needs are framed as much by men's behavior as by women's, I have used "gender relations" in the title.

[2] Rosaldo's theory may be criticized for it's universal scope. It should be remembered, however, that she considers it to be a series of empirical generalizations rather than logical deductions. Regardless of whether she is empirically accurate on this universal level, I am using it only insofar as it seems to accurately portray relevant aspects of Latin American societies.

adult life is spent giving birth to and rearing children leads to a differentiation of "domestic" and "public" spheres. While women are generally given a social role by their age or relationship to men and engage in child-rearing activities and the biological maintenance of life, men define and interact in groups, statuses, and hierarchies that cut across domestic lines, constitute the public social structure, and fashion the system of public cultural symbols (Rosaldo 1974, 24).

The nature of this social and cultural sphere, says Rosaldo, is such that there is more room for variation (see also Berger and Luckmann 1966, 47ff; Geertz 1973, 45-46) in its construction than in the methods of child-rearing and biological maintenance; witness the relative diversity of the former versus the relative similarity of the latter in cross-cultural comparisons. The definition of the public sphere on the basis of male experiences and needs affects the way women are perceived. "Since women must work within a social system that obscures their goals and interests, they are apt to develop ways of seeing, feeling, and acting that seem to be 'intuitive' and unsystematic..." (Rosaldo 1974, 30).

Thus, Rosaldo sees women's general lack of authority and status arising from the division of labor in two ways. First, perception of status is contained in symbol systems that are publicly constructed and maintained. As such symbol systems are defined by men, they tend to favor the status of men (see for instance Chafetz 1991, Huber 1991). Secondly, as the considerable power that women often exercise takes place within public social and cultural structures that obscure their interests, they will often not follow approbated paths. As a result, they are often seen as deviant, manipulative, or anomalous.

The result of these tendencies is a seemingly universal asymmetry in cultural evaluation. "Women may be important, powerful, and influential, but it seems that, relative to men of their age and social status, women everywhere lack generally recognized and culturally valued authority" (Rosaldo 1974, 17). However, Rosaldo distinguishes between *power*, the ability to get others to follow your desires, and *authority*, the legitimate holding of power. While she concentrates on women's lack of "generally recognized and culturally valued authority" she understands that "male authority might be mitigated, and, perhaps rendered almost trivial, by the fact that women...may have a good deal of informal influence and *power*" (Rosaldo 1974, 21; see also Lamphere 1974).

Others have taken up this distinction between "culturally valued authority" and "informal influence and power" as it comes into play in gender relations and carefully analyzed its elements. Carole Rogers (1975) maintains that men and women have roughly equal measures of power in peasant societies characterized by the following six conditions:

1. Men are occupied with extra-domestic activities and have access to formal societal rights and positions.
2. Women are primarily associated with the domestic sphere.
3. The domestic sphere is of central importance in the given society.
4. Most important interactions are face-to-face in which informal relationships and authority are at least as important as formalized relationships and authority.
5. Men and women are approximately equally dependent on each other.
6. Men's activities are given more esteem (Rogers 1975, 729-730).[3]

Rogers is writing about rural France, but these conditions can be nicely applied to the "household economy," or traditional division of labor in Latin American hacienda or peasant society. While a number of suitable frameworks could be used, I will use this one throughout the rest of the section to analyze the changes gender relations have undergone in Latin America's economic development.

(1 & 2) In the traditional "household economy" of Latin America, men work in the fields, work for and have contact with the patron, sell their services with animals and implements: plowing, loading, and transporting. Women maintain the home, take care of the animals, keep gardens, prepare agricultural produce, such as shucking corn and making dairy products, and, of course, rear the children. While men are more likely to fill formal posts in the politics or religion of the community, women often assume the responsibility for many aspects of these forms of association (Rothstein 1983, 19).

(3) Peasant communities are "domestically oriented" insofar as this is the realm over which they actually have control and efficacy. Their channels of political power often have little effect on the government policies that affect them: farm prices, taxes, social security, and so on. In addition, peasants are often distrustful of any social institution that operates beyond the level of the immediate neighborhood (Torres 1970, 506-512; Rogers 1975, 745). Rogers summarizes, "If, as is clearly true in most peasant societies, the family is the most significant social unit, then the private rather than the public sector is the sphere in which relative attribution of power is the most important" (Rogers 1975, 734). It is here that women tend to have the most power, significantly contributing, at times controlling, decisions regarding family production and the allocation of family resources.

(4) Above the household level, it is the frequent, intimate, personal, informal contacts on the village level that are most important (Torres 1970, 504). The typical routine of women has them in the neighborhood throughout

[3] I have altered Rogers' formulation for concision and clarity in the following presentation, but all six of her essential elements are present and used in the same way.

the day and in frequent contact with each other in the course of their ordinary activities. They are in a position in which they can monitor and sanction behavior, and disseminate information. Torres summarizes for the case of Colombia, "The neighborhood and the family constitute the most efficient institutions for social control within present [peasant] society. The approval or disapproval of the neighborhood has a great influence on the behavior of the peasant" (Torres 1970, 507).

(5 & 6) "Virtually everywhere," writes Rogers on peasant society, "it is observed that male and female peasants perform very different, but equally essential and mutually interdependent tasks" (Rogers 1975, 744; see also Rothstein 1983; Brusco 1986b). Women's position tends to give them as much or more *de facto* power as men. Yet, "the fact remains," she writes, "that high prestige *does* accrue to these male activities, whether they are actually 'important' or not" (Rogers 1975, 746). She terms this the "myth of male dominance." Rogers writes that peasant men and women do not try to overthrow the myth because they each get what they want. The myth "gives the latter [men] the *appearance* of power and control over all sectors of village life, while at the same time giving to the former [women] *actual* power over those sectors of life in the community which may be controlled by villagers" (729). The myth of male dominance and the relative equality of power can persist as long as the above conditions exist.

Of course, these conditions change with social and economic changes. Different combinations of changes alternately tilt the scale of power and autonomy towards males or females. The social and economic changes that Latin America has experienced have complex implications for gender relations. The following brief description should suffice to explain how such changes affect gender relations in the classes most highly represented among Evangelicals.

Since the end of World War II the most important demographic characteristic of Latin American development has been mass "urbanization," taken to mean not only mass migration to and concentration in urban centers, but "the spread of [urban] lifestyles and the technology and conditions that make them possible into the rural hinterland" (Butterworth and Chance 1981, ix). Capitalization of agriculture in rural areas has resulted in the decline of self-sufficiency and concomitant expropriation of renter's land or purchasing of peasant plots. These changes, plus rapid population increase, generate a rural proletariate of wage laborers, many of whom migrate to the urban centers where, of course, industrial growth is radically insufficient to absorb them. In the urban centers the net effect is an increase in the size of the population in the "informal," or "small-scale" sector. The work in this sector tends to be temporary and unstable, entailing shifts from ill-equipped workshop to petty-merchandizing to selling services, etc. (Roberts 1978, 120-22). The rapid turnover of work engagements and the fact that job opportunities must be scouted out weeks in advance of the current job end produces an atmosphere of perpetual job hunt (Roberts 1978, 129). The highly competitive environment and low margins of profit limit possibilities of rapid improvement (124). The implications for gender relations can be broken down using Rogers' schema.

(1 & 2) Kristina Bohman (1984) identifies three characteristics of male employment in this environment. First, men generally need to be engaged in several different kinds of activities at the same time. Second, unemployment or underemployment is a constant prospect and reality. Third, occupations tend to be fluid over time, that is, men move in and out of different economic activities over the course of a life time. For women, Bohman found that while being a housewife was still the cultural ideal, more than two thirds had outside remunerated activities. Others have found percentages as high as 80% (Perlman 1976, 153). In addition, it has been shown that, in general, the poorer the social stratum, the less gender inequality in earnings (Neuhouser 1989, 689).

(3) The domestic sphere becomes less important for production (Brusco 1986b, 152-153). Yet important aspects of economic survival, such as food preparation, still take place in the home. Neuhouser also points out that the gender division of labor gives women control over the most important material possessions of the family, such as appliances and the house itself.

(4) Despite the diminishing importance of the home as an economically productive unit, networks and informal contacts are of utmost importance. The volatility of the small-scale economy makes family and friendship networks of trust essential for information on jobs and assistance in time of scarcity (Roberts 1978, 128). Thus the traditional image of the socially isolated rural-urban migrant is, for the most part, inaccurate. Neighborhood and city-wide networks are quickly formed and maintained for help and information. And here, as in rural areas, women are at the center of such networks and use them more effectively than men (Bohman 1984, ch.11).

(5) Men and women are no longer interdependent to the degree they were in the peasant economy insofar as their tasks are less complementary. More than before, they perform similar remunerated tasks. However, those on the lower end of the social scale are in a sense mutually dependent because it is difficult to survive without pooling incomes (Neuhouser 1989, 694).

(6) Under the pressure of these economic changes, the myth of male dominance, comes under serious strain. The behavior of males whose efficacy, dominance, and importance is challenged day after day is one of the principal sources of gender problems and conflict. In her work on Haiti, Karen McCarthey Brown (1991) gives a felicitous description of the effect these socio-economic changes have on men in contrast with women. She notes that market women are called *Madan Sara* after the black finches of the

island, the female species of which will work herself into exhaustion hunting for food to feed her young. She contrasts this to male adjustment.

> Men and women have different ideas about what constitutes dignified labor, and these differences affect their economic and social roles. Whereas women draw on the *Madan Sara* model for a style of earning a living that depends on constant work, high energy, and the ability to exploit several small and often erratic sources of income simultaneously, men usually find it demeaning to emulate the *Madan Sara*, and they consequently have less flexibility in weaving an economic safety net than women do (Brown 1991, 158).

Men, says Brown, are caught in a double bind. "They are still reared to exercise power and authority, although they have few resources with which to do so. When their expectations run up against a wall of social impossibility, men often veer off in unproductive directions" (Brown 1991, 235). These "unproductive directions" often sap already scarce resources from a man's family commitment. John Burdick shows that residents of the urban periphery in Brazil are unanimous in their view that compared to the rural areas from which many of them migrated, there is more tension within their households. Two of the major issues are "the threat to male authority represented by urban unemployment," and "the heightened competition for expenditures between the male prestige sphere, on the one hand, and children's education and the insecure urban household, on the other" (Burdick 1990, 156).

The complex of male behavior described in these accounts is commonly referred to as *machismo*. Perhaps the most careful analysis of *machismo* has come from Elizabeth Brusco. Traditionally, the ideal male has been the man who effectively provides for the family and who through his courage is in control of all situations that effect it. The fluctuating, unstable capitalist economy precludes this sense of control among those in the lower rung of the work force, thereby impeding the development of the "positive" traits of the male ideal. The traits of ideal manliness are traded for the characteristics of "*machismo*." Courage becomes exaggerated aggressiveness and intransigence in male to male relations; effectiveness and control becomes sexual aggressiveness and condescension in male to female relationships (Brusco 1986b, 140). Status acquisition for males becomes individualistic. The classic example is the male spending the family budget drinking at the *cantina* talking of his sexual prowess, perhaps falling into violence (Brusco 1986b, 137-138; Bohman 1984). As Rosaldo states, "failure [of men] to perform as providers and symbols of status" may undermine their relationship to the family (Rosaldo 1974, 26).

In sum, part of the process of social and economic change in Latin America is a change in gender relations. This leaves women with two problems. First, while their situation demands greater autonomy on their part, they lack cultural legitimation for these activities. Second, *machismo* can seriously undermine a family's economic well-being. Both problems are matters of great urgency for Latin American women.

Gender and the Dual Ethic of Christianity in Latin American Evangelicalism

Historian and theologian Ernst Troeltsch (1931) has argued that Christian monotheism contains competing conservative and revolutionary elements. On one hand, it is revolutionary insofar as it transcends "the world" and therefore "will possess and reveal the radicalism of an ethical and universal ideal in face of all existing conditions" (Troeltsch 1931, 85). This, writes Troeltsch, is the first and most outstanding sociological characteristic of Christianity, its unlimited, unqualified individualism and equality, based on the individual call to fellowship with a transcendent God and the eternal value of the individual soul (55). On the other hand, it has a conservative element,

> just because it is a religious faith which believes that the whole world and its order is being guided by God, in spite of devils and demons, just because it means submission to the Will of God who predestinates and allows all kinds of human differences to exist, it can never be a principle of revolution (Troeltsch 1931, 85).

Non-religious institutions that embody inequality, insofar as they do not rely on openly sinful foundations, might be accepted as divinely ordained with equality relegated to the religious sphere (Troeltsch 1931, 75). Even further, worldly inequality may be given a positive value as the arena in which religious equality receives special stimulus. Thus, belief in a God of love who radically transcends the world can lead the statuses, hierarchies, and differences of this world to be seen as distinctions to be overcome in union with the Other, or as the divinely ordained order in which Christian love and equality is carried out. At root the tension is a sociological version of the problem of theodicy: all humans are equal before God, but what attitude is to be taken toward inequality in this world? Does the reason for its existence lie in the sin of humans or the will of God? (74). These are the stubborn problems of Christianity which have not merely produced difficult theological problems, writes Troeltsch, "They have also become basic coefficients...of social thought which have lasted for centuries" (73). And they find solutions not merely by argument, but by the weight of social conditions and imperatives.

The poles of Troeltsch's revolutionary-conservative opposition can be exemplified, respectively, by the egalitarianism of the Primitive Church and the hierarchical character of the medieval Roman Catholic Church. However, it must be remembered that these are not logical opposites but poles on a continuum that may, and usually do, co-exist in tenuous compromise. For example, while Pauline Christianity preserves many radical elements, such as manifestations of spiritual power, it also displays a conservative tendency toward "Christian patriarchalism," the willing acceptance of existing inequalities as the arena within which to carry out ethical personal relationships (Troeltsch 1931, 78).

This conservative attitude is expressed in Paul's view of the family. Troeltsch writes,

> The existing patriarchalism, with the predominance of the husband, is accepted as the natural order, and submission to it is demanded as an ethical duty....The wife and the child, ...are regarded as equal to the husband and the freeman in the religious and moral realm, and this actually, even if not in the eyes of the law, deepens and spiritualizes the whole of family life (Troeltsch 1931, 81).

In the following section, the guiding thought is that Latin American Evangelicalism represents a move away from traditional Catholicism *towards* Troeltsch's "revolutionary" pole, albeit not in its most radical form (Troeltsch 1931, 433, n. 164). This move can be seen in three areas: the domestic sphere, sexual relations, and participation within the church.

The Domestic Sphere

Forms of Christianity that lean toward the revolutionary pole have a tendency to accord greater esteem to the domestic sphere. Hannah Arendt (1958) argues that in the ancient world Christianity was instrumental in reversing the values attached to the public and private realms. Rather than a realm of "privation" that existed for the sole purpose of reproducing and sustaining humans for activity in the public realm, among early Christians the household became the sphere of primary importance to which political activity was merely a means (Arendt 1958, 60). Because of the eschatological focus of early Christianity, the construction of objects that would endure in this world was seen as a vanity that detracted from true faith. Christianity avoided manifestations that could possibly lead to an "earthly immortality," thereby diminishing the importance of the public sphere (see also Elshtain 1981; ch.2). Troeltsch states well the paradox of its impact:

> For the conservative attitude was not founded on love and esteem for the existing institutions, but upon a mixture of contempt, submission, and relative recognition. That is why, inspite of all its submissiveness, Christianity did destroy the Roman State by alienating souls from its ideals, and it has a

> disintegrating effect upon all undiluted nationalism and upon every form of exclusively earthly authority (Troeltsch 1931, 82).

In Latin America as well, Evangelicalism valorizes the domestic sphere.

Above we looked at the problem of *machismo* as a result of men being unable to fulfill the traits of ideal manliness. Key to understanding these ideals of masculinity in the case of Latin America is the idea of *honor*, the estimation of one's worth in terms of a society's values.[4] In terms of honor, *masculinity* means authority over the family, the desire for precedence, the refusal to submit to humiliation, and the willingness to defend reputation. Peristiany says "honour is at the apex of the pyramid of temporal social values and it conditions their hierarchical order" (Peristiany 1966, 10). As honor is an estimation of one's worth in the world, obvious lack of esteem from, and efficacy in, the world can lead to *machismo* as outlined above. Conversion to Evangelicalism leads to an ideological[5] movement away from temporal, societal standards of value through "the melting down of earthly smallness and worldliness in the Fire of the Divine Love" (Troeltsch 1931, 56). Evangelicalism allows the male to step out of the position in which he loses face for his lack of efficacy in the public world, and into a situation in which he gains status by simply providing for his family as well as he possibly can. It *erodes* the separation of male and female spheres, championing the household as the locus of status-acquisition for both sexes (Brusco 1986b, 197).

In a monograph on Pentecostalism in Colombia, Cornelia Butler Flora likewise argues that Evangelicalism valorizes the domestic sphere, and she gives data to support her case. While she found no evidence of greater material success among Pentecostals, she found some striking patterns of consumption (see Table 2.1). The data, argues Flora, show a greater orientation towards the household among Pentecostals. Ownership of a radio, she maintains, indicates a degree of orientation to the outside world, while ownership of a dining room table means the family eats together rather than the more typical pattern of the individual taking the meal from the stove when

[4] One must exercise caution in generalizing from Mediterranean to Latin American societies as Levine points out (Levine 1992, 327). I think it justified to make this move insofar as I accept Pitt-Rivers' view that "honor" possesses a general structure which gets appropriated in particular ways in different societies (Pitt-Rivers 1966, 21). It is certainly recognizable in Latin America.

[5] I use the term "ideological" because while Evangelicals explicitly come out against societal standards of value, the norms and values they develop are usually those of "bourgeois respectability" (see Willems 1967).

ready and eating alone (Flora 1976, 221; on eating patterns see also Willems 1967, 172).

The family structure that develops in Pentecostalism is, as Troeltsch calls it, a "Christian Patriarchalism" that reasserts the place of the male as the God

Table 2.1 Consumption Patterns

Item	% of **Catholic** Households Possessing:	% of **Pentecostal** Households Possessing:
1. Radio	96.6	66.3
2. Television	6.5	2.5
3. Sewing machine	64.4	56.3
4. Electric or gas stove	17.2	21.3
5. Set of Living room furniture	28.8	42.5
6. Dining room table	47.5	82.5

(Flora 1976, 222-23).

ordained head of the family. Flora writes that Pentecostal households are characterized by men who dominate and by women who believe this is the way it should be. Even women who are active in the life of the church are expected to fulfill their household duties first, then their religious ones (Flora 1976, 199). In research on lower-class urban Pentecostals in Sicily, a situation quite similar to the Latin American case, Salvatore Cucchiari maintains that the notion of "family" they champion looks much like the traditional Sicilian family, which the members understand as God-ordained. However, Cucchiari points out that despite emphasis on the patriarchal family as God-ordained, these Pentecostals emphasize that all members are equals before God. "This egalitarian sense of family," says Cucchiari, "is reflected in the redemptive dogma of Sicilian Pentecostalism, in which men and women come before God as abstract 'souls' shorn of all hierarchical social identities, including gender" (Cucchiari 1990, 696; for Colombia see Bohman 1984,

298). These internal contradictions between conservative and revolutionary tendencies permit negotiation about the specifics of gender relations.[6]

While this reaffirmation of Christian patriarchalism is hardly what we normally consider women's liberation, it should be understood on its own terms. Michelle Rosaldo argues that there are three ways in which women's situation can be improved. First, women may take on men's roles. However, "Women in men's roles" she says, "constitute an elite segment of female humanity." Alternately, "women may win power and value by stressing their differences from men. By accepting and elaborating upon the symbols and expectations associated with their cultural definition, they may goad men into compliance, or establish a society unto themselves." Lastly, women's situation can improve when societies "place positive value on the conjugal relationship and the involvement of both men and women in the home..." (Rosaldo 1974, 39). In Latin America, Evangelicalism functions to improve women's lot primarily in the two these ways.

Sexuality

The ideal of feminine spirituality and purity that developed in medieval Catholic Europe reached its apex in Latin America. The term *Marianismo* denotes the secular cultural constructions surrounding the veneration of the Virgin Mary. Evelyn Stevens defines it as "the cult of feminine spiritual superiority, which teaches that women are semi-divine, morally superior to and spiritually stronger than men" (Stevens 1973, 91). Women are characterized by abnegation, and "infinite capacity for humility and sacrifice" (94). In addition, the ideal "dictates not only premarital chastity for all women, but postnuptial frigidity" (96). Good women neither seek sex nor enjoy it.

While traditionally the Marian image has provided women a modicum of respect and power within the household, it currently encourages a destructive double standard for men's behavior. The harmful sequence of male intemperance, violence, and infidelity, met with female long-suffering and resignation, is expected by both parties and society at large. In addition, the ideal of female frigidity makes it not unexpected that males will pursue passion outside of their conjugal relationship.

[6] We should not think however, that women who become Evangelical simply make a "trade off," accepting the patriarchal elements in exchange for the beliefs in individual charisma and equality. It is well documented that, around the globe, women have been actively engaged in the revival of religious traditionalism that contain no charismatic element (for an overview see Hardacre 1993).

The intolerance of Evangelicals for the double standard of male and female sexual behavior is well known (see Willems 1967, 169ff). Brusco points out that, in addition, there is an important redefinition of conjugal sexuality. She notes that a basic text used by Evangelicals for discussing sexuality and marital relations is Paul's first letter to the Corinthians which teaches that humans by nature desire sex, and that reproduction is the primary goal of neither sex nor marriage (Brusco 1986b, 194-197).

In the seventh chapter of I Cornninthians, Paul gives an "eminently practical" argument against both libertainism and undue continence (see Verhey 1984, 117-118). He writes that each person has gifts from God, but not everyone has the gift of celibacy. It is better not to marry and to stay celibate, "but if they cannot control themselves, they should marry, for it is better to marry than to burn with passion" (I Corinthians 7:9). Thus, Evangelicalism simultaneously serves to remoralize sexual behavior and to champion sexual desire as an important part of marriage. Together these changes undermine important aspects of *machismo* and contribute to a renewed focus of both members on the conjugal bond.

Associational Participation

Max Weber long ago noted the equality given to women in charismatic religion when their "pneumatic manifestations of charisma are valued as hallmarks of specifically religious exaltation" (Weber 1968, 489). He states:

> The great receptivity of women to all religious prophecy except that which is exclusively military and political in orientation comes to very clear expression in the completely unbiased relationships with women maintained by practically all prophets, the Buddha as well as Christ and Pythagoras (Weber 1968, 489).

Cornelia Flora shows how the ideology of spiritual equality has moved Colombian women into roles previously unavailable to them (Flora 1976, 195). In her study she found that almost all Pentecostal churches have women's organizations while only about half of the Catholic churches do. In the Pentecostal organizations women, often for the first time, take part in organizing and leading prayer meetings and proselytism. Often they travel to other parts of the country on church functions (195-196). Here as elsewhere there are both "conservative and revolutionary tendencies;" the ideal of the priesthood of all believers competes with formal patriarchalism. Women's participation in religious activities can coexist with the most conscious domination of formal authority by men. Cucchiari notes that in Sicilian Pentecostalism, women exercise much influence and receive esteem for their charismatic manifestations. The religious roles of women are acceptable because of the way they are defined:

> Women are said to have 'gifts' but not 'ministries:' they may have the 'gift of Evangelism' but not be evangelists, have the 'gift of the Word' but not be preachers, have the 'gift of prophecy' but not be prophets...however, the gift/ministry distinction is a fiction when used to distinguish what established prophetesses do from what their male counterparts do (Cucchiari 1990, 694).

Cucchiari argues that the gift/ministry distinction defines an arena of struggle over the definition of patriarchy, "of which the two fixed boundaries are that men will have formal authority and that women will not be excluded from important religious roles" (Cucchiari 1990, 695). In my own fieldwork I have seen how even these boundaries can be negotiated. In Caracas, Venezuela, I met a middle-aged woman who became a Pentecostal pastor after she felt the spirit had called her. Originally, "Elena"[7] intended to carry out her mission within her church; however, the male pastor would not allow it. There was, she explained, no recourse other than to start her own church. This church is now quite successful and she is a respected member of the Caracas community of Pentecostal pastors. Indeed I met her at a conference of Evangelical pastors where she was treated like every other pastor. She related to me what she tells the girls and women of her church: "Never hope to become a pastor for that is the job of a man. However, if you are called by God to do so, you have no choice" (Smilde 1992).

Continuity and Change in the Turn to Evangelicalism

As mentioned above, the predominance of women in Latin American Evangelicalism bears much continuity with their predominance in all Latin American religion. The Virgin Mary is perhaps the most important role model for Latin American Catholic women (Bohman 1984, 295). Kristina Bohman argues that *La Virgen* is a polysemous symbol the interpretation of which depends on the actual conditions of women. Among the lower classes, the Virgin is believed to receive her power from God the Father for her unconditional willingness to take suffering upon her self as the most obedient servant of God (305). Bohman describes the role of the Virgin and her cult for women in the Colombian barrio she studied as follows:

> The Virgin is thus the exemplary believer, who obeys even when she does not understand -- she is an ideal for women who should learn to *aguantar* (endure), show *paciencia* [patience] and have faith in God who will finally reward their suffering if not on this earth then in the after-life.
>
> The Virgin is said to 'speak to the heart' and her cult is suffused with mystical dimensions. Some women relate how they become transposed to an

[7] Names of all Evangelical leaders have been changed.

> other-worldly reality when praying to her -- they go into ecstasies when contemplating her suffering or when they invoke her as the all-knowing and all-forgiving great Mother (Bohman 1984, 305-306).

In traditional Catholicism, these feminine ideals and forms of religiosity are indeed respected, but in the official cult they are, as Troeltsch would say, "mere factors in the system," not "ruling principles" (Troeltsch 1931, 336). Troeltsch writes that the more the Church attempts to become a universal church in control of great masses of people, the more Christianity becomes an institutional form and less a subjective form:

> The more that Christendom renounced the life of this supernatural and eschatological fulfillment of its universal ideal, and tried to achieve this end by missionary effort and organization, the more it was forced to make its Divine and Christian character independent of the *subjective* character and service of believers; henceforth it sought to concentrate all its emphasis upon the *objective* possession of religious truth and religious power (Troeltsch 1931, 335).

In official Catholicism, the "subjective" elements that are associated with "female," as outlined above, have not been ruling principles. Speaking of the beliefs of Colombian Catholicism, Bohman says

> These ideas sustain the notion that women and men are basically very different kinds of human beings. Men and women should complement one another, but they could never 'be the same.' The barrio priest, in his 'classes for married couples' elaborates on this view and teaches that 'the man is the head of the family, the woman is the heart.' Although each organ is said to be equally essential for the functioning of the body, the head is the superior one for 'it reasons and decides' (Bohman 1984, 306).

In Latin American Evangelicalism, where "blessed are the meek" is, in essence, preached at every service and a spiritual, emotional faith is propagated as the norm, these "feminine" qualities are no longer secondary factors typifying women but become ruling principles for all. While there might still be a good deal of patriarchalism, spiritual equality, the "sameness" of "God's children," is at the center of the Evangelical message (see Bohman 1984, 298).

Brusco points out that part of the Marian role is the female as reformer of the male. Bohman finds that while women do voice opposition to some of the misogynic tendencies of their social setting, their complaints are mainly directed against "abuses within the system," with little questioning of the basic system of sexual differentiation (Bohman 1984, 294). Evangelicalism appeals to such women as it does not attempt to overthrow the system but rather undermines the ideals of *machismo*, remoralizes the male ideal, and refocuses the male on the household. Brusco describes a typical sequence in which the woman reformer seeks out Evangelical groups and then tries to get her man to come. She concludes that Evangelicalism in Colombia can be seen as "a 'strategic' women's movement, aimed at fundamentally altering sex role behavior," or "an intensely pragmatic movement aimed at reforming those aspects of society which most affect their lives" (Brusco 1986b, 221; see also Brusco 1986a).[8]

While it certainly is correct to highlight these pragmatic aspects, they should not be reduced to "strategic action." In recent fieldwork in Colombia and Venezuela, I met only a few Evangelicals, male or female, who had followed the ideal sequence Brusco lays out: woman converts, becomes member of church and then prods male into attendance. I did meet many women who had suffered from *machismo*. Most, however, were still without a husband though many had varying degrees of hope for his return (Smilde 1992).[9]

A more complex understanding of religion can be of some help here. As Leslie Gill (1990) argues in her work on Bolivia, not only does Pentecostalism modify aspects of male behavior harmful to women, it "is a means by which these women reinterpret past gender-based problems, as they struggle to identify themselves..." (Gill 1990, 709). In this sense, Evangelical religion may serve the purpose of helping women to understand what happened to them as much as developing a plan for "strategic action." Put differently, the religious problem of suffering is not only how to avoid suffering, but *how* to suffer, how to make pain, loss, and defeat sufferable (Geertz 1973, 104). Defining new gender relations, even for those women who remain alone, can offer an interpretation of what went wrong that helps them to continue on.

[8] The connection between women's involvement in Evangelicalism and their involvement in magical religions and demon possession should also be noted. I.M. Lewis most clearly articulates it in the case of East Africa. He shows the average profile of the woman maligned by spirits "is that of the hard-pressed wife, struggling to survive and feed her children in this harsh environment, and liable to some degree of neglect, real or imagined, on the part of her husband" (Lewis 1989, 67). In his research the affliction provides an opportunity for women to pursue their interests in a context of male dominance, and in some cases obtain a larger slice of the domestic budget. As the woman is subject to an affliction outside of her control, her demands may be met without the husband losing face (see also Brown 1991 on Vodou in Haiti, and Lerch 1982 on Umbanda in Brazil).

[9] It is indicative that in the case history Brusco gives of a woman driven to Evangelicalism, the woman was still in her broken home hoping her husband would come back (Brusco 1986b, 170-180).

The Potential Impact of Protestantism on the Status of Women in Latin America

The rise of Evangelicalism in Latin America has drawn considerable attention from social scientists because of the large role that many of them attribute to Protestantism in the development of democratic political institutions and the capitalist economy (cf. Halevy 1924, 1925; and Weber 1958). In an even closer parallel to the situation in Latin America, many scholars believe that the early nineteenth century U.S. (the Second Great Awakening) spurred greater participation in public life by women and contributed to the rise of the women's rights movement later in the century. That apparent connection suggests the possibility that Latin America's Pentecostal movement might have a similar impact on women there (see Martin 1990, 181).

Women in the Second Great Awakening as a Precedent for Latin America?

The Evangelicalism of the Second Great Awakening pushed an ideology of domesticity that represented an expansion of women's roles. Women were to be the moral backbone of the family and "the guardians of traditional Christian virtues such as service and self-sacrifice" (Marsden 1990, 83). It was a logical step for them to join the moral reform movements. "Ideologically, this new activity was inherent in the conception of separate spheres: if women were to be effective guardians of the home and its morality, then they might well find it necessary to act in the world in order to protect the home and to preserve its morality" (Degler 1980, 298).

Prayer meetings of women developed into social and benevolent societies. Few men objected to them as long as they stayed well within the "female" sphere; however, as Degler notes, "the moral character of these early benevolent societies and concerns encouraged women who worked in them to slip over into activities with a stronger aura of social reform about them" (Degler 1980, 302). The social cause that first animated women was the abolition movement. The form and spirit of the revival meetings, formerly used to save souls, was now applied to the antislavery campaign. The appeal they made was Evangelical: the "moral conquest of the world" (Rossi 1974, 261ff). Not long afterward, the first meeting for women's rights in America was held in a Methodist church in Seneca Falls, New York. Alice Rossi provides convincing evidence of the overlapping membership of revival groups, abolition and temperance movements, and women's rights groups. Says Rossi, "The crusading zeal stimulated by the religious revivals had been expressed in the abolition cause, and within a short time it flowed into the movement to expand women's rights" (Rossi 1974, 263). Rossi summarizes the influence of revivalism by saying:

> The women who attended the first woman's rights meetings in 1848, at Seneca Falls in July and at Rochester in August, were not novices to meetings of this kind. While the topic was a new one for many, most of those attracted to the cause of woman's rights had been active in other reform movements themselves, or they had grown up in families where such movements were discussed and often supported by their parents. Revival and temperance meetings in the 1820s and abolition societies in the 1830s paved the way for woman's rights conventions in the 1840s and 1850s (Rossi 1974, 274).

Revivalism provided patterns which women followed to channel discontent into social organization.

One cannot help noticing some striking similarities between nineteenth century American revivalism and in the current Evangelical movement in Latin America (Ryan 1981, 1978; and Cott 1977). Could the "logic of participation" provide a base for greater associational participation on the part of Latin American women as it did for women in the nineteenth century United States? David Martin argues in *Tongues of Fire* (1990) that changes which would not initially be accepted on the societal level can sometimes take place in the realm of culture, then gain autonomy, solidify, and have an influence on society. This possibility is consistent with Max Weber's theory of charisma. In ideal form, "charisma transforms all values and breaks all traditional and rational norms" and "shapes material and social conditions according to its revolutionary will" (Weber 1968, 1115-1116) though he emphasized that the actual impact of the novel cultural formulations depends on the social and cultural context.

Weber argued that the principle that the sexes are equal before God may become equality in fact during a period of charisma. But when the charismatic outbreak begins to subside, "when the tide that lifted a charismatically led group out of everyday life flows back into the channels of workaday routines," charismatic forms of authority will wane and become institutionalized, sometimes forming new structures, often falling back into old ones (Weber 1968, 1121). Consequently, it is common for the religious equality women achieve to evaporate if the charismatic movement becomes institutionalized in traditional patriarchal structures. Says Weber:

> ... only in very rare cases does this practice (unbiased relationships) continue beyond the first stage of a religious community's formation, when the pneumatic manifestations of charisma are valued as hallmarks of specifically religious exaltation (Weber 1968, 489).

Thus, to speculate about the potential significance of this charismatic movement, we need to consider both the ideology that develops out of it and the social settings of its carriers.

Ideological Differences

Both nineteenth century North American revivalists and twentieth century Latin American Evangelicals justified the participation of women based on the "priesthood of believers." If what is most important about a person is his or her relationship to God, then whether that person is male or female is of little importance. But there may be a subtle difference between the two movements in their attitude toward the preponderance of women. Degler writes about the Second Great Awakening, "Not surprisingly, churchmen liked the interest women showed in religion, and they recognized and praised the affinity. Many believed women had a special gift for religion and morality" (Degler 1980, 299). It was part of thc developing ideology of separate spheres that women were the moral strength of humanity. Thus their preponderance in religion was not seen as an aberration, but as evidence of their moral superiority.

In Latin America, on the other hand, there is a tendency to expect, or hope, that the numerical preponderance of women is a temporary phenomena. In my own field work, interviews with Evangelical leaders revealed this attitude. When asked why so many more women than men come to the Evangelical churches, Manuel Arango, leader of an Evangelical umbrella group, answered:

> One of the reasons is that, [laugh] women are less difficult to convince [laugh]. But also because they are more open to the work of God in their lives. And often when we evangelize door to door, women are those at home. They respond more to the campaigns. When there are conflicts on the family level, they more readily seek help. And when a women converts she is more likely to open her mouth to say to another person that she is a new creature in Christ (Smilde 1992).

Jaime Perez, pastor of one of the largest churches in a major Colombian city and a leading Evangelical figure leader, answered the same question.

> On the one hand, there are more women for the reason that it is men who fight wars. Here you see every other day that the guerrillas killed twenty policemen, the army killed twenty guerrillas. These are always men. Thus, naturally, if men are killed, the [relative] number of women increases. On the other hand, there has been a teaching in our Western humanist culture that religion is for the weak. This idea has grown and together with certain sociological circumstances, has led to a feminine tendency in the church. But we are struggling to have a more masculine leadership. Not because we do not recognize the contributions of women, but because the man ought to take his appropriate place (Smilde 1992).

In these two answers we see the presence of some of the elements of the Second Great Awakening's idea of "women's special susceptibility." But there is also an element of happenstance. Men have been killed; women answer the door; religion is seen as for the weak. The predominance of females appears as something to be overcome. It is hoped that when the Evangelical church is more successful and established, there will be as many men as women and the leadership will become more masculine.

A second important aspect of ideology is the attitude it takes towards the world. Martin argues that despite the escapist, privatist ideology of Evangelicalism, a logic of participation develops that later becomes essential in the development of the associations essential to democracy. While this causal sequence is certainly evident and represents a clear parallel between the cases of the Second Great Awakening and current Latin American Evangelicalism, there was clearly less privatism in the Second Great Awakening. From the beginning, the notion of conversion had an outward direction: "...individual salvation was no longer the result of passive patience waiting for the spirit to descend, but of morally responsible contributions to the community through individual efforts or concerted social action." Charles Finney preached that conversion was the result of the right use of God-given abilities and that a convert's faith should be tested through moral reconquest not just of the person but of the world (Rossi 1974, 253-62).

For the most part, this outward direction is absent from Latin American Pentecostalism. Reception of the spirit is seen as conditioned on the moral purity of the individual. Flora shows tht there is little evidence that the expanded options that Pentecostal women experience lead to greater secular participation. Pentecostal women, says Flora, "have learned the self-confidence and organizational skills to be effective in the secular sphere," but see any organization oriented to social change or reform "as reflecting worldly interests and therefore taboo" (Flora 1976, 201-202). Thus Latin American Evangelical women are developing a logic of participation that could provide the basis for change at the social level, but at this point it does not seem to have the outward direction which, as in the Second Great Awakening, makes this a likely possibility.

Class Differences

In research on Jamaican Pentecostals, Diane Austin argues that whether cultural reformulations have a creative impact on social institutions or simply "routinize" with no impact is determined more by the structural location of its carriers than the profundity of the cultural change. In other words, cultural changes are more likely to produce social changes when "the changed" have social power. And here lies perhaps the biggest difference between the women of the Second Great Awakening and those in Latin America's Evangelical churches.

The regions that experienced the Second Great Awakening were undergoing rapid social changes due to prosperity. Those who moved from the revivals to reform movements were small-town, middle-class women, not the women of the more charismatic camp meetings of Kentucky and Tennessee. When the Awakening ended, these women had the free time and the moral authority, in their own and the larger society's minds, to form associations to change society.

In Latin America, Evangelical women are more commonly the marginalized who are fighting for material survival, with little freetime and little prospect for influencing the major institutions of society. It is, therefore, that much less likely that this religious form will provide a base for societal change in a way analogous to the Second Great Awakening.

Reference List

Arendt, H. 1958. *The human condition.* Chicago: University of Chicago Press.

Austin, D. J. 1981. Born again...and again and again: Communitas and social change among Jamaican Pentecostalists. *Journal of Anthropological Research* 37(3): 226-426.

Berger, P. 1990. Forward. In *Tongues of Fire,* D. Martin, vii-xi. Oxford: Basil Blackwell.

Berger, P., and T. Luckmann. 1966. *The social construction of reality: A treatise in the sociology of knowledge.* New York: Anchor Doubleday.

Blumberg, R. L. 1991. *Gender, family, and economy: The triple overlap.* London: Sage Publications.

Bohman, K. 1984. *Woman of the barrio: Class and gender in a Colombian city.* Stockholm: Stockholm Studies in Social Anthropology 13.

Brown, K. McCarthey. 1991. *Mama Lola: A vodoo priestess in Brooklyn.* Berkeley: University of California Press.

Brusco, E. 1986a. Colombian Evangelicalism as a strategic form of women's collective action. *Feminist Issues* Fall: 3-13.

________. 1986b. The household basis of Evangelical religion and the reformation of *machismo* in Colombia. Ph.D. Diss. City University of New York.

Burdick, J. 1990. Gossip and secrecy: Women's articulation of domestic conflict in three religions of urban Brazil. *Sociological Analysis* 50 (2): 153-170.

Butterworth, D., and J. K. Chance. 1981. *Latin American urbanization.* Cambridge: University of Cambridge Press.

Bynam, C. Walker. 1987. *Holy feast and Holy fast: The religious signigicance of food to medieval women.* Berkeley: University of California Press.

Chafetz, J. Saltzman. 1991. The gender division of labor and the reproduction of female disadvantage: Toward an integrated theory. In *Gender, family, and economy: The triple overlap*, ed. Rae Lesser Blumberg. London: Sage Publications.

Cott, N. F. 1977. *The bonds of womanhood: "Woman's sphere" in New England, 1780-1835*. New Haven: Yale University Press.

Cucchiari, S. 1990. Between shame and sanctification: Patriarch and its transformation in Sicilian Pentecostalism. *American Ethnologist* 17(4) (Nov.): 687-707.

Degler, C. 1980. *At odds: Women and the family in America from the revolution to the present*. New York: Oxford University Press.

Drogus, C. A. 1992. Popular movements and the limits of political mobilization at the grassroots in Brazil. In *Conflict and competition: The Latin American church in a changing environment*, eds. E. L. Cleary and H. Stewart-Gambino, 63-86. Boulder: Lynne Rienner Publishers.

Elshtain, B. 1981. *Public man, private woman: Women in social and political thought*. Princeton: Princeton University Press.

Flora, C. Butler. 1976. *Pentecostalism in Colombia*. Cranbury, N.J.: Associate University Presses, Inc.

Geertz, C. 1973. *The interpretation of cultures*. New York: Basic Books.

Gill, L. 1990. "Like a veil to cover them": Women and the Pentecostal movement in La Paz. *American Ethnologist* 17(4) (Nov.): 708-721.

Hardacre, H. 1993. The impact of Fundamentalism on women, the family, and interpersonal relations. In *Fundamentalisms and society: Reclaiming the sciences, the family, and education*, eds. M. Marty and S. Appleby, 129-150. Chicago: University of Chicago Press.

Huber, J. 1991. A theory of family, economy, and gender. In *Gender, family, and economy: The triple overlap*, ed. R. L. Blumberg,. London: Sage Publications.

Lamphere, L. 1974. Strategies, cooperation, and conflict among women in domestic groups. In *Woman, culture and society*, eds. M. S. Rosaldo and L. Lamphere, 97-112. Stanford: Stanford University Press.

Lerch, P. B. 1982. An explanation for the predominance of women in the umbanda cults of Porto Alegre, Brazil. *Urban Athropology* 11(2): 237-261.

Levine, D. H. 1992. *Popular voices in Latin American Catholicism*. Princeton: Princeton University Press.

Lewis, I.M. 1989[1971]. *Ecstatic religion: A study of shamanism and spirit possession*. New York: Routledge.

Marsden, G. M. 1990. *Religion and American culture*. Chicago: Harcourt Brace Jovanovich.

Martin, D. 1990. *Tongues of fire: The explosion of Protestantism in Latin America*. Oxford: Basil Blackwell.

Neuhouser, K. 1989. Sources of women's power and status among the urban poor in contemporary Brazil. *Signs: Journal of Women in Culture and Society*. 14(3): 685-702.

Peristiany, J. G. 1966. *Honour and shame: The values of Mediterranean society*. Chicago: University of Chicago Press.

Perlman, J. 1976. *The myth of marginality*. Berkeley: University of California Press.

Pitt-Rivers, J. 1966. Honour and social status. In *Honour and shame: The values of Mediterranean society*, ed. J. G. Peristiany, 19-77. Chicago: University of Chicago Press.

Roberts, B. R. 1978. *Cities of peasants: The political economy of urbanization in the third world*. Beverly Hills: Sage Publications.

Rogers, S. C. 1975. Female forms of power and the myth of male dominance: A model of female/male interaction in peasant society. *American Ethnologist*. 2: 741-754.

Rosaldo, M. Z. 1974. Woman, culture, and society: A theoretical overview. In *Woman, culture and society*, eds. M. Z. Rosaldo and L. Lamphere, 17-42. Stanford: Stanford University Press.

Rossi, A. S. 1974. *The feminist papers: From Adams to de Beauvoir*. New York: Bantam Books.

Rothstein, F. 1983. Women and men in the family economy: An analysis of the relations between the sexes in three peasant communities. *Anthropological Quarterly* 56(1): 10-23.

Smilde, D. A. 1992. Colombia and Venezuela, Field Notes. Fall.

________. 1978. A woman's awakening: Evangelical religion and the families of Utica, N.Y., 1800-1840. *American Quarterly* 30(2) (Winter): 602-623.

Stevens, E. P. 1973. Marianismo: The other face of machismo in Latin America. In *Female and male in Latin America*, ed. A. Pescatello, Pittsburgh: University of Pittsburgh Press.

Stoll, D. 1990. *Is Latin America turning Protestant? The politics of Evangelical growth.* Berkeley: University of California Press.

Tinker, I. 1990. *Persistant inequalities: Women and world development*. New York: Oxford University Press.

Torres Restrepo, C. 1970. Social change and rural violence in Colombia. In *Masses in Latin America*, ed. I. L. Horowitz, 503-546. New York: Oxford University Press.

Troeltsch, E. [1931] 1992. *The social teachings of the Christian churches*. Olive Wyon transl. Louisville: Westminster/John Knox Press.

Verhey, A. 1984 *The great reversal: Ethics and the New Testament*. Grand Rapids: Eerdmans Publishing Co.

Weber, M. 1958. *The Protestant ethic and the spirit of capitalism*. New York: Charles Scribner's Sons.

________. 1968. *Economy and society*. Berkeley: University of California Press.

Willems, E. 1967. *Followers of the new faith: Culture change and the rise of Protestantism in Brazil and Chile.* Nashville: Vanderbilt University Press.

Chapter 3

Orality and Power in Latin American Pentecostalism

Quentin J. Schultze

In the summer of 1991, I was in Vancouver during the same weekend that North American televangelist Jimmy Swaggart was scheduled to conduct a three day crusade in the city. There was greater than usual media interest in Swaggart's appearance because of the televangelist's recent sex-related scandal. I went to the crusade to see for myself how well the televangelist was surviving the bad publicity. Only about 800 people attended the opening evening service, and in spite of massive leafletting in the city, the small arena was never filled to capacity. Nor did Swaggart discuss his personal problems with the media. By and large, the event was not very newsworthy -- at least not for mainstream media.

In fact, there was an important story behind the Vancouver crusade, though it was outside of the purview of contemporary news investigation. Nearly all of the people attending the crusade were Hispanic. As I sat in the arena, listening to snatches of Spanish conversation among attendees, I felt like I was back in Central America, eavesdropping on people at the market in downtown Guatemala City or at the square in San José. It was a strange situation: a white, old-style Pentecostal from the Southern United States singing a Methodist hymn to a group of Hispanics in a hockey arena in Western Canada.

The cultural incongruities of that event raise many interesting questions. Foremost among them is the reason for the enormous popularity of old-style Pentecostalism in Latin America. According to recent estimates, about 75% of Latin American Protestants are Pentecostal (Núñez and Taylor 1989, 159). Although there are exceptions, the Pentecostal trend in Latin America is clear and highly significant for the region. David Stoll's book *Is Latin America Turning Protestant?* (1990), could have been just as appropriately titled, *Is Latin America Turning Pentecostal?* or, in a global perspective, *Is Protestantism Turning Latin American and Pentecostal?* As Stoll shows, the "third wave" of Evangelical missionary activity in Latin America during the 1960s and '70s was Pentecostal; it rapidly eclipsed 19th-century mainline Protestant missions and even the more recent Evangelical missions (Stoll 1990, 101). The Assemblies of God, Swaggart's own denomination at the time, was the major player in this third wave. By 1984, 9.9 million of the Assemblies' adherents resided in Latin America, primarily Brazil (Stoll 1990, 101, 107). The title of David Martin's excellent work *Tongues on Fire: The Explosion of Protestantism in Latin America* (1990), more clearly captured the Pentecostal impulse in Latin America. Edward Norman has gone so far as to claim that Latin American Pentecostals, unlike the historic Protestant denominations, are the "true" churches of the "disinherited" for those "seeking an alternative either to Catholicism or to the radical secular politics...." (Norman 1981, 67). Similarly, Guillermo Cook suggests that Pentecostals, more than "members of any other Protestant movement, are in a position to challenge Catholic popular religiosity and Afro-Brazilian Spiritism...." (Cook 1985, 227).

My purpose in this essay is not to shed any further light on the extent of Pentecostal expansion in Latin America. Nor will I examine the likely impact of Pentecostal growth on economics, politics, or established churches in the region. Martin and others have established some provocative theses that must be debated as well as tested in the light of everyday, empirical realities (Martin 1990). Instead, I am interested in one fundamental question: Why is there such an obvious affinity between traditional Pentecostalism, as it has evolved in the United States, and the poor of Latin America? Moreover, I wish to ask this question as a student of communication studies, especially the branch of communication studies known as "cultural studies."

Cultural studies examines how human beings use language and other symbolic activities, including the mass media, to create, maintain, and change culture. The field focuses on symbols because of the primacy of "meaning" in all cultural activity. It assumes that human action, including the action of "becoming a Pentecostal," or at least in Latin America an *Evangélico*, is not ***primarily*** reducible to political, economic, psychological, or any other "factors," but is, like all basic cultural activity, a search for individual and collective meaning that takes place within social settings which provide both opportunities and limitations. In other words, communication studies is an interpretive discipline or a hermeneutical task, not a predictive science. I shall leave it to the social scientists to help us understand the measurable factors that may have precipitated the Protestantization of Latin America as a Pentecostal victory. I will offer social "facts" only as they might help contextualize distinctly cultural phenomenon.

My thesis is as follows: the primacy of oral over literate culture among poor Latin Americans nearly guarantees that any existing Protestant impulses will move these people toward old-style Pentecostalism. Oral cultures (really "oral-aural cultures") are predicated on the primacy of the spoken word. By contrast, mainline Protestantism and even "mainstream Evangelicalism," represented in Latin America by such groups as the Latin American Mission and Central American Mission, are the products of a more literate (chirographic or typographic) culture, which has a very different symbolic sensibility. Indeed, the orality of North American Blacks and Southern Whites is culturally similar to the indigenous orality of much of Latin America, but especially like the culture of the urban poor who immigrated from rural areas in hopes of employment and social stability. These urban poor are, culturally speaking, Latin America's Blacks and Southern migrants. Swaggart was raised in this type of oral culture and appeals to people who have had similar cultural experiences, even if they speak a different language and reside a thousand or more miles to the south.

Various scholars have offered sociological, psychological, and economic explanations for Pentecostalism's success in the region. Sometimes these arguments are not really idiosyncratic to Pentecostalism but could just as easily be applied to other, unsuccessful Evangelical missionary activities. Stoll suggests that the Assemblies of God's growth resulted from fishing "in the streams of rural-urban migration," from the group's "expectation that every member evangelize," and from its "transfer of leadership to Latin Americans" (Stoll 1990, 108-109). Willems cites, somewhat similarly, "the primacy of the laity, local autonomy, freedom of disquisition, egalitarianism, and the absence of ecclesiastical hierarchies" (Willems 1967, 250, 252). He adds that the Pentecostal sects, especially in Chile, maintain "a value system apparently consistent with the way of life of the lower class." Christian Lalive d'Epinay's largely functional explanation posits that although traditional Protestant groups and Pentecostals share the same "credo," the latter is much more able to translate the credo into the cultural language of the country (Lalive d'Epinay 1969, 222-223). Westmeier locates Bogotá's Pentecost upsurge in its "outstanding healers," its "secure relationship with the supernatural," its "eagerness to distribute and explain the Bible," and the ability of Protestant pastors "to guide their faithful into an experience where the supernatural can actually be 'touched'" (Westmeier 1986, 372-373).

Lancaster believes that Pentecostalism's "religious rationalization....*simplifies* the core of belief, *centralizes* spiritual authority around the Godhead, and *decentralizes* the church's political authority and bureaucratic organization...." (Lancaster 1988, 113). He adds that such rationalization is kept in check by the "irrational" components of Pentecostalism, including healing and personal blessings. Brown and Cooper, citing "historical factors" rather than "contemporary sociological phenomena," suggest that the most important considerations in Brazil are the erosion of Catholic doctrine and practice by syncretism, the limited number of Catholic clergy, and the rise of a "familial and formal Catholicism guided by clerics more interested in secular than religious pursuits" (Brown and Cooper 1980, 388). Into that context, continue Brown and Cooper, came Pentecostalism, which took advantage also of existing Brazilian traits, including "innate warmth and hospitality, resignation in the face of periodic natural calamities, a flexibility of spirit producing toleration, enchantment with charismatic personalities, individualism, and a distinct turn to emotionalism and mysticism." Read and his colleagues attribute Pentecostal growth to "native genius," particularly aggressive public evangelism, and more generally a creative energy that takes advantage of indigenous cultural patterns" (Read, Monterroso and Johnson 1969, 324). Norman believes that Pentecostalism's social solidarity appeals almost exclusively to rural and especially urban poor, where social change has greatly disturbed traditional relationships (Norman 1981, 67). Arias and Arias (1980) and Núñez and Taylor (1989, 156) cite anthropological reasons (hunger for God), spiritual factors (the free action of the Spirit), sociological elements (shelter, security, identity, community), pastoral methodology (lay participation), and finally cultural factors (freedom of worship and emotion, folk music and instruments). Finally, Glazier concludes from his analysis of others' case studies of the Caribbean and Latin America that the Pentecostal Church has become a "logical substitute for the extended family ties temporarily or perhaps permanently severed by migration" (Glazier 1980, 2). He adds that "behavior patterns in the new Church are based on the same norms of reciprocity and mutual aid inherent in relations among kin and fictive kin."

Four authors -- Martin (1990), Walter Hollenweger (1986), and co-authors Trevor Beeson and Jenny Pearce (1984) -- have addressed the North-South connection between Pentecostalism and Latin America in the context of oral culture. Beeson and Pearce wrote in *A Vision of Hope* that Latin American Pentecostalism "has a greater affinity with the independent African churches than with the charismatic movements in the USA or Europe" (Beeson and Pearce 1984, 44-45). Although this argument is probably true, it wrongly assumes that there is no North American Pentecostalism which is similar to Latin American Pentecostalism. They mistakenly confuse the orality of Latin American Pentecostalism -- "an oral theology of song, story and dance, prayer for the sick, exorcism and speaking in tongues" -- with indigenousness. Orality never guarantees indigenousness; it is only a cultural sensibility with a particular kind of symbolic capacity that can be filled indigenously or with imported versions of oral culture. As they recognize, the oral culture in Latin America predates the region's Roman Catholicism. Obviously Catholicism was not indigenous, but was adapted to the existing contours of community life and took advantage of the propensity toward oral or "folk" theology. In my view, the best parallel in Latin America to the charismatic movement in the United States is the upper-middle class "megachurch" in large cities. These churches, such as *El Verbo* and *Fraternidad Cristiana* in Guatemala City, are not the product of an oral culture, but are a far more literate style of worship and community with greater rationalization and individualization. At best, the charismatic megachurches are meager attempts to resuscitate orality in the midst of disorienting urban bureaucratization and rapid upward mobility.

Hollenweger, in his influential summary of twenty years of scholars' research on Pentecostalism, concluded that its "black roots" included "orality of liturgy," "narrativity of theology and witness," a participatory community, dreams and vision in worship, and an understanding of "body/mind" relationship that was manifested in "the ministry of healing by prayer" (Hollenweger 1986, 6). He also observed that these classic characteristics of oral culture were not always present in middle-class expressions of Pentecostalism in the Third World. Based partly on this observation, Hollenweger divided Pentecostalism into "three main streams": classical Pentecostal denominations (including their mission churches), the "charismatic movements" within traditional churches, and "indigenous non-white churches" primarily in the Third World. He even suggested that the overwhelming growth of the third category of Pentecostalism indicated that "the numerical and perhaps also the spiritual centre of Christianity will shift from *white western* [my italics] forms to this new type of Christianity. Christianity as a whole will no longer be a predominantly white person's religion" (3). Then, most interesting of all, Hollenweger argued that these Pentecostals' religion "is not a primitive but a prime and highly complex mode of communication.... This...system is vital for pre- and post-literary cultures (10-11). As these cultures become more and more important, it becomes imperative for western thinkers to be able to read these 'oral books,' to tune into these socio-psychological information systems and to communicate with the theologians of these oral cultures."

Finally, Martin has called Latin American Pentecostalism a "system of communication" integrated "around the key notion of transformation" (Martin 1990, 163). In his view, Pentecostalism's orality has the explosive potential to unite ancient and modern practices in the restored life of the local community. "Whereas the older Protestant denominations stressed literacy," writes Martin, Pentecostals "work with the oral tradition aided sometimes by the visual icons of religious television and the cinema" (Martin 1990, 167). Pentecostalism thereby takes the hope and methods of change directly to the people, using ordinary language to "empower" them for personal and social transformation. Without the intermediary of the printed page, Pentecostal orality has "spontaneity, power and immediacy" (177). "What we see in the movement," concludes Martin, quoting the South African Pentecostal, David du Plessis, "is a restored emphasis on our oral tradition, spoken spiritual autobiographies" (178). The result is "indigenous expressions of faith, couched in the vernacular and spread by ordinary men...and women" (180).

These four observers share a belief in the value of understanding Latin American Pentecostalism as a form of spiritual communication predicated on oral culture. Nevertheless, none of them has examined closely the communicative character of orality; they have simply asserted that an oral culture exists and identified a few apparent characteristics of oral communication. I now turn to the subject of "oral culture" in hopes of elucidating the situation in Latin America and comparing it to traditional Pentecostalism in the United States and other literate cultures.

Oral-Aural Cultures

In the introduction to the classic work, *Literacy in Traditional Societies*, Jack Goody discussed the difficulty of locating *any* purely oral cultures in the modern world (Goody 1968). Taking to task both anthropologists and sociologists for their loose use of the terms "oral culture" and "literate society," Goody argued that even Redford's legendary studies of Mayan civilization were skewed by false assumptions about the level of literacy in a traditional society. There are few purely oral cultures, he argues, and no purely literate societies, because orality is not eliminated by writing or the printed word. Many traditional societies are predominantly oral, but rarely exclusively oral, since the messages of the printed world are spread orally even in countries with low literacy rates. In other words, "pre-industrial" societies are a kind of ideal type, not a social reality (Goody 1968, 6-7). As Goody and his colleague Ian Watt put it in another essay, there is simply no radical dichotomy between "primitive" and "civilized" thought and culture (Goody and Watt 1968, 68). Walter Ong distinguishes among cultures which are *radically* oral, *largely* oral and *residually* oral, depending on the level of distinctly oral forms of thought and expression as well as on the extent of literacy (Ong 1967, 22). It is entirely possible that the forms of communication (and culture) within a large nation may vary more greatly from place to place than do the literacy rates between nations. The newer electronic media complicate matters even more, delivering identical programming to different cultures and making "literate" information available to non-literate people.

Nevertheless, it is possible to compare and contrast identifiable subcultures in terms of the *degree* of orality. This can be accomplished by using the ideal type of an oral culture as a yardstick. In *The Presence of the Word* and *Orality and Literacy*, Ong used historical records and contemporary cultural analysis to articulate some of the more salient features of oral cultures (Ong 1967; 1982). I have organized, summarized, and somewhat restated his conclusions, using my own key terms:

> ***powerful immediacy*** -- Since verbalization has no connection to writing, it is generated in and limited to oral-aural communication; sound is active, dynamic, an "evanescent effluvium," always changing, a "real" happening (Ong 1967, 22, 42, 111); words have "great power," even a "magical potency" (Ong 1982, 32).
>
> ***presentness*** -- Culture exists in the here and now because there is little abstract and analytical thought; history is inseparable from the present life situation (Ong 1967, 23-24, 33); in this "homeostatic" culture, people live in the present by "sloughing off memories which no longer have a present relevance" (Ong 1982, 46).
>
> ***playfulness*** -- Verbal communication is more like celebration or play than like work (Ong 1967, 30).
>
> ***performance*** -- Gifted communicators are dazzling "performers," especially of narratives, who can affect an audience by adjusting *how* they communicate, not *what* they communicate (Ong 1967, 31; Ong 1982, 140); originality is evident in the speaker's ability to "manage" a particular interaction with a specific audience, adapting the story uniquely for each situation (Ong 1982, 42; Bauman 1986, 4).
>
> ***parabolic morality*** -- Oral narratives tend to be examples of standing moral truths, creating an "oral sensibility"; speakers and listeners interpret life in terms of pre-determined "commonplaces" organized especially around "virtue and vice" (Ong 1967, 82-85); knowledge is "agonistically toned" within a "context of struggle;" "praise expressions" are commonly part of the "highly polarized" world of good and evil (Ong 1982, 43-45).
>
> ***conventionality*** -- Messages are highly conventional and formulaic, and often very repetitious and even redundant (Ong 1967, 30; Ong 1982, 40); public communication is often characterized by minor variants of an established myth (Ong 1982, 42).
>
> ***commonality*** -- Because sound unites groups as nothing else does, relationships are close, and local experience is deeply shared (Ong 1967, 122); people are

"empathetic and participatory" (Ong 1982, 45); there is a communal identification with the known (Havelock 1963, 145-146).

As Ong sees the history of the Western world, this primary orality is reduced but not eliminated by writing and particularly printing. Typography especially helped create the literate culture of the Enlightenment, in which the individual became an isolated thinker, separated from his community as a detached observer. Written words objectified language and thought, including religious faith (Ong 1967, 54). According to Ong, 18th-century Deists reflected this triumph of the print-culture view of the universe, where man becomes a "kind of stranger, a spectator and manipulator in the universe rather than a participator...." In chirographic and especially typographic culture, God is "no longer a communicator, one who speaks to man, but...a Great Architect" (Ong 1967, 73). This "devocalization" of culture, says Ong, took hundreds of years and was never entirely successful because of the tenacity of oral forms even in the literate West.

The current situation in the West is even more confused because of the development of the "electronic" media -- e.g., broadcasting, computers -- which reactivate orality but also enhance the communication of images. These latest media, like their print-oriented predecessors, "do not cancel out one another but build on one another." The result is not Marshall McLuhan's "global village," a romanticized "retribalization" of humanity on an international scale, but a "supercharging" of visual *and* aural senses (Ong 1967, 89-91). Electronic media validate voice and ear once again, while simultaneously heightening the visual sense. Thus, says Ong, the print-oriented, visualist mentality still exists behind the contemporary oral-aural mentality created by the electronic media (Ong 1967, 260). In the electronic age, however, the "new" orality is necessarily only "secondary," although it has "striking resemblances to the old orality in its participatory mystique, its fostering of a communal sense, its concentration on the present moment, and its use of formulas" (Ong 1982, 136). Examined on an international, national, or even local scale, "contemporary" culture is a highly dynamic world of conflicting symbols and opposing media forms. Some groups are forging ahead electronically, while others are trying to reclaim oral traditions or promote literacy. Even religiously conservative movements, such as Fundamentalism, can become very technologically sophisticated, often giving very little thought to the long-term effects of communications technology on their lives.

In summary, oral and to some extent electronic media produce an oral culture that is significantly different from a literate culture. While the alphabet and printing tend to individualize, objectify, and rationalize life, orality promotes powerful immediacy, presentness, playfulness, performance, parabolic morality, conventionality and commonality. Perhaps two metaphors would help: oral culture is an *organism*, whereas more literate culture is an *organization*. Again, these are ideal types, not immutable laws of social life under one communications system or another.

Orality and Religion

Orality has significant implications for religion. Orality should support culture which is more or less conducive to particular religions as well as to various expressions of those religions. Within Christianity, for instance, Roman Catholicism and Protestantism were established under significantly different cultural conditions maintained by contrasting media. Similarly, Calvinistic (highly typographic) and Anabaptist Christianity (highly oral), although they emerged during roughly the same period in Western history, placed considerably different emphases on literate and oral culture and communication -- emphases which shaped their respective developments down through the contemporary period. Similarly, Black churches in the United States created pulpiteer-orators who were "sonorous," "thrilling," and "forceful." Their "rhythmical and musical culture" was highly dramatic, with "role-playing, humor, imagery, music, dance, and story-telling...." As Stone describes it, Black orality created "the sermon-story as plot," and the preacher became the "principal performer in this "church-theatre" (Stone 1980, 21-23). He nicely summarized the orality of Black worship: "Call and response, humor and imagery, song and dance, imagination and improvisation..." (26). Black preaching was often spontaneous, without manuscript or even notes (Rosenberg 1988, 11-12).

Goody distinguished between "religions of conversion" and "magico-religious" faiths. In his view, conversionary religions are also "religions of the book" which exclude particular people from membership and are less tolerant of change. Literacy leads such religions to rationalize and bureaucratize faith by including authoritative documents which articulate the nuances of acceptable belief and practice. Literacy also enables religions to establish organizations that maintain the documents. These literate religions are, in Goody's perspective, more conversionary or "salvationist" because they place greater emphasis on "individual paths to righteousness." By contrast, "magico-religious" faiths are "singularly eclectic in that shrines and cults move easily from place to place." In other words, without objectifying the faith through the written or printed word, these faiths are enormously fluid and localized. As a result, they are also "more universalistic" and less "particularistic;" they simply lack the cultural mechanism necessary for establishing nuanced dogma regarding belief and practice. Without writing, a religion could not "rescue" itself from the "transitoriness of oral communication." With printing, the same faith might be plunged into "complex bureaucratic organizations" (Goody 1968, 1-2). In Ong's view, contemporary Fundamentalism is oral in its insistence on preaching the word, but typographic in its emphasis on the "literal meaning" of texts (Ong 1967, 275). Such are the confounding complexities of the modern age.

When Ong examined his own Catholic tradition in these cultural terms, he found considerable weight on the literate mode even though the church had expanded to predominately oral cultures. For one thing, the Latin language for over a thousand years had been a "chirographically controlled language in which all oral performance had been forced to conform to written models" (Ong 1967, 65). The Roman church had become heavily dependent on the language that was used for learned thinking and expression in Western Europe through the Middle Ages and the Renaissance. Indeed, Latin was so dependent on script that it was not spoken by anyone who could not write it. While other Romance languages, including Spanish, evolved as spoken vernaculars, Latin became increasingly a purely literary system of symbols. The result, says Ong, was a "sight-sound split" between the oral tongues of the vernaculars and the imaged script of Latin. Asian and African cultures remained far more oral than those of the West, except for indigenous western cultures such as American Indians (Ong 1967, 75-79). Meanwhile, the Roman Catholic Church, under the weight of an enormous bureaucracy extending around the globe from Rome, and with an "oral" liturgy based in a literary language, tried to maintain its province over a myriad of localized cultures, many of them primarily oral cultures in the Third World.

With the advent of electronic communication, especially broadcasting, literate religions were in even greater trouble. Electronic media introduced a new, "secondary" orality, which puts less of a premium on typographic thought, but does not fully embrace orality. "Many of our liturgical problems," writes Ong, "are indentifiable in terms of adjustment to the new orality of our era...., to ... the secondary orality as contrasted to the primary orality of preliterate cultures" (Ong 1992, 182). As Goody and Watt put it, radio and television, without any limit of time or place, produced yet another kind of culture: "less inward and individualistic than literate culture, probably, and sharing some of the relative homogeneity, though not the mutuality, of oral society" (Goody and Watt 1968, 63). The electronic media centralized communication even more than did printing, creating vast new monopolies or at least oligopolies of image and word. But they have little of the permanence essential to much cultural activity, including religious faith and practice. As Canadian scholar Harold Adams Innis argued, oral traditions, in spite of their localized nature, are slow to change when they go unchallenged by other media cultures. They provide a necessary countervailing force to modern communications, whether print or electronic (Carey 1989, 172). It might be that the resurgence of orality in contemporary Christianity, especially in the charismatic movement, is partly a natural human response to the rationalization of literate religious cultures. To put it differently, the emergence of the charismatic culture in mainline, middle-class churches could be a serious oral challenge to literate religious bureaucracies, including mainstream denominations, unless the orality is harmonized with typographic creeds, church organization, and literate modes of church education.

In Latin America, the two most prominent and probably most influential Protestant movements are traditional urban Pentecostalism and the newer-styled, upper-middle-class charismatic movement. As mentioned earlier, the latter is more or less equivalent to the charismatic mega-church movement in the United States. Oddly enough, the pastor of the large *Fraternidad Cristiana* in Guatemala City humorously told me that visitors from the United States compare his worship services to Calvary Chapel of Los Angeles, even though he has never been to that church. Urban Pentecostalism in Latin America is most similar to the storefront churches in Black and Hispanic neighborhoods in the urban United States. In both places the Pentecostals are less literate than their charismatic counterparts and their indigenous cultures are considerably less rationalized and far more oral.

Pentecostal Orality

Given the broad historical context, it is now possible to estimate the extent of orality in Latin American Pentecostalism as well as to assess the relative importance of such orality in the growth of Pentecostalism. This is partly a comparative issue: How oral is Pentecostalism relative to other religions vying for adherents and authority in the region? In addition, it is an historical issue: what religions has Pentecostalism had to compete with during its ascendancy? Because no one has done a systematic study of orality in Latin American Pentecostalism, but many scholars have examined the phenomenon from other perspectives, I will use these other scholars' findings to support my own thesis. More specifically, I will compare other scholars' findings with the characteristics of orality listed earlier.

Powerful Immediacy and Presentness

Perhaps no two characteristics of an oral culture are more obviously present in Latin American Pentecostalism than immediacy and presentness. These Pentecostals experience the faith not principally as a set of objective doctrines or abstract theological tenets, but as the living, dynamic work of the Holy Spirit in their everyday lives. God is present in their midst both as a community and, more directly, in each of their lives. In this sense, as MacRobert has argued in his study of the history of North American Pentecostalism, especially in the Black community, this expression of Christianity is principally about "experiencing the power of God in a personal, subjective and highly exciting way" (MacRobert 1988, 14). God is not the doctrinal Christ of the historic Protestant churches or even the ritual of Roman liturgy and folk practices, but the fiery Holy Spirit of *this* moment. As Torres has observed, even within Roman Catholicism in the region the "fundamental tension...occurs between fidelity to the founding event of Christology (the Spirit) and fidelity to the historical praxis of the institutional Church...." Pentecostalism's immediacy and presentness "trump" other movements' attempts to create popular religiosity, even Liberation Theology (Torres 1992, 70).

Pentecostal liturgy and belief deeply reflect this spiritual orality in Latin America. As transitional events in the life of the believer, both religious conversion and spirit baptism, manifested in speaking in tongues or simply "ecstatic speech," are immediate experiences of the personal presence of God (Westmeier 1986, 13-15; Martin 1990). Similarly, the loud, spontaneous prayers uttered personally but simultaneously in Brazilian worship are divine communication, not planned statements or prose from manufactured prayer books (Goodpasture 1989, 276). As Read has described it, Pentecostal worship is "uninhibited and spontaneous." Moreover, he reports that new Chilean converts are encouraged to "give immediate expression to their faith by preaching on the street corners" (Read, Monterroso and Johnson 1969, 315-316). In other words, there is no basis for waiting to see if one's faith is doctrinally correct or propositionally accurate -- the standards and expectations of literate faith; the overwhelming concern is simply immediate experience. One group of Pentecostals explained their growth in these words:

> We grow because we preach in the open air. We do not wait until men are interested in going to church. We go to them to interest them. Anyone who would try this same method would also grow. Men are interested in what we say on the street corner because we are not talking about *cold theories* but about what we ourselves have *experienced*. We tell them how God has helped us and healed us. We talk of victorious life and describe the joy we feel. We sing happy music that confirms our words. When we show men how God has promised to do the same for anyone who will ask him, many of them meet God. By the next service they are with us to give their testimonies (Read, Monterroso and Johnson 1969, 317-318). [italics mine]

The "magical" or "supernatural" character of Latin American Pentecostalism, which creates a sense that spoken words have power, is thoroughly consonant with the culture dominated by orality. Norman (1981, 59) describes Pentecostalism's strong "miraculous" element, while Westmeier (1986, 373) explains how pastors in Bogotà guide the faithful to an experience where the "supernational can actually be 'touched.'" This type of spirit-ecstasy, says Westmeier, "palpably relates man with the supernatural world...once more into a context of cosmic meaning" (Westmeier 1986, 374). Willems suggests even more directly that Pentecostalism promises the supernatural "coming of the deity here and now to the individual believer" (Willems 1967, 249). This type of Pentecostal spirituality is fundamentally at odds with the literate theology of traditional historic Protestantism, which objectifies belief and thereby transforms faith into a more or less logical consent to "non-subjective" doctrinal statements. Indeed, literate culture tends to take faith out of the individual believer and isolate it in written documents to which believers must pledge fidelity. In this way the "priesthood of all believers" is strongly checked by confessional orthodoxy that provides little room for spontaneous outworkings of the Holy Spirit. The "emotionalism and mysticism" of the Brazilian Pentecostals, as described by Brown and Cooper, are highly problematic to many observers reared in typographic culture (Brown and Cooper 1980, 388).

Strangely enough, as Martin suggests, this non-literate emphasis in Latin American Pentecostalism is actually a union of pre-literate and post-literate cultures (Martin 1990, 183). While worship announces that "God is here" (Beeson and Pearce 1984, 45), the church ignores "centuries of church evolution since apostolic times," attempting "to return to the simplicity and power of the early church" (Read, Monterroso and Johnson 1969, 322). Catholic observer Enrique Dussel wrote in 1976 that the church was "coming to realize that faith is not necessarily a matter of educated self-awareness" (Dussel 1976, 163). But the Pentecostal church does this *after* 2,000 years of church history have taken place, after millions of books, documents, and conventions in which groups tried to determine the precise meaning and contours of the faith, after several hundred years of academic theology, after formulated and reformulated liturgies, after prayer books and hymnals -- in short, after literate Christianity seems to have run its course in the region. Moreover, the Pentecostal churches reclaim their own version of Christian primitivism in the age of electronic media, using radio and television, even satellites and cable, to spread their primitive spirituality in the face of modern, literate skepticism (Rose and Schultze 1993).

It might be that Latin American Pentecostalism is not anti-literate, but simply a-literate; perhaps its orality has no place for the major questions and concerns of the modern West and the Enlightenment worldview. Ong writes that oral culture "simply does not deal in such items as...abstract categorization, formally logical reasoning processes, definitions, or even comprehensive descriptions or articulated self-analysis, all of which derive not simply from thought itself, but from text-formed thought" (Ong 1982, 55). As Lancaster has suggested in the Nicaraguan context, Pentecostals resist the rationalization of their faith, preferring the "practico-magical" (Lancaster 1988, 113). Martin persuasively argues that this type of non-literate religion eschews the stability of history and the wisdom of the past for the dynamic theme of transformation (Martin 1990, 163). God is not the stability of literate doctrine, but the present hope of immediate change. Interpreting the work of Rolim (1978, 85-86), Cook asserts that local Pentecostalism, unlike even popular Catholicism or traditional Protestantism, gives these Latin Americans "direct access to the means of religious production" (Cook 1985, 226). In a predominantly oral culture, it could not be any other way.

Playfulness and Performance

When Martin compares Pentecostal worship to a fiesta, he identifies another important aspect of orality represented in this Latin American movement: playfulness. Such playfulness is widely evident in oral cultures, and often part of a "performance" by a gifted communicator in a public square, at a family meal, or during a worship service (Martin 1990, 83). Goodpasture describes a two-hour Pentecostal service in São Paulo as "lively, joyful," and says that the mood is "even *hilarious*...." [italics mine] (Goodpasture 1989, 276). Aided by an ad-hoc orchestra, the worshipers were not experiencing the short, sequential service of literate Protestantism, but a joyous celebration marked by much spontaneity, delight, and fun. A more rationalized service would undoubtedly have offered much less appeal to members of this culture.

Pentecostal pastors, as conduits of the oral culture, are known more for their ability to move a congregation emotionally than for their knowledge or education. As McGavran and colleagues suggest, Pentecostals' "qualifications for the ministry are spiritual rather than academic" (McGavran, Huegel and Taylor 1963, 119; cited in Read et. al. 1969, 319). Núñez and Taylor cite the lack of formally trained Pentecostal ministers as a significant problem in Latin American Protestant leadership (Núñez and Taylor 1989, 157). No doubt this is a legitimate concern for the church as an organization, but it is a distinct cultural advantage for the church as a dynamic witness to faith in the context of orality. Literate understandings of Christianity tend to create a rationalized decorum that shifts the emphasis in worship from playful celebration to religious "work." Pentecostal leaders implicitly oppose this by seizing the dramatic moment and directing the congregational performance. Although the service is more or less predictable in overall structure, each performance is playfully its own non-duplicatable event. According to Martin, even though the Spiritualists similarly appeal to an oral culture, their expression of power is less of a "dramaturgical mode" (Martin 1990, 171).

Most interesting of all, however, is the comparison of Catholicism and Pentecostalism in terms of both playfulness and performance. Catholic rituals such as Mass and holy-day processionals are undoubtedly somewhat appealing to an oral culture that values symbolic enactments shaped by well-known narratives such as the death of Christ and the first Christmas. But they are too well organized and not adequately improvisational for deep orality. Bogotá's "outstanding healers," as Westmeier calls them, are far more attractive partly because of their ability to "perform" instead of merely their ability to conduct (Westmeier 1986, 37). Even the Mass, assuming a priest is available, offers no real "performance," only the enactment of the same ritual. Healing services, by contrast, are always new performances with at least moderately unpredictable outcomes. Who will come forward? Who will be healed? What will the congregants see and hear on this day? The answers depend on the performance, and in Pentecostal terms the performance is controlled by God even if orchestrated by the pastor. This game-like approach to liturgy turns the service into a far more interesting and impressive -- not to mention "fun" -- activity to those who either can or do not have to suspend their literate mentality of objective doubt and scientific suspicion.

Part of the reason for the popularity of some North American Pentecostal broadcasters and revivalists in Latin America, I believe, is their highly polished and technologically sophisticated approach to oral performance. Jimmy Swaggart, by far the most popular gringo on Latin television, and probably the most popular stadium revivalist (at least prior to his fall), has learned how to translate his playful oral performances into effective televisual communication (Rose and Schultze 1993, 435; Schultze 1991, 83-85). Although he acts as if the cameras were not present, the cameras and editors are carefully capturing his highly expressive face and body, while the microphones sensitively reflect Swaggart's resonant voice. Ong believes that the new electronic orality tends "to promote spontaneity...with the existential focus on the present that comes naturally to the sound media...." (Ong 1992, 172). The result is a seemingly unplanned service at which all viewers sit in the front seats. In order to insure the "authenticity" of the performance, the cameras regularly capture the very close-up images of emotionally moved attendees in the "real" audience. This, too, mirrors an "oral service," where participants can see each other and be convicted by the convictions of others. Contrasted with a Presbyterian TV minister such as D. James Kennedy or even a Southern Baptist T.V. preacher like Charles Stanley, Swaggart is far more oral and much less literate. No doubt this clash of cultural sensibilities is precisely what either maddens or simply frustrates some of Swaggart's northern competitors who went to respected seminaries and can recite the fine points of theology, but are unable to move an audience with the skill of a performer such as Swaggart.

Parabolic Morality and Conventionality

Orality supports highly formulaic communication which often takes the form of narratives that "speak" moral truths. This sharply contrasts with literate forms of communication which are much more discursive and propositional. Of course there are many apparent contradictions, from novels and short stories to collections of humorous anecdotes. Writing can and has supported narrative forms and has even given birth to a few distinctly literary genres, most notable the novel. Nevertheless, writing and speaking are distinct modes. Speech is primary, while writing is derivative. Without the written records made possible primarily by alphabets, oral communication is necessarily formulaic and often narrational. The narrative form organizes thought thematically for both memory and effective presentation. Writing, on the other hand, opens up the world of detached record-keeping, and with it the modes of scientific and reportorial communication. It should not surprise thoughtful observers, then, that worship communication is considerably different in Pentecostal services than it is in other, more "traditional" (i.e., imported, literate), Protestant services in Latin America.

As Martin has observed, Pentecostal worship makes considerable use of testimonies, or "spoken spiritual autobiographies" (Martin 1990, 163, 178). These personal narratives help communicate the truths of Pentecostalism by experientially validating community beliefs. Personal testimonies, which can be told over and over again, are like contemporary hagiographies that reflect the real-life work of God in the lives of individual believers. In an oral culture, the assumption is that such tales must be truthful, if not literally then thematically. Indeed, the issue of their *literal* truth is largely irrelevant. This is not to say that testimonies are fictional, or worse yet that they are intentional fabrication. Truthfulness resides, in an oral culture, in the belief in the message, not in the literal components of the message. As Ong reminds us, in an oral culture you "know what you can recall..." (Ong 1982, 33). The oral mind is largely uninterested in "outside" truth, such as definitions, but focuses on present meanings (Ong 1982, 47). The most effective and usually the most popular preachers will be able both to recite effectively the Bible's stories and to elicit personal testimonies, particularly spoken autobiographies, that support the theme of the sermon.

Moreover, the themes of worship narratives in an oral culture tend to be organized conventionally around clearly oppositional values. Stories divide the world into right and wrong, good and evil, and especially vice and virtue. Complexity and nuance are the province of the literary mode, not the oral mode which lacks the luxury of parchment or paper. In order for speakers to recall narratives, and listeners to make sense of them, stories are built around oppositional values. This makes oral rhetoric rather Fundamentalistic, where black and white are clearly distinguishable. Lancaster discovered, for instance, that Nicaraguan Pentecostals tend to "simplify" the core belief, often around a virtuous faith that gets results (Lancaster 1988, 113). Cook supports this as well by suggesting that Pentecostals see themselves as "participating in a holy combat against 'the power of the world'" and the "domination of the Evil One" (Cook 1985, 228).

As in North American Pentecostalism, the Latin American version directs this Fundamentalistic rhetorical style at the common evils of the average people. To the extent that these overlap in the two societies, someone such as Swaggart can be enormously popular in Spanish-speaking nations as well as in Hispanic and Black sectors of the United States. Willems reported the fairly obvious fact that Latin American Pentecostalism seems to be a "solution to various personality problems manifest in the practice of 'vices'" (Willems 1967, 249). Drunkenness is certainly one of the major vices, but among the urban poor there are many practices that both reflect the poor social and economic conditions and also exacerbate them: alcohol, wife abuse, sexual immorality, and the like. Lancaster believes that Pentecostalism's approach to Christianity "ultimately combats the culture of despair by causing the poor to lead more exemplary lives" (Lancaster 1988, 115). If this is true, and I believe it is, the oral style of communication is not only more effective, but it is also the most culturally beneficial style in the Latin American context. In other words, oral conventions promote beneficial cultural invention.

On the negative side, however, the deep orality among the poor of Latin America also makes them particularly vulnerable to rhetorical manipulation by politicians and religious orators. Ong examined this problem decades ago, concluding that the new mass media were open to "overt personal polemics" that sometimes ran "completely wild." He hoped that as the region's literacy expanded and deepened, the culture would be less susceptible to oratorical propaganda which "overplayed" the "virtue-vice polarity." According to Ong, radio was the biggest offender both because it was cheaper than television and because it "exploits to the maximum the old oral-aural structures, building up around the hearer the resonances, personalist loyalties, strong social or tribal feelings and responses" characteristic of oral culture (Ong 1967, 256-257).

Commonality

Perhaps the most obvious and significant characteristic of an oral culture is the high level of shared life. While print tends to enhance individualization, specialization, and rationalization, orality necessarily promotes localized common cultures. The Latin root for the word communication literally means "to make common" -- a root that undoubtedly stems from oral culture, where "community" can indeed be measured by common experience and not just close proximity (Williams 1976, 62). Many authors have pointed out the relationship between Latin-American Pentecostalism and the improvement of family and community life (Maldonado 1993). However, few authors see, apparently, the direct relationship between orality and the resurrection of community in the region. One of Pentecostalism's major contributions to Latin America is a widespread resuscitation of social bonds through spiritual language. Pentecostalism has been a boon to the re-creation of orality and, thus, community.

Using the language of the people, free of ecclesiastical intermediaries and status differences, Pentecostalism linguistically helps to empower its adherents to rebuild community life (Martin 1990, 83, 171, 175, 180). The result is what Martin calls a "substitute society," a "revolutionary reversal" of the social order (258, 287). Many of these urban Pentecostals left their extended families in the country to find work in the city, thereby keeping alive their dreams of a better life (Westmeier 1986, 372; Glazier 1980, 2). Such urban migration not only uproots them from local culture, but just as importantly it plunges the immigrants into a new "mass" society where social bonds are impersonal and tenuous, and where the omnipresent mass media, especially radio and television, are diversionary forms of re-socialization. Unable to address satisfactorily the needs of these immigrants, due both to a shortage of clergy and to inflexible ecclesiastical structures, the Roman Catholic Church cannot easily compete with the communal thrust of Pentecostalism. As late as 1961 only two Catholic parishes served Managua's 200,000 residents (Lancaster 1988, 110). As Willems put it, Pentecostalism, more than other faiths, has turned into a "symbolic subversion of the traditional social order" (Willems 1967, 249). Norman suggests that Latin American Protestantism has generally "served as a protest against the *Hispanidad* values of traditional society, and as a rejection of the influence of the Catholic Church" (Norman 1981, 65). However, such subversion and rejection are always the contemporaneous result of the new Pentecostal community, which collectively reinterprets personal experience.

Perhaps another way of putting it is that Pentecostalism in particular makes faith meaningful and relevant to the people of this largely oral culture, establishing an alternative community of vision. As Cook has concluded, even mainline Protestant churches and Catholic base communities are not grassroots communities compared to Pentecostal ones (Cook 1985, 224-225). He and Brandão believe the small Pentecostal sects, with at most a regional radius of influence, have their own "supernational protection, community *identity*, [and] experience of *power* over the sacral world that mainline Pentecostals are leaving behind" (Brandão 1980, 139-141). Indeed, the lack of centralized, bureaucratic authority gives the small Pentecostal groups a cultural edge. It may not help them directly solve their social problems, which probably require more organizational expertise and political power than they have, but Pentecostalism provides the organic energy, the communal impetus necessary for individuals to act collectively on behalf of the community. Lancaster perceptively argues that these Evangelicals and the Catholic liberation movements are both Evangelical discourses" that "renounce the formalism of clerical practice" and "entail a strong conception of Christian praxis in daily life" (Lancaster 1988, 104). But in my judgment he fails to make the crucial cultural distinction between grassroots Pentecostalism, which is driven internally by the quest for a new communal identity, and Liberation Theology, which tries to create a popular vision of a new community by imposing communicative methods from the outside. In other words, the spread of Liberation Theology requires fairly rationalized techniques, whereas small-church Pentecostalism is unplanned and internally driven.

Pentecostalism's orality is unfortunately also a stumbling block to its communal endeavors. As Read and his colleagues observe, there is no single Pentecostalism in Latin America (Read 1984, 313). Instead, there are multiple Pentecostalisms which share orality but often disagree with each other over particular matters of belief, especially with regard to which vices are acceptable or condemnable. Without the rationalization provided by written standards of faith and practice, Pentecostalism's centripetal forces for community are often battling opposing centrifugal forces that regularly create new leaders and churches. Even so, the localized community is crucial to social and economic change in the region, regardless of all of the schismatic tendencies.

Conclusion

It appears that Latin American Pentecostalism is highly oral, and that its orality has meshed extremely effectively with the indigenous orality of the region as well as with the particular needs of the urban poor. This is not to say that orality *caused* the explosion of Pentecostalism in Latin America. Rather, I wish to argue that the largely oral character of culture among Latin America's poor is a necessary but not sufficient prerequisite to the growth of traditional Pentecostalism. In my judgment, the necessity of orality is an important aspect of the Latin American situation precisely because orality is now establishing the potential *and* the limits of Protestant development. These potentials and limitations, in turn, have important implications for political and economic changes and conflicts. In other words, the explosion in Pentecostalism is both a religious awakening and a cultural force reasserting orality, and with it immediacy, presentness, playfulness, performance, parabolic morality, conventionality, and commonality. As Pentecostalism grows, so too will these cultural sensibilities spill into other areas of life outside of the church. Over the long run I see three possibilities in Latin America.

First, Pentecostalism's possible literate success could also signal its eventual decline. According to this scenario, Pentecostals will increasingly organize and professionalize their communities, achieving enough "religious" success to gain upward mobility. They will increase literacy in their ranks, partly through increased Bible study and improved Christian schooling, and perhaps even overcome their schismatic tendencies as they merge into national or at least regional church organizations (Rose and Schultze, 1993). Eventually Pentecostalism will be less of an organism, and more of a rationalized and bureaucratized organization. This may not be all bad, especially considering the doctrinal strengths that might result from articulating their faith on paper, commensurate with the historic Protestant churches. Nevertheless, it is possible that this type of success, which already somewhat characterizes some of the neo-Pentecostal churches imported from North America, would actually co-opt Pentecostalism so that it becomes merely another "legitimate" player in the official political and economic establishment. Of course a model for this already exists among the upper-middle class charismatic churches in some urban areas, especially Guatemala City. In addition, there is probably little doubt that some of the traditional Protestant churches would aid this process if they had access to the ears and hearts of local Pentecostal leaders.

A second possibility is also in evidence at some Pentecostal churches. By avoiding any chirographic or typographic opportunities, Pentecostalism could implode orally, driving itself into ever more schisms, personality cults and, worst of all, a playful faith that is little more than a temporary escape and catharsis from the realities of daily existence. Listening to some Pentecostal worshippers in the *bárrios* of Guatemala City, I wondered if this were not a real possibility. Orality is not an outward-looking basis for cultural life; it can and does become a kind of ecstatic tribalism concerned only about in-house matters or inter-tribal squabbles. Moreover, the parabolic morality of oral cultures is sometimes open to exploitation from oratorical propagandists within or even outside of the tribe. Since Latin American Pentecostalism is significantly post-literate as well as pre-literate, the broadcast media are likely to be important influences. It will be interesting to see who will control these media, and for what purposes.

As things now stand, Pentecostals are using their orality to seize cultural power for their tribes. As the tribes grow, so does the potential power. But this power is dynamic and unpredictable, and by virtue of the nature of oral culture it must remain so unless it finds a new kind of power in more literate expressions of the faith. Pentecostal orality is the power of spiritual organism without the authority of literate organization and rationalization. It thrives on charismatic authority as expressed in "the words" of gifted Pentecostal orators and the personalized testimonies of responsive congregants. Martin seems to celebrate this orality, believing that it will necessarily produce a more productive market economy and a more stable and egalitarian social order (Martin 1990). I am not nearly so optimistic. A literary revolution is necessary to convert oral dynamism into stable, rational democracy.

The third and most likely possibility is that the Protestantization of Latin America will continue to create contradictory religious tendencies marked by social class. Traditional Pentecostalism will spread in the *bárrios* and some rural areas, but without literacy it will never organize sufficiently for denominational cohesion or structural social change. Meanwhile, some Pentecostals will achieve enough economic success to move into the middle class, join the neo-Pentecostal churches, and perhaps even assume influential roles in industry or government. As this happens, however, they might not look back to the Pentecostal world they left behind.

Swaggart's own career symbolically represents the opportunities and dangers facing Latin American Pentecostalism. Raised a piano-playing, Bible-preaching dynamo, he learned by experience how to convict large audiences of their sins. But as his organization grew from tents to arenas to satellites, the movement of the Spirit was increasingly transformed into weekly financial accounts and monthly audience ratings reports. The charisma still flowed effortlessly, but behind the scenes was an increasingly rationalized operation that resembled an industrial park, not an urban Pentecostal church. His ministry was an unusual combination of oral performance and rationalized organization. To the faithful in Vancouver on that weekend in July, the charisma was all that mattered. However, I cannot but wonder about the empty seats and the people who never came to fill them.

Reference List

Arias, M. and E. Arias. 1980. *The cry of my people: Out of captivity in Latin America.* New York: Friendship Press.

Bauman, R. 1986. *Story, performance, and event: Contextual studies of oral narrative.* Cambridge: Cambridge University Press.

Beeson, T. and J. Pearce. 1984. *A vision of hope: The churches and change in Latin America.* Philadelphia: Fortress Press.

Brandão, C. R. 1980. *Os daises do povo.* Rio de Janeiro: Editora Brasilense.

Brown, L. C. and W. F. Cooper. 1980. *Religion in Latin American life and literature.* Waco, TX: Markham Press Fund.

Carey, J. W. 1989. *Communication as culture: Essays on media and society.* Boston: Unwin Hyman, Inc.

Cook, G. 1985. *The expectation of the poor: Latin American base ecclesial communities in Protestant perspective.* New York: Orbis Books.

Dussel, E. 1976. *History and the theology of liberation: A Latin American perspective.* New York: Orbis Books.

Glazier, S. D. 1980. *Perspectives on Pentecostalism: Case studies from the Caribbean and Latin America.* Washington D.C.: University Press of America.

Goodpasture, H. M. 1989. *Cross and sword: An eyewitness history of Christianity in Latin America.* New York: Orbis Books.

Goody, J. 1968. *Literacy in traditional societies.* New York: Cambridge University Press.

Goody, J. and I. Watt. 1968. The consequences of literacy. In *Literacy in traditional societies,* ed. Jack Goody, 27-68. New York: Cambridge University Press.

Havelock, E. A. 1963. *Preface to Plato.* Cambridge: Belknap Press.

Hollenweger, W. J. 1986. After twenty years' research on Pentecostalism. *International Review of Mission.* LXXV: 2-12.

Lalive d'Epinay, C. 1969. *Haven of the masses: A study of the Pentecostal movement in Chile.* London: Lutterworth Press.

Lancaster, R. N. 1988. *Thanks to God and the revolution: Popular religion and class consciousness in the new Nicaragua.* New York: Columbia University Press.

MacRobert, I. 1988. *The black roots and white racism of early Pentecostalism in the USA.* New York: St. Martin's Press.

Maldonado, J. E. 1993. Building 'Fundamentalism' from the family in Latin America. In *Fundamentalisms and society: Reclaiming the sciences, the family, and education*, eds. M. E. Marty and R. S. Appleby, 214-239. Chicago: University of Chicago Press.

Martin, D. 1990. *Tongues of fire: The explosion of Protestantism in Latin America.* Oxford, UK: Basil Blackwell Ltd.

McGavran, D., J. Huegel and J. Taylor. 1963. *Church growth in Mexico.* Grand Rapids: Eerdmans.

Norman, E. 1981. *Christianity in the southern hemisphere: The churches in Latin America and South Africa.* Oxford: Clarendon Press.

Núñez C., E. A. and W. D. Taylor. 1989. *Crisis in Latin America.* Chicago: Moody Press.

Ong, W. J. 1967. *The presence of the word: Some prolegomena for cultural and religious history.* New Haven: Yale University Press.

________. 1982. *Orality and literacy: The technologizing of the word.* New York: Methuen.

________. 1992. *Faith and contexts: Selected essays and studies 1952-1991.* Vol. 2. Atlanta: Scholars Press.

Read, W. R., V. M. Monterroso and H. A. Johnson. 1969. *Latin American church growth.* Grand Rapids: Eerdmans.

Rolim, F. C. 1978. Abordagem sociológica de religiosidade popular. In *A religião do provo*, eds. Beni dos Santos, et al., 81-91. Sao Páulo, Brazil: Edicões Paulinas.

Rose, S. and Q. J. Schultze. 1993. The Evangelical awakening in Guatemala: Fundamentalist impact on education and media. In *Fundamentalisms and society: Reclaiming the sciences, the family, and education*, eds. M. E. Marty and R. S. Appleby, 415-451. Chicago: The University of Chicago Press.

Rosenberg, B. A. 1988. *Can these bones live?: The art of the American folk preacher.* Rev. Ed. Urbana: University of Illinois Press.

Schultze, Q. J. 1991. *Televangelism and American culture: The business of popular religion.* Grand Rapids: Baker Book House.

Stoll, D. 1990. *Is Latin America turning Protestant?: The politics of Evangelical growth.* Berkeley: University of California Press.

Torres, C. A. 1992. *The church, society, and hegemony: A critical sociology of religion in Latin America.* Westport, CT: Praeger.

Westmeier, K. W. 1986. *Reconciling heaven and earth: The transcendental enthusiasm and growth of an urban Protestant community, Bogotá, Columbia.* New York: Verlag Peter Lang.

Willems, E. 1967. *Followers of the new faith: Culture change and the rise of Protestantism in Brazil and Chile.* Nashville: Vanderbilt University Press.

Williams, R. 1976. *Keywords: A vocabulary of culture and society.* New York: Oxford University Press.

Chapter 4

The Dynamics of Latin American Pentecostalism

Everett A. Wilson

Introduction

Scholarly observers of contemporary Latin American Protestantism identify a number of circumstantial reasons for the movement's rapid growth. Most of them are especially applicable to the Pentecostal groups, whose adherents now make up as many as three-quarters of the total number of Latin American Evangelical Christians (Wagner 1988; Barrett 1990). Observers agree that Pentecostalism has had a special appeal for the region's poor and powerless, the populations most affected by changing economic patterns, by migration to the cities, and by the misfortunes common to those who occupy the bottom rungs of a highly stratified society. Protestantism in Latin America thus acquires more the appearance of a mass movement than of a programmed extension of American or European denominations overseas. Accordingly, sociological and cultural considerations are often given more attention in the literature than are theology and missiology (Lalive d'Epinay 1969; Willems 1967; and Nida 1974).

Recognizing the apparent reasons for some Latin Americans' adoption of a new faith, however, leaves many questions still unanswered. In order to emphasize what Pentecostalism is producing -- in changed customs, values and institutions -- investigation is needed to identify the dynamics of the movement's growth. This chapter seeks to explain the movement's empowering, its institutional structures, its resources, and its resilience. It concludes that Pentecostalism represents a truly popular and indigenous movement; one with great potential to shape the future of Latin America, not only in terms of personal religion but in many other areas as well.

Scholars have only recently recognized the potential of popular Latin American religious movements for assuming an important role in forging the region's future. Attention throughout the 1980s on Liberation Theology, the popular church, and ecclesial base communities, as well as on cultural analysis and the self-empowerment of indigenous, women's, and other underrepresented and submerged groups, has set the stage for a closer look at the region's popular Evangelical Protestant movements (Boudewijnse, Droogers and Kamsteeg 1991). In 1990, Latin American Protestantism was given a revised assessment in two book-length studies which focused primarily on Pentecostals (Martin 1990; and Stoll 1990a). While current estimates of Pentecostal adherents reach upwards of 25,000,000 (Wagner 1988; and Barrett 1990), having approximately doubled their numbers each decade since the 1950s (Woodward 1986), analysis and interpretation of these and other popular religious groups in the region (*e.g.*, the Mormons and Afro-Brazilian spiritism), have not kept pace. Current scholarly investigation does, however, significantly alter previously held assumptions about these groups and the nature of their influence.

First, scholars increasingly view these movements as a distinctly Latin American, grassroots phenomenon, a popular insurgency that depends little on North American or other foreign influences (Stoll 1990a; Martin 1990; and Glazier 1980). Research has failed to established a direct correlation between Pentecostal growth, on the one hand, and foreign personnel, resources, and strategies, on the other. The frequently repeated assertion that Evangelical Protestant churches have been directed and financed from outside the region has lost much of its credibility, at least for its Pentecostal expressions (Cleary 1992). While North American groups have invested a great deal in missionary ventures (Stoll 1990b), for the most part membership growth has occurred in groups that are "indigenous" that is, nationally underwritten, directed, and promoted (Martin 1990; Stoll 1990a).

Second, Pentecostalism is no longer viewed as an escapist religious movement without significant social implications. Rather than considering Pentecostalism as a "theology of desperation," as was sometimes the case in the past (Lalive d'Epinay 1969), observers have increasingly recognized that, while Pentecostals have not distinguished themselves by political activism or specific humanitarian services, their entire movement may be viewed as a social program (Gros 1987). David Martin persuasively attributes Pentecostal growth to the irrepressible demands of Latin Americans for a better life for themselves and their children (Martin 1990). Far from being a passive escape from reality, Pentecostalism mobilizes its adherents to address temporal as well as spiritual needs. While Pentecostals often cling to tradition, they also appear to be pragmatically heading full tilt into the future (Glazier 1980; Boudewijnse, Droogers and Kamsteeg 1991).

Third, Pentecostals, the largest and the most rapidly growing sector of Latin American Protestantism, seem to hold promise for bringing some measure of moral renovation to Latin America. While rank-and-file Pentecostals are not always sufficiently aware of the implications of their faith to assert such claims, its relevance to entrepreneurship, consumerism, "good-government" campaigns, and ecumenism, among other issues, has been recognized by non-Pentecostals who covet the movement's support (Brusco 1986; Gill 1988; Castro 1972; Marcom 1990; "Latin America's Protestants" 1990).

This potential for mobilizing the masses has led some observers to offer broader assessments of Pentecostal social roles, including comparisons of Evangelicalism with Liberation Theology (Stoll 1990b). Writers are now acknowledging that Pentecostals are indeed addressing the social needs of the people among whom they work, not only in building morale and creating self-help associations, but in fostering education and other social services and in providing links to the larger world and a power base for future political action (Boudewijnse, Droogers, and Kamsteeg 1991; Stoll 1990b; Martin 1990).

Whether Pentecostalism in the region can measure up to these opportunities and expectations remains to be seen. Much has yet to be investigated about the numerous and varied Pentecostal movements in Latin America, especially if projections about their capacity for continued growth and for effecting substantial change are to be regarded seriously. Since Pentecostals have generally been studied as generic subjects, rather than as members of particular movements, each of which has emerged from a unique social milieu, questions remain about their willingness to work together, their persistence, their resilience in confronting difficult social situations, and their capacity for perpetual renewal.

While the thesis at hand -- that Latin American Pentecostalism arms individuals in the popular sector for effective participation in modern life -- does not address directly the issues of economic and political restructuring, it does speak to the absence of morale and initiative that are widely believed to impede national development. This essay attempts to show that though the world of day-to-day reality is decidedly unfavorable to the vast majority of Latin American Pentecostals, their Evangelical faith provides them with means for addressing the ills of their families, their communities, and their nations.

Background

Given the often inchoate appearance of Pentecostalism, some additional preliminary words need to be said about its nature. As recently as fifty years ago, Pentecostalism, in the United States and elsewhere, was generally considered exotic, if not bizarre. Out of step with both the "historic" Protestants, Pentecostals were often considered marginally Christian in doctrine and practice, and were thought to consist largely of disaffected social elements. That Pentecostals, in addition to being "irresponsible," tended also to be irrepressible, did not make them any more endearing, above all to conservative Protestants with whom Pentecostals shared many affinities of origin, theology and practice. While the charismatic movements within the historic denominations in the 1960s and 1970s provided an avenue of understanding, that phenomenon also alienated Protestants who were loyal to traditional practices or who resented the aggressiveness and divisiveness of persons caught up in "renewal." Even with impressive numerical growth (Pentecostals/Charismatics may now constitute the largest single branch within the Protestant tradition worldwide) and the increasing acceptance of Pentecostal beliefs and practices, Pentecostal growth has yet to be explained adequately.

Pentecostalism apparently remains suspect in part because of its spontaneity and unpredictability. Even apart from the spectacle of televangelists with outrageous presentations and scandalous personal conduct, simply the unrestrained emotionalism, the expressive freedom, and the popular taste that adheres to much of the movement discredits it with large numbers of theologically conservative Protestants. Perhaps even more disturbing is an intuitive feeling experienced by many Christians that Pentecostalism is threatening because of the diffusion of authority implicit in its emphasis on spiritual gifts.

Pentecostalism, though generally adhering to a conservative Christian theological tradition and a cluster of characteristic beliefs and practices, defies easy definition. Perhaps because theological sophistication has been regarded by Pentecostals as at least slightly suspect, adherents have not been forced to adopt a specific confession, nor, probably, could they. Early public opprobrium of identifying oneself as a Pentecostal ensured that few people would identify with the movement unless they were sincerely persuaded; hence strict doctrinal standards seemed superfluous. The desire to be a part of a Pentecostal congregation, with its sometimes rigorous demands on the member, was long taken by the faithful as sufficient evidence of one's having a validating experience of "the truth." Yet, despite its originality, modern Pentecostalism draws its theological positions almost intact from Wesleyan perfectionism, specifically from the Holiness and Keswick movements of the nineteenth century, and exhibits numerous similarities to many other historical Christian renewal movements (Jones 1990).

While twentieth century Pentecostalism is a sprawling, decentralized movement that lacks unity of polity and doctrine and has many differing worship styles, at its root lies the assertion that Christian faith, biblically and historically understood, no matter how orthodox or pietistic, must be existential. Though typically buoyant and enthusiastic, Pentecostals are basically skeptical of human intentions, efforts, and institutions. However, their movement views human brokenness not with despair, but with hope, recognizing redeemable man's human potential. Hence the emphasis on divine empowering of morally (and physically and intellectually) frail human beings. After all is said and done, Pentecostalism may offer very little that is novel beyond a focus on the actualization of the gospel in the experience of the person who recognizes his or her own need.

Pentecostals are probably best considered Protestants -- especially in Latin America where the vast majority of indigenous Pentecostals are suspicious of Catholics. Nevertheless, their spirituality, expressed in periodic fasting or other self-denial, intense devotion, concern for their brothers and sisters in the faith, sacrificial generosity of time and resources, and the expectation of miracles, displays many resemblances to Roman Catholic practices that are deeply rooted in Latin American popular culture.

While it may be argued that Pentecostals owe much to the radical Reformation, some observers see a more immediate affinity with the restorationist tradition that gave rise also to the Campbellites and Mormons in nineteenth century America. Even while Pentecostals give a prominent place to glossolalia, the miraculous, and the prophetic, they are not characteristically mystical or ascetic. They are clearly more concerned with God's immanence than with His transcendence. They derive emphases from a wide range of Christian experience, yet uniquely they succeed in making their movement perpetually new, remarkably orthodox, culturally relevant, personally expressive and, above all, dynamic.

For people who are supposed to be expecting the imminent end of the world, Pentecostals are inveterate optimists. Not only do they exhibit a buoyancy that enables them to survive and even thrive in adversity, they are adept -- even if only by rationalization -- at making everything come out alright. As Martin Marty pointed out in *A Nation of Behavers*, Pentecostals used to say that their doctrine was "'true' because it was small and pure, now it is 'true' because so many are drawn to it" (Marty 1976). Pentecostals often see themselves as "earthen vessels" whose transparent weakness permits the demonstration of God's power. Now that their movement has grown, however, adherents tend to boast of their size and resources, their proprietary claim to virtue and spiritual insight, and even their access to temporal power. Marty correctly recognizes that Pentecostals cannot have it both ways. But if, in fact, the Pentecostal movement has spread globally primarily among constituents who are humble and vulnerable but who are spiritually sensitive, we must not be surprised to find men and women who are often rustic and undistinguished while possessing, nevertheless, remarkable spiritual insight and purpose (Pretiz 1988).

Moreover, as a corollary, we are likely to see God's handiwork primarily in the personal experience of adherents who believe intensely that their lives have been remarkably reordered. Their testimonies relate examples of their changed attitudes, physical healings, favorable turns of events, and unanticipated resources. Even where there may be little objective evidence to support such assertions, observers -- employers, neighbors and family members -- may attest to the subject's vitality by offering examples of strength of character or some remarkable act of faith. That is, since transcendence, like the Spirit, is by definition concealed, elusive, and transient, we are likely to observe much that is human and perhaps only traces of what is divine.

Pentecostals derive their recognizable character largely from their origins among socially marginal populations and from a protean formula that enables individuals and like-minded groups to express their yearnings for legitimacy, realization, recognition and power. The great mass of Pentecostal phenomena look pretty ordinary to an outside observer. One sees men and women who are very average in appearance, and of very average moral character, who are convinced of their own worth and willing to make strong commitments because of their own or others' climactic experience, but who are not always or even frequently able to explain well -- beyond their own subjective experience -- reasons for their unshakable confidence. In other words, if one proposes to see the divine in the Pentecostal movement, one must expect to sift through what is very Latin American, or very African, or very Korean, or very working class, or very popular. One may need to listen carefully to the often emotionally moving personal accounts of adherents who believe that they are recipients of divine grace. One may need to sit -- or stand -- through meetings that seem too long, too loud, too unplanned, too low brow, and too boisterous.

Latin American Pentecostals share with Pentecostals generally an immediate, subjective, personal, vindicating sense of divine presence which translates behaviorally into a recurrent and reproducible cluster of beliefs, practices, and organizational patterns appropriate to the host culture. In practice, Pentecostalism appears as a tendency within a conservative Christian framework for believers to arrogate some measure of power. Stated theologically, Pentecostal groups carry the doctrine of immanence accepted by all Christian believers beyond the usually accepted boundaries, since the grace, gifts, and power attributed to the church are believed to be accessible, at least on occasion, to every believer.

Our North American experience, religious and otherwise, has not prepared us very well to understand the dynamics of the Pentecostal movement. Pentecostalism is simply too emotionally unrestrained, too expressive, and too crass. We will have to dispossess ourselves of some assumptions and plunge into popular Latin American culture. We will have to identify Latin Americans in respect to their feelings, their desire for freedom to express themselves, and their wish to gain respect for themselves and their values. If Pentecostalism has indeed produced remarkable Evangelism and spiritual renewal, then we have to investigate what may be difficult for North American Protestants to understand the impulse toward popular association, personal expressiveness, a profound disengagement from the past, and a deep longing for a better future, which are the most distinguishing characteristics of Latin American culture (Nida 1974).

Latin American Pentecostalism is not a new phenomenon; it began before World War I, almost as early as did Pentecostalism in the United States. Yet, the movement is generally believed to have acquired its familiar character in the years following World War II, when the process of agricultural modernization set off vast migrations of rural people, resulting in the proliferation of sprawling, improvised settlements around the major cities. This wrenching process produced popular cultural responses, including, apart from Pentecostalism, such spontaneous religious movements as Afro-Brazilian Umbanda and Afro-Cuban Santería. The coincidence between large population movements accompanied by changed conditions of life on the one hand, and the emergence of popular religious groups on the other, suggests some correspondence, if not a causal relationship between urbanization and religious transformation.

The human aspiration for betterment, a concept in the Western cultural legacy that in Europe and North America has played an important role in social cohesion and development, has often been frustrated in Latin America. There, while the same utopian dreams of the Enlightenment persist with probably more meaning than in North America, most peoples have been left to fashion for themselves, within the resources of their own experience, responses to insecurity, rejection, and injustice, often reverting to traditional beliefs and organizational structures.

Yet, despite the air of crisis that pervades academic discussions of contemporary Latin American life, Latin Americans themselves are hardly demoralized. The spiritual, mystical, heroic, optimistic, transcendent, and surreal are all quite evident in Latin American culture, nourished apparently by profound inner resources of patience, hope, and imagination. Numerous examples of the sensitivity and resilience of Latin Americans can be cited, many of them derived from their captivating musical styles and dramatically expressive painting, design, and architecture, as well as in the highly acclaimed literary output of twentieth century authors whose novels and short stories often deal with the philosophical themes of injustice, hypocrisy, pride, and patience, as well as the transcendent issues of death, fate, and the supernatural. According to Richard Rodriguez, a Mexican-American writer whose commentaries are syndicated in American newspapers, we should not pity the common people of Latin America.

> Five hundred years after Christopher Columbus set foot on the Americas, Indians are alive and growing in number from the tip of South America to the Arctic Circle. If you do not believe me, look at brown Mexico City! In 1992 it is Europe that has lost its God. The religion of Spain -- I mean Roman Catholicism -- is now centered in the Latin Americans. Christianity is an Indian religion. The Indian has stolen your God! In fact, the Americas are alive with Indians. Go to the Guatemalan mountains and you will see Indians who are Evangelical Protestants. They are headed this way; they are coming to the secular United States to convert you (Rodríguez 1993, 4)!

It is against a backdrop of betrayal and frustration, in a surge of irrepressible impatience and hope, that Pentecostalism -- sometimes like new wine in old bottles -- has appeared.

Pentecostalism and Exponential Growth

Church-growth studies link quantitative growth ("evangelism") to qualitative belief, conviction, and dedication ("renewal"). According to these studies, a church should grow, given sustained levels of intensity (of belief, initiative, and adaptability to internal and external changes) at a fixed rate of reproduction. This fixed rate, moreover, will "generationally" (the rate at which cohorts of converts gain other converts) produce exponential growth that appears, when graphed, as a steeply ascendant curve.

This theory (whatever its merits or inadequacies) recognizes that a group may remain large or even continue to grow in absolute numbers without, however, maintaining the original rates of growth. Such a relative "decline" may indicate conditions that impede sustained rates of growth (*e.g.*, the inability to resolve internal problems or the constituents' desire to limit the extension of the group to certain populations). Sustained rates of numerical growth, on the other hand, should indicate qualitative strengths such as satisfactory incorporation of new members, periodic renewal of intensity, and effective leadership formation, which have inherent importance for the well-being of the church. Concern with "qualitative" development, as opposed to simple numerical growth, is of special concern to a religious movement that asserts claims of spiritual renewal, the exercise of divine power, and personal transformation. A mechanism for analyzing these "qualitative" features of Pentecostalism in the light of practical institutional results exposes the movement to at least some measure of empirical scrutiny.

Recognizing that Pentecostal constituencies are dynamic -- even ephemeral -- associations, assessment of these groups should include analysis of the phases of their development to determine as precisely as possible why and in what ways they are effective in gaining adherents, structuring their congregations, and perpetuating and extending their beliefs and practices. The number of adherents in a growing Pentecostal fellowship does not represent mere numerical increase but rather a net growth (converts less lapsed members) and, as well, an increasing ratio of "pillars" to uncommitted constituents.

Since the proportion of Pentecostals who are likely to move frequently or to have uncertain employment (given the adherents' social origins) is frequently high, congregations tend to be unstable. If Pentecostals succeed in registering sustained growth, it is because they have managed to replace the adherents who leave (for whatever reason) with new converts or migrating members who have left other congregations. Despite this "revolving door" phenomenon, it is evident that enough people have found Pentecostal churches rewarding for net growth to have occurred. Moreover, the evident success of Pentecostal churches in recruiting new members has inspired or compelled in any non-Pentecostal congregations to imitate their style, reducing somewhat the differences between them as more and more Evangelicals become "Pentecostalized."

The question rises, are Pentecostals simply the vanguard of secularization, people who question tradition and disregard established mores? Clearly, they are too innovative to be traditionalists. They are in some measure radicals who are contesting the existing social system. Nevertheless, they are neither secular nor merely nominally religious. Moreover, while Protestant Pentecostalism in Latin America might be considered antithetical to the Roman Catholic faith, it appears to have gained much of its strength from individuals who, before becoming Pentecostal, were already strongly religious (Boudewijnse, Droogers and Kamsteeg 1991). Latin American popular society, a mosaic of ethnic minorities, peasants, marginal urban workers, small rural landholders, entrepreneurial small businessmen, market women, independent professionals, and skilled workers, has not produced many options for the restless and aspiring. In a society where few alternative social roles exist, agents of change may channel their aspirations and creative energies into the promotion of an alternative religious movement.

Not only did the "fertile soil" of Latin American social upheaval give rise to a variety of religious alternatives, the responses of these movements to the overwhelmingly difficult problems of personal survival and group identity are not without some similarities. One may conclude that Latin American popular religions, whatever their metaphysical claims, have grown because they serve as surrogates for disappearing extended families, communities, and associations. Whether one looks at Umbanda or Pentecostal congregations, ecclesial base communities or a number of quasi-religious political or indigenous movements, the immediate concern is the formation of popular associations in the interests of protecting vulnerable individuals.

In order to maintain high levels of credibility and to develop institutionally, all of these groups must face problems of legitimation, structuring, adaptability, and moral accountability. If Pentecostal growth in Latin America is in some sense assured, it is also still precarious. Having gathered large followings, Pentecostal churches must now demonstrate continuing leadership in the resolution of severe human problems.

The Process of Pentecostal Growth

The next section of this chapter identifies and assesses seven strategic "moments" in the process of Pentecostal emergence, with emphasis on process rather than on historical or structural analysis. These moments are characteristics of collective Pentecostal belief and experience. They occur continuously within the group, but come as identifiable phases in the individual adherent's development. Their effectiveness relies in large part on the subjective motivation of the constituents, as religious dedication regularly does not bring material compensation commensurate with the adherent's investment of time, effort, and resources. Specifically, these moments are the experience of powerlessness or vulnerability, when the (potential) convert's (1) crisis leads him or her to opt for radical religious change, followed by acceptance within an inclusive (2) community which endorses and encourages her (3) personal confirmation by means of an intense subjective emotional experience and promotes belief in the accessibility of (4) supernatural power, often beginning with physical healing and increasingly extending to the resolution of personal problems. Association with the group tends to (5) mobilize the adherents by providing opportunities for recognition, influence, and extended relationships. Internal mechanisms of control, meantime, ensure (6) moral discipline, as well as the accountability of the leadership. The group's organizational and cultural (7) adaptability enables it to overcome restrictive internal and external conditions in order to ensure ongoing institutional development.

Crisis

> The Pentecostal creed is . . . almost ideally adapted to the aspirations and needs of the lower classes.
>
> --Emilio Willems (1967, 133)

> The creative minority (to use Toynbee's phrase) which is reshaping Latin [American] life has its origin primarily in the upper lower class and the lower middle class, the very groups to which Protestantism has directed its approach.
> --Eugene Nida (1974, 94)

Though Pentecostals have emerged most frequently from among the popular groups whose lives are typically precarious (suggesting deprivation as a "cause" of the movement), they represent a small fraction of Latin America's dispossessed, an apparently select faction among the millions caught up in the process of social transition. If, on the one hand, "modernization" has stripped large numbers of people of their emotional security, leading them to question their world view and to seek religious and associational alternatives; it has, on the other hand, left them by proximity, commercialization, and the mass media, within view -- though often out of reach -- of the material and social benefits of established groups. Whether symbolically or literally, Pentecostals are asserting a claim to a better life.

Assuming more or less equal access to this novel religious alternative, why do some people, but not others, find Pentecostalism appealing? While the answer may lie in a complex of motives, perceived opportunities, and compulsions, certain individuals apparently feel compelled to make a critical decision. They must defy the majority around them, either from a sense of alienation or from the belief that change offers them something preferable. In either case, the individual must be assertive and must risk losing whatever benefits derived from his or her previous associations. They are, in comparison with their peers, apparently more philosophical, more suspicious, more resilient, and more volatile. They harbor aspirations and, with increasing impatience, they demand fulfillment. In large numbers, though remaining still a small proportion of the entire Latin American population, they have found in this form of Evangelical Christianity a means of acquiring the personal satisfaction for which they have longed. It is scarcely an overstatement to say that beyond finding a faith, they have, in their own experience, forged it.

Although adherents have often been described as being passive and otherworldly, in fact many appear to be decisive, practical persons faced with real problems that demand solutions. Their assertiveness suggests the attraction of strong-willed, iconoclastic persons, who, regardless of personality type or conformity in other respects, are mounting a personal protest against the world of their experience. And in fact, according to available descriptions, Pentecostals are typically young, detached, disillusioned, or uncommitted to tradition and inclined to seek alternative solutions (Roberts 1968).

Many people become Pentecostals after having experienced a crisis of identity, a threat to their security, or some emotional deprivation. Many have become Evangelicals during times of civil turmoil and natural disaster. They refuse to accept passively the suffering and deprivation imposed on them and in a religious or symbolic way they revolt. The hardiness and resourcefulness of Pentecostals who are thrust into entrepreneurial and leadership roles suggest that they seek alternative, perhaps more rational, associations to guide them toward a more secure and rewarding future (Boudewijnse, Droogers, and Kamsteeg 1991).

Reviewing the historical growth of Pentecostalism in country after country, it is clear that they are not "bewildered, alienated masses." In disposition, converts may be more pragmatic and activist than reflective and deliberate. Yet, it would not be easy to overemphasize the tenacity, persistence, inner strength, and determination Pentecostals display in the process of establishing their influence (Butler Flora 1978). Ostracism and abuse occurred with enough frequency in the beginning stages to suggest that these people were either very determined or masochistic. As persons who assert leadership (at various levels) with decisiveness and credibility, in their own individualistic way Pentecostals are protesting their condition. While such persons under normal circumstances should be unable to mount an effective social movement, they have apparently developed one by sheer determination.

Community

> [Pentecostal] groups are visible and available forms of association. The doors of the . . . churches are always open.
> --Bryan Roberts (1968, 767)

> Where traditional social organization is breaking up, Evangelical churches constitute new, more flexible groups . . which are therefore more adaptable to rapidly changing conditions.
> --David Stoll (1990a, 331)

> The contours of the [coming social] revolution . . . can already be perceived in that 'free space' which the Protestant communities are carving out for themselves.
> --Peter Berger (1990, ix)

Emphasis on Pentecostalism's alleged revivalist origins in the United States and Europe has obscured one of the most important features of the movement's growth, the local congregation (Marty 1983; Martin 1990). While the stereotype of the North America televangelist or the large stadium crusade persists, the Pentecostal movement in Latin America owes little to either one. Apart from a few highly visible churches housed in large or imposing facilities, Pentecostal congregations characteristically have a nucleus of two or three dozen proprietary members, often essentially an extended family or several families that in effect, serve as the congregation's patrons. In order to visit the vast majority of Pentecostal churches in Latin America, one must find the back street, the remote mountain village, the unlandscaped, cinder-block building at the edge of town. The land is often donated by a patron, often, but not always, a member of the congregation. Church buildings in rural areas are frequently in an unfinished stage of construction, as it may require several years for the congregation to raise funds for its completion. Pentecostal denominations have an aggregate of upwards of 25,000,000 adherents, congregated in as many as 250,000 small groups.

While the Bible (as interpreted by the pastor and congregational elders with the affirmation of the individual members) is the standard of faith and practice among Pentecostals, in practice the group's constitution is the belief that the church is the spiritual, social, and material possession of the faithful. Access to divine grace is assured to the humblest member or prospective convert, since salvation and the illumination of the Holy Spirit are immediate and socially indiscriminate. Thus, in an effective, religiously sanctioned manner, Latin American Pentecostals have asserted their claim to a place of their own. This congregational feature of Pentecostal churches is more familiar to rural Latin Americans than might at first glance appear. Emilio Willems argues that the patterns of association in Evangelical churches correspond closely to the reciprocal labor arrangements traditional in Brazil and elsewhere (Willems 1967). Others see in these congregations surrogates to replace the fictive kinship or the patron-client relationship characteristic of the traditional *hacienda* (Lalive d'Epinay 1969). The decline of such traditional arrangements has left many people vulnerable; voluntary associations provide an accessible alternative. Such studies simply document what is already apparent: the openness and lack of social distinctions make Pentecostal churches especially effective agents of group formation, in contrast to the historic Protestant groups whose mission is primarily to extend (or protect) the patrimony of a given confession or an ethnic tradition *e.g.*, North American Baptist or German Lutheran (Manning 1980).

Entirely apart from the use that is made of an Evangelical church, the fact of its existence and accessibility speaks warmly to Latin Americans, not only to those from humble origins, but increasingly to the insecure or aspiring elements of the middle sectors as well. To people who possess few material goods and who live in modest, functional housing, the church (*templo*) immediately becomes their community center. Many congregations meet nightly, providing their members with moral guidance, a sense of community, and a locale where they are recognized and respected.

Experience

> Pentecostal teaching legitimized the expression of intense feelings for which there was so little opportunity otherwise.
>
> --Bryan Wilson (1970, 72)

> Within the Pentecostal vocabulary the term *gozo* [enjoyment, pleasure] recurs with frequency.
> --Emilio Willems (1967, 109)

A third moment in the development of a Pentecostal believer is a peak emotional experience, usually, but not always, that of baptism in the Holy Spirit. It is possible to overstate the importance of tongues and healing in the conversion process, but without a doubt subjective confirmation contributes greatly to Pentecostal growth and survival. Small, marginal, and disparaged congregations have been extraordinarily persistent, apparently deriving sufficient confidence from their personal spiritual experience to withstand the rejection of the larger community. The feeling of personal worth derived from an intense spiritual experience may be decisive in making possible a break with the past and may result in the adoption (or recovery) of values that would be unlikely without a peak experience.

After an emotional initiation, however, the individual is likely to lose the immediate subjective rewards of a such a climax if it is not in some way renewed. While the discovery that many Pentecostals have never experienced such a peak experience for themselves has surprised some observers, adherents are nevertheless inclined to view the experience (even if vicariously) as important. Beyond the "boundary maintenance" function of such experiences, the freedom of expression, the legitimizing of one's needs (often expressed publicly as prayer requests), and a confirming sense of justification by the group's approval is important in sustaining the believer's sense of worth (Butler Flora 1978). Functionally, spiritual climaxes serve to integrate the group in a therapeutic, culturally familiar manner, which, in the process, is validated by the meeting's religious context. Persons who have had such experiences, often overwhelming in their intensity and beauty and accompanied by an integrating sense of their own spiritual self, are not likely to be satisfied thereafter by more formalistic, liturgical, or stylized forms of religion.

In practice, individual Pentecostals tend to find a level of emotional expression consistent with their own personality and the expectations of the group. The growth of the movement must be viewed as the result of the vicarious ratification of the intense experiences of some communicants by other members of the group. Children may follow their parents with dedication even though their confidence lies less in their own experience than in that of a given parental model. The same tendency may also apply to relatives or other role models, especially a pastor or other elder. Accordingly, it is generally the case that a given Pentecostal congregation will include a large proportion, even a majority, who have not frequently had climactic spiritual experiences.

It is not merely coincidental that Pentecostalism finds expression in the "soulish" or lively music included in their services. Here the optimum opportunity for participation and expression are found, though in a somewhat regulated way, as the leader, invariably equipped with a public address system, encourages a hearty, rhythmic concert of voices. Adapting modes of popular improvisation, repetition, variation, and, increasingly, the use of electronic keyboards and drum sets, public worship permits the congregants to express themselves without inhibition. If verbal and kinetic expressions are spontaneous they are also typically stylized and appropriate to the type of service. At occasional retreats or in other situations where attendance is sufficiently restricted to permit greater freedom, stronger displays of emotion or verbal ejaculations occur without causing offense. The freedom to shout, weep, embrace, or express other strong feelings, far from representing a loss of control, is extended deliberately in such settings because all present regard such behavior as sincere and appropriate forms of expression (Marty 1976).

Power

> A powerful God is above all a God who heals. Innumerable conversions have been preceeded by a cure.
> --C. Lalive d'Epinay (1969, 47)

> Jesus not only saves, but he saves **now** and **here** in this world.
> --Emilio Willems (1967, 121)

Demonstrations of power, especially as reflected in some tangible, inspiring form such as physical healing, remains a distinguishing feature of Pentecostal groups in Latin America and a major basis of their religious faith and commitment. Trapped in a hand-to-mouth existence, large numbers of Latin Americans have attempted to refashion their world by recourse to a variety of inner and transcendent strategies. These efforts to escape everyday "reality" range from development of an "informal economy" to the appearance of large and influential Afro-Brazilian religious movements, from the formation of self-help burial and labor associations to the use of magical cures for illness and depression.

The religious creations may be the most important of these popular efforts to construct institutional means of survival and hope because they represent the deepest reality to large portions of the Latin American population. In a culture that draws simultaneously from modern, rationalized economic and political concepts and from traditional African, medieval Christian, and indigenous notions of the spirit world, millions of people have turned to Pentecostalism. Originally owing at least some debt to North American and European Pentecostals, this Evangelical alternative was viable because it lent itself immediately and on a mass scale to appropriation by Latin Americans. The spiritual rewards of the faith were translated into culturally compatible demonstrations of power, providing an answer to a sense of personal and institutional impotence. Comparisons of Pentecostal growth with that of non-Pentecostal churches seems to document the fact that Latin Americans are seeking power in religion. However tentative and unreliable it may be in fulfilling this promise, Pentecostalism represents a serious contender for the confidence of large numbers of adherents.

While political power is both a possibility and, increasingly, within reach of some Pentecostal groups in Latin America (Martin 1990; Stoll 1990a), their primary use of "power" is more personal. Observers attribute many Pentecostal conversions to physical healings. Where these healings meet the recipients' criteria for recuperation, however different these may be from the clinical criteria of outsiders, they sustain the faith of members and prospective adherents. Typically, such people testify to the resolution of some specific need as a result of prayer. It makes little difference that the healings are often unverifiable. Such claims to physical healing become the basis for establishing a new life with recovered health and energy, altered perspectives, a new set of associates, and widened expectations and opportunities. The most important common variable in these myriad testimonies is the subject's personal affirmation of worth, dignity, and acceptance. The stories become the climactic episode in the teller's otherwise difficult and demoralizing existence. The healing of a child or other family member whose illness was the cause of profound concern becomes the repeated reminder of divine intervention for the entire community and, not infrequently, the reason given for the conversion of non-Pentecostal members of the family.

Healings are not the only topics of these testimonies to divine power. Employment, a better housing arrangement, the solution of the problems of a family member, apparent preservation from an accident or illness, for example, may be considered miraculous and worthy of a testimony. The fact that opportunity is given at public worship for such testimonies heightens their value both to the subject and to other members of the congregation. The overcoming of personal vices, control of one's explosive anger or jealousy, the improvement of relationships between spouses or estranged family members may likewise be considered miraculous. After concluding that circumstances are hopelessly unfavorable, any positive development may be attributed to God's intervention.

While such beliefs and practices require a great deal more scholarly attention than they have received, there is little reason to doubt the sincerity of such testimonies or the wide-ranging effects of putative healings and miracles. The theme of power, belief in one's access to power, accounts of supernatural intervention, and the fear of another's power, are all familiar parts of the emotional and cultural life of Latin Americans. Pentecostals simply use an idiom to which they and their communities are accustomed. Pentecostalism, it might be said, is effective, not because it introduces novel ideas about spiritual power, but because it employs familiar notions in more morally responsible ways.

Mobilization

> Pentecostal sects found means and ways to mobilize their vast human resources to the last man.
> --Emilio Willems (1967, 149)

> The strength of the structure is the participation of everyone.
> --Eugene Nida (1974, 141)

> In the Pentecostal congregation the initiate finds he is given a place which carries rights and duties.
> --C. Lalive d'Epinay (1969, 49)

Converts to Evangelical churches typically find themselves involved in a great deal of structured activity. Beyond the opportunity for expression, neophytes have demands imposed upon them that not only affect their time and resources, but strongly encourage the development of communication and organizational skills. Recognition of one's leadership and other contributions to the survival and growth of the congregation become circular, as members are encouraged to invest increasingly in the "work" (*la obra*) and assume still greater responsibility for its development. Whether such opportunities exist elsewhere (as apparently often they do not), at least for persons involved in the process, community life brings the realization of latent personal abilities and rewarding opportunities to exercise them. Observers have often remarked on the weakness of Pentecostal groups because of the lack of formal training of pastors and their rapid rise to positions of responsibility. This alleged weakness, however, often appears to be the reason for the Pentecostals' vitality. The doctrine of spiritual gifts (charismata), provides justification for diffused leadership, widely shared labor, and the right to contest (at least in some forms) organizational authority.

Much of the routine work of caring for the church building, overseeing regular services, and dealing with the needs of the congregation requires a considerable amount of organization, activity, and the development and exercise of the members' skills. Pentecostal congregations provide social welfare services to needy families, the sick, and the aged. If assistance is limited, it nevertheless provides members who are without a family or are deprived of a livelihood, some minimal social guarantees. In addition, the community provides adult role models and surrogate parents for children. In churches where vision for progress exists, the members often attain extraordinary levels of cooperation and reliability. Planning, projection of programs, decision-making, allocation of resources, and many other roles appropriate to associational life, are part of the members' participation in an Evangelical community. While ascription remains determinative in most Latin American social situations, in Evangelical churches, especially in Pentecostal congregations where persons of humble social status predominate, achievement is the rule. Not only does this policy permit persons of little standing to find social opportunity, but it permits the full use of everyone's talents and energies.

An important feature of organization is acquisition of legal recognition in the form of *personería jurídica*. Threatened with reprisals or discrimination, the members of legally recognized Pentecostal congregations may assert their legitimacy even while they remain a small minority in the community. While Pentecostals have sometimes been viewed as tools of reactionary political regimes, their sometime support of dictatorships is largely a matter of recognizing the state as the agency that guarantees their legitimacy and protects their right to an independent existence. More often, as has also been observed with concern, Pentecostals appear simply to withdraw from political participation in their efforts to remain independent and uncompromised.

A landmark study of Pentecostalism was published by Luther Gerlach in 1974. According to his analysis, Pentecostals as groups ensure their survival by being "segmentary" (cellular), "polycephalous" (possessing collegial leadership) and "reticulate" (networked). The basic unit of this organization is the congregation, which is free to form new cells by splitting or creating entirely new entities, each with an existence of its own. A second characteristic is the tendency to be "many headed," without a paramount leader but with a "first among equals" who can retain his office only by continually proving his worth. "Any member of the small group is a potential leader and many indeed strive to be actual leaders since they feel that they have a duty to help the group succeed" (Gerlach 1974, 680). A third characteristic of Pentecostal organization is that it is reticulate, a network of overlapping memberships sharing a common cause, ideology, and opposition. Gerlach explained the versatility of such a system by noting that it defies efforts to rationalize its organization and, in the process, creates a system "highly adapted for exponential growth and for generating and promoting revolutionary change" (Gerlach 1974, 681).

> First, it promotes coping in new environments, maximizing cellular variation, innovation, entrepreneurship, and trial-and-error experimentation and problem solving. The failures of the group do not cause the whole to fail, but the successes help the total movement. Second, it permits a movement to penetrate and recruit from a broad societal range. An individual who is attracted by what he perceives to be the general purposes of the movement can find within the myriad of cells a group of peers whose goals, tactics, personal

> life styles, and backgrounds appeal to him. Third, it prevents effective suppression or cooptation of the total movement through its redundancy, multiplicity of leadership, and self-sufficiency of local groups. Fourth, it generates an escalation of effort and forward motion through the rivalry and competition among its various segments and leaders (Gerlach 1974, 681).

The system encourages individual and group persistence, risk-taking, and sacrifice for the cause. It tends to provoke an unjust opposition, strong enough to challenge but eventually be overcome by the group, and it compels its members to take bridge-burning acts that cut them off from the established order and often from past associations.

The skills and roles learned in the context of the congregation may not easily apply to other areas of life, but there is undoubtedly some transfer. Recognition of their accomplishments by individuals outside the congregation draws some Pentecostals to become involved in political and administrative functions in the larger community. Despite their usual reluctance to take part in many community events, churches often organize marches or other outdoor events that are designed to heighten their visibility. The approval of the larger community, even if conceded reluctantly in the form of respect for persons with strong convictions in a *machista* society, places the members of the Evangelical church on a platform not generally available to unaffiliated Latin Americans. Evangelicals, it has been argued, have essentially created their own separate community not for the purpose of remaining aloof, but in order to establish for themselves a staging area from which they can more effectively operate in a hostile world.

Increasingly, it is clear that Pentecostals' intentions are not narrowly limited. While the movement has often been considered irrelevant to the communal life of Latin America, it provides a serious institutional alternative for many people who have few other opportunities to exercise leadership or participate responsibly in their communities.

Moralism

> [Pentecostal] groups are effective moral communities [that] stress the importance of their moral code. Offenders are disciplined.
>
> --Bryan Roberts (1968, 767)

> As they see it, a person's Christian quality . . . is certified by changes which occur in his moral life, rather than by his doctrinal loyalties.
>
> --Byron Wilson (1970, 72)

Another key moment in the process of Pentecostal institutional development may be found in the insistence that the members conform to the often rigid demands of personal integrity and group loyalty. Although many of the functions of the Evangelical congregations could be met by other voluntary associations, the emergence of congregations as "moral communities" is an important reason for their success and an inherent function of the groups' religious commitment. Their doctrinal positions and the solemnization of the investiture of offices sacralize the various social functions of the group, implicitly invoking divine sanctions against members who betray the group's purposes or other members' expectations. Through an extended process of setting boundaries, enforcing codes of behavior, creating an expectation of acceptable behavior both inside and outside the group, rewarding loyalty to the group's tenets, and administering justice with reasonable firmness and compassion, the system evokes a great deal of internal loyalty that serves to bind members not simply to a church, but to a set of internalized values.

Their role as "moral communities" explains much about the growth of Pentecostal groups. Characteristically they promote the same values found in the family: reciprocity, respect for elders and others in authority, faithfulness to each other in a variety of relationships including marriage, chastity, care for children and others needing special care, asylum for persons who have been taken advantage of by outsiders, identification in a society where isolated individuals are often especially vulnerable, and admission to a "family" of persons disposed to share both joy and grief. This moralism makes Pentecostal and other Evangelical churches distinctive in Latin American popular culture where one finds considerable tolerance for violation of ideal morality.

Such high behavioral expectations are likely to result in frequent lapses. Mechanisms for accepting less than ideal conduct, or for the restoration of the lapsed, are an important feature of Pentecostal groups. They are designed to direct the progress of new converts toward full status until there are reasonable assurances that the individual will conform to the established norms. In the relatively brief history of Latin American Pentecostalism, the distinctiveness of the members' doctrines and practices have been enough to repel all but the fully committed. Thereafter, water baptism, usually preceded by a catechism and a probation sufficiently long to establish the neophyte's commitment to the group, further assures the community of his or her sincerity.

When there are lapses, the penitent's acceptance of the group's ethical demands in the process of restoration to the community tends to renew the entire group's commitment to those standards. Individuals who persist in defying the group's code or who demonstrate disregard for its sanctions are disciplined or expelled, purging the group of persons who are not wholehearted in their commitments. What tends to remain is a group of highly committed persons whose involvement is based on demonstrated loyalty to the group and its beliefs and code of conduct.

Studies of Pentecostals' attrition rates have suggested that groups sometimes experience large losses. Undoubtedly the number of persons who remain active over a prolonged time is far less than those who are initiated into the churches. Ultimately, the effectiveness of the system lies not in quantitative growth of the adherents, but in their qualitative development. When too many constituents fail morally, the group loses its sense of purpose, its credibility and, likely, its membership declines. Where a dedicated, enthusiastic nucleus emerges, a growing church is bound to follow, if not in numbers, at least in the persistence and tenacity of the remaining members.

Versatility

> The genius of Pentecost is to be free to find new methods,... to adopt and adapt practices which reflect their cultural heritage.
>
> --William R. Read (1969, 324, 321)

> Pentecostals tend to be adventurous; [they] have more new congregations and they *trust them more.*
>
> --Donald McGavran (1977, 98-99)

> Freedom implicit in the Spirit's gifts confirms them in exercising individual freedom that a rigid confessional orthodoxy could never countenance.
>
> --Emilio Castro (1972, 956)

The Pentecostal movements of Latin America have grown in diversity as well as in size. Springing from a variety of situations, the fertile soil of contemporary crisis and change has led to a broad range of movements, including those that reflect the different aspirations of ethnic groups, those built largely on diverse regions or social classes, and those that accommodate diverse doctrinal, organizational and denominational emphases. Moreover, an important feature of each of these movements is its capacity for development and change. Considering that all of the groups tend to incorporate the features previously identified, they adjust to them in a variety of ways and continue to adapt to internal and external circumstances after reaching an advanced stage of development.

This tendency to adapt, besides contributing importantly to Pentecostal survival and growth, gives the movement a progressive posture that sometimes appears incongruous. For example, while many Evangelical groups resisted the use of folk instruments and musical styles, Pentecostals readily accommodated these cultural forms. Technological innovation is another interesting aspect of Pentecostal versatility. If few Pentecostal churches have pianos, to say nothing of pipe organs, they have readily adopted the electronic keyboard, a standard instrument of secular entertainers.

The pragmatic willingness of Pentecostals to break with outworn tradition is nowhere better displayed than in the prominent place which women have assumed in the movement. Beyond some leadership roles, including that of pastor, women invariably control the selection of the (usually male) pastor through their majority vote and they control all congregational policies indirectly through their offerings. Some observers view Pentecostal churches as essentially a protest mounted by women against the disabilities that Latin American women face in a machista culture (Butler Flora 1986; Brusco 1986).

Pentecostals are no less inclined, if not always astutely, to seek novel ways of addressing other problems, such as giving a greater political voice to disadvantaged popular groups by displays of organizational strength (Garma Navarro 1984). Often appearing pragmatic, they use a variety of means to advance their cause, generally, without abandoning their principal reason for being, and without unduly committing themselves politically. Their political independence, as well as their tentativeness and a wide variety of mechanisms for instrumenting change, permits a variety of approaches and strategies.

The often-criticized tendency of Pentecostal groups to fragment serves as an extremely effective means of applying a variety of different approaches to difficult problems. This "speciation," as in the biological analogy, ensures that some groups will survive even as others fail, resulting in the perpetuation of the movement (Gerlach 1974). While pragmatism and adaptability may gravely weaken Pentecostal distinctiveness, flexibility must be recognized as an organizational characteristic which is, on balance, a strength.

Conclusion

The internal structure of Latin American Pentecostal groups, articulated by successive "moments," helps explain the groups' dynamic development. Moving from a large "pool" of potential adherents, many of whom bring with them considerable vision, abilities and material resources, and at least latent commitment to an enterprise of a socially redemptive nature, Pentecostals have formed themselves into voluntary associations that reproduce some strategic features of traditional social organization. Beyond the immediate benefits of a surrogate extended family or community, including acceptance and a proprietary interest in a legally constituted, property-owning collective, the congregation enhances the further development of the initiates by encouraging and validating an intense subjective experience and morally reinforcing their values, beliefs, and conduct. In a society where status is largely ascribed, the adherent is presented with the opportunity for personal growth, peer recognition, and extended influence, in addition to the acquisition of skills that have broad application outside the church community. Moreover, the church provides opportunities for extending one's associations, often through a network well beyond the constituent's family, village, city and nation.

While various other voluntary associations and networks could theoretically provide similar benefits, the Pentecostals' motivation and moral discipline contribute indispensably to the survival and growth of their churches. Recurrent cycles of recruitment, constituent formation, and institutional development over a period of time produce a dynamic, effective popular institution uniquely appropriate for orienting and mentoring contemporary Latin Americans in a time of great change.

The organizational effectiveness of these groups, however, appears to lie in large part in their religious propensities. Without the intense, morally vindicated efforts of their adherents, congregations would lack much of the incentive, personal discipline, and sacrificial effort that are necessary for institutional success. According to Luther Gerlach,

> The very characteristics of ecstatic religious behavior -- ceremonial dissociations, decentralized structure, unconventional ideology, opposition to established structures -- which might appear to be makers of a sect of misfits and dropouts, are indeed the features which combine to make Pentecostalism a growing, expanding, Evangelistic religious movement of change. It is a movement which is likely to disturb those who wish religion to maintain established ways and values. We have examined Pentecostalism as an example of a religious movement which, in spite of conventional interpretations of its seemingly bizarre features, is in fact a movement for change, not a collection of sects, an opiate, or an anchor for tradition (Gerlach 1974, 686).

At each developmental moment there are "spiritual" motivations that advance the movement. Converts typically enter the process with enthusiasm originating from intense aspiration and relief that sustains their commitment and differentiates them from the non-Evangelical community. The immediate results of adherence to a Pentecostal group are often quite positive -- adoption into a community dedicated to the well being of its members. Longer association imposes burdens on the adherents as their fraternal relations require altruistic conduct, honesty, good will, and even sacrifice, but in large measure reciprocity ensures that even here there is little net cost to the individual. Ultimately, the growth of Pentecostalism in Latin America as an authentic expression of popular sentiment, appears to depend on this continued spiritual sensitivity and aspiration.

Reference List

Anderson, R. M. 1979. *Vision of the disinherited: The making of modern Pentecostalism.* New York: Oxford University Press.

Barrett, D. B. 1990. Statistics, Global [Pentecostal]. In *Dictionary of Pentecostal and charismatic movements*, eds. S. M. Burgess and G. B. McGee, 810-830. Grand Rapids: Regency (Zondervan).

Berger, P. 1990. Introduction. In *Tongues of fire, the explosion of Protestantism in Latin America*, ed. David Martin. Oxford: Blackwell.

Boudewijnse, B., A. Droogers, & F. Kamsteeg. 1991. *Algo más que opio.* San José, Costa Rica: Editorial Dei.

Brusco, E. 1986. The household basis of Evangelical religion and the Reformation of machismo in Colombia. Ph.D. Diss. City University of New York

Butler Flora, C. 1978. *Pentecostalism in Colombia: Baptism by fire and spirit.* Cranbury, NJ: Associated University Presses.

Castro, E. 1972. Pentecostalism and ecumenism in Latin America. *Christian Century* (September): 955-957.

Cleary, E. 1992. Report from Santo Domingo. *Commonweal* (20 November): 7-8.

Corral Prieto, L. 1984. Las iglesias Evangélicas de Guatemala. Master Thesis. Universidad Francisco Marroquin.

Deiros, P. A., ed., 1986. Los Evangélicos y el poder político en America Latina. Grand Rapids, MI: Eerdmans.

Dominguez, R. 1971. *Pioneros de Pentecostés en el Mundo de Habla Hispana.* 2 vols. Miami: Literatura Evangelica.

Escobar, S. 1973. What is happening to the fastest growing church in the World? *His* (October): 8-11.

Garma Navarro, C. 1984. Liderazgo Protestante en una lucha campesina en México. *América Indígena* 44(1): 127-141.

Garrison, V. 1974. Sectarianism and psychosocial adjustment: A controlled comparion of Puerto Rican Pentecostals and Catholics. In *Religious movements in contemporary America*, eds. I. I. Zaretasky and M. Leone, 298-329. Princeton: Princeton University Press.

Gaxiola-Gaxiola, M. J. 1975. *The serpent and the dove: A history of the Apostolic Church of the faith in Christ Jesus in Mexico (1914-1964)*. South Pasadena: William Carey Library.

Gerlach, L. 1974. Pentecostalism: Revolution or counter-revolution. In *Religious movements in contemporary America*, eds. I. I. Zaretsky and M. P. Leone, 669-699. Princeton: Princeton University Press.

Gill, L. 1988. Bolivia: Pentecostals fill a gap. Series on Women in Poverty in the Andes, part II, *Christianity and Crisis*, 395-397.

Glazier, S. D. G., ed. 1980. *Perspectives on Pentecostalism: Case studies from the Caribbean and Latin America.* Lanham, MD: University Press of America.

Gros, J., FSC. 1987. Confessing the apostolic faith from the perspective of the Pentecostal churches. *Pneuma* 9(1) (Spring): 5-16.

Hoffnagel, J. C. 1980. Pentecostalism: A revolutionary or a conservative movement? In *Perspectives on Pentecostalism: Case studies from the Caribbean and Latin America*, ed. S. D. Glazier, 111-123. Lanham, MD: University Press of America.

Hoover, W. C. 1931. *Historia del avivamiento Pentecostal en Chile.* Santigago: Comunidad Evangelica de Chile.

Howe, G. N. 1980. Capitalism and religion at the periphery: Pentecostalism and Umbanda in Brazil. In *Perspectives on Pentecostalism*, ed. S. D. Glazier, 125-141. Lanham, MD: University Press of America.

Huntington, D. 1984. God's saving plan. *NACLA Report* 18(1): 23-33.

Jones, C. E. 1990. Holiness Movement. In *Dictionary of Pentecostal and charismatic movements*, eds. S. M. Burgess and G. B. McGee, 406-409. Grand Rapids: Regency (Zondervan).

Kessler, J. B. 1967. *A study of the older Protestant missions and churches in Peru and Chile, with special reference to the problems of division, nationalism and native ministry.* Goes: Oosterman and Le Cointre.

Lalive d'Epinay, C. 1969. *Haven of the masses: A study of the Pentecostal movement in Chile.* London: Lutterworth Press.

Latin America's Protestants: A potent force for change. 1990. *Business Week* (4 June): 79.

Manning, F. E. 1980. Pentecostalism: Christianity and reputation. In *Perspectives on Pentecostalism*, ed. S. D. Glazier, 177-187. Lanham, MD: University Press of America.

Marcom, J., Jr. 1990. The fire down South. *Forbes* (15, October): 56-71.

Martin, D. 1990. *Tongues of fire: The explosion of Protestantism in Latin America.* Oxford: Blackwell.

Marty, M. 1976. *A Nation of Behavers.* Chicago: University of Chicago Press.

________. 1983. Baptistification take over. *Christianity Today* (2 September): 33-36.

McGavran, D. 1977. What makes Pentecostal churches grow. *International Bulletin of Church Growth* 13(3) (January): 97-99.

Mello, M. de. 1974. Participation is everything: Evangelism from the point of view of a Brazilian Pentecostal. *International Review of Mission* 60(238): 245-248.

Nida, E. A. 1974. *Understanding Latin Americans; with special reference to religious values and movements.* Pasadena, CA: William Carey Library.

Pretiz, P. 1988. The gospel people. *Latin America Evangelist*, (October): 18-19.

Protestants create an altered state. 1990. *Insight* (16 July): 9-17.

Read, W., V. Monterroso, and H. A. Johnson. 1969. *Latin America church growth*. Grand Rapids: Eerdmans.

Roberts, B. 1968. Protestant groups and coping with urban life in Guatemala City. *American Journal of Sociology* (May): 767.

Rodriguez, Richard. 1993. Don't pity the Indian in the year of Columbus. *Chapel Hill, North Carolina Herald*, (12 October): 4.

Shepperd, J. W. 1990. Sociology of Pentecostalism. In *Dictionary of Pentecostal and charismatic movements*, eds. S. Burgess and G. B. McGee, 794-799. Grand Rapids: Regency (Zondervan).

Stoll, D. 1990a. *Is Latin American turning Protestant?* Berkeley: University of California Press.

________. 1990b. A Protestant reformation in Latin America. *The Christian Century* (17 January): 44-48.

Taylor, W., and C. Emilio Nuñez. 1989. *Crisis in Latin America: An Evangelical perspective*. Chicago: Moody Press.

Wagner, C. P. 1988. Church growth. In *Dictionary of Pentecostal and Charismatic Movements*, eds. S. M. Burgess and G. B. McGee, 180-195. Grand Rapids: Regency (Zondervan).

Willems, E. 1967. *Followers of the new faith.* Nashville: Vanderbilt University Press.

Villapando, W. L., ed. 1970. *Christian Lalive d'Epinay and Dwain C. Epps: Churches of the transplant.* Buenos Aires: Centro de Estudios Cristianos.

Wilson, B. 1970. *Religious sects: A sociological study.* New York: McGraw-Hill Book Company.

Wilson, E. A. 1983. Sanguine saints: Pentecostalism in El Salvador. *Church History*, 52 (June): 186-198.

________. 1988. The Central American Evangelicals: From protest to pragmatism. *International Review of Mission* 77 (January): 94-106.

_______. 1990. Identity, community and status: The legacy of the Central American Pentecostal pioneers. In *Earthen vessels: American Evangelicals and foreign missions, 1880-1980*, eds. J. A. Carpenter and W. R. Shenck, 133-151. Grand Rapids: Eerdmans.

_______. 1991. Passion and power: A profile of emergent Latin American Pentecostalism. In *Called and Empowered: Global Mission in Pentecostal Perspective*, eds. M. Dempster, B. D. Klaus and D. Petersen, 67-97. Peabody, Mass: Hendrickson Publishers.

Wonderly, W., and J. Lara-Braud. 1964. *¿Los evangélicos somos así?* México: Casa Unida de Publicaciones, S.A.

Woodward, K. 1986. The Protestant push. *Newsweek* (1 September): 64.

Wuthnow, R. 1984. *Cultural analysis: The work of Peter L. Berger, Mary Douglas, Michel Foucault and Jürgen Habermas.* New York: Routledge and Kegan Paul.

Yinger, J. M. 1970. *The scientific study of religion.* New York: The Macmillan Company.

SOCIAL AND POLITICAL IMPLICATIONS OF PROTESTANT GROWTH IN LATIN AMERICA

Chapter 5

Protestant Presence and Social Change in Latin America: Contrasting Visions

Guillermo Cook

Introduction

Christianity was long taken for granted in Latin America. Roman Catholicism in particular was a given -- socioculturally and politically -- and a religious force to be reckoned with. It was, as it were, part of the spectacular scenery. The pageantry and the color attracted the attention of foreign visitors who rarely even noticed the presence of Protestant churches. Protestantism was simply not considered a significant factor in society. All of this has changed in the last 30 years.

In the 1970s and 1980s, observers of the religious scene turned their attention to the revitalization movements within the Catholic Church -- in particular the Charismatic Renewal and the Base Ecclesial Communities. In the 1990s, their focus has shifted to the startling growth of Latin American Protestantism. This latest phenomenon has been studied from a number of methodological perspectives by scholars in Europe and North America. Most notable among them are David Martin, of Britain, and David Stoll, a North American -- whose works have drawn considerable attention to the social and political implications of the Protestant growth. In Latin America, secular social scientists and Catholic missiologists are also focusing upon the growing Protestant presence. A key issue for nearly all of these observers is the potential impact of Protestantism on Latin America's long-festering social, economic, and political problems. David Stoll asks, "Could the surprising Evangelical groundswell affect the course of events in Latin America?" (Stoll 1990, 182). Some scholars view Protestants as too apolitical to permit an affirmative answer to Stoll's question. Others fear an affirmative answer because they expect Protestants to align themselves with an already ascendant reactionary tide. Such possibilities are real, but the record of Protestantism in Latin America indicates that other outcomes are quite possible as well. Indeed, if there is one leson to be learned from the last several decades it is that Latin American Protestants are quite capable of surprising the most knowledgable of observers with unanticipated developments.

The Context of the Protestant Presence

Beginning around the middle of this century, events in Latin America have brought about dramatic changes in both Protestantism and in the society of which they are a part. Perhaps we could think of them in terms of two concurrent explosions -- the social explosion and the religious explosion.

The Social Explosion

The majority of early Evangelical converts came from the urban and rural working classes. There were, of course, notable exceptions. The first Protestant missionaries to Guatemala and Brazil came at the invitation of chiefs of state who hoped that the religion from the North might weaken the power of the Roman Church in their lands and bring the intellectual and material benefits of Western Europe and North America. These missions focused initially on winning converts from among the liberal elite. Nonetheless, the majority of Protestant converts were poor. Their ancestors had been poor since the time of the Conquest. If anything, their lot worsened after the Latin American nations became independent from Spain and Portugal. In Guatemala, to pick a notable example, the modern assault on native American land and labor began in 1870 when General Justo R. Barrios, the "reformist" president who brought Protestantism to Guatemala, tried to introduce modern production methods, along with cash crops such as coffee. The eventual result was the removal of millions of acres from Indian ownership and the expansion of the national army to silence any objectors. He built railways and a secret police that was so effective that a British consul described Guatemala as "one of the most cruel despotisms the world has ever seen" (Wright 1992, 265). Today's poverty is even more acute. The statement "the rich are growing richer and the poor are becoming poorer," while trite, yet accurately describes the social and economic reality of contemporary Latin America. The social crisis of Latin America can be seen in unequal distribution of land, capital losses to the wealthy nations, huge masses of displaced people, an unpayable foreign debt, hundreds of thousands of street children, corrupt politicians, festering shanty towns, drug cartels, spiraling violence, and deadly epidemics.[1] This explosive social environment provides the context within which Latin American Protestantism is growing.

The Religious Explosion

Accompanying the social explosion is a religious explosion which includes the growth of Protestantism, but which also encompasses pseudo-Christian sects and nativistic African and Amerindian religious movements. To grasp this second phenomenon it is necessary to understand the interaction and competition between newly prominent Protestantism and the hitherto predominant Catholicism. One way to assess their relationship is to focus on the various strategies which the Catholic Church has adopted in its 500 year effort to direct the religious life of the Latin American people.

Ivan Vallier pointed out some time ago that the survival strategy of the Catholic Church has consisted of "maximization of short-term gains when conditions are favorable, and exercising of restraint in periods of uncertainty, and an ever present willingness to be inconsistent if the situation demands it" (Vallier 1970, 23, 26). The Vatican, adds David Martin, has tried three strategies in its efforts to defend its interests in Latin America: 1) *Christendom*, church and state successfully merged their self-interests during the Colonial era; 2) *Political realignments*, after the national independence movements of the nineteenth century had separated church and state, the church empahsized indoctrination to maintain social control; and 3) *Liberation Theology and the base church communities*, these were tolerated in the '70s and 1980s in hopes of regaining the allegiance of the masses. None of these "strategies" has worked (Martin 1990, 7, 8). Rome is now attempting a fourth strategy, *Lumen 2000*, the "new evangelization" of Latin America. The need for this strategy was proclaimed by pope John Paul II and recognized at the Santo Domingo Conference of Bishops (CELAM IV, October, 1992). Taken together, the sequence of strategies give unmistakble evidence that the relgous monopoly which the Catholic Church once enjoyed in Latin America has weakened considerably.

[1] By the end of 1992 the number of cholera sick in Latin America reached a staggering 324,345 (Latin America Newsletters, Jan. 28, 1993).

Some Catholic observers view this development in an insidious light. Left-of-center Catholics have tended to explain the extraordinary Protestant growth in Latin America in terms of a U.S.-based right wing conspiracy while conservative Catholics -- who years ago equated Protestants with "communists" -- now hint that the Evangelical presence is part of a U.S. imperialist plot. Rome needs to take another look at the evidence. David Stoll makes the case that Protestant growth is, in considerable measure, a result of the growing conservatism of Rome. As Catholics find less and less room for freedom of the spirit, they are turning to other alternatives, including to Protestantism. He insists that to blame Evangelical growth on extraneous influences implies a profound distrust of the poor and of their ability to "turn an imported religion to their own purposes" (Stoll 1990, xvi).

Rome is not the only one to suspect a plot; conspiracy theories are also rife among Protestants. While "progressive" Protestants join some Catholics in suggesting that traditional Protestants are at least unwitting tools of U.S. imperialism, "right wing" Protestants point accusing fingers at their "leftist" and "liberal" brothers and sisters. As they see it, the nefarious influence of Liberation Theology and of the Base Ecclesial Communities (BECs) has undermined the very foundations of the Gospel. Hence, people in search of the *real* gospel turned to Protestantism.

In actual fact, the interaction between the Catholic BECs and grassroots Protestantism is too complex to fit neatly into the conspiracy theories of either the Left or the Right. And there is no certainty that recent trends which have favored Protestantism will continue indefinitely.

> Dealing with people as a part of a great mass instead of attending to their individual needs is a temptation that often follows success. Many pastors deal with the crowd and not with the individual.... People are starved for personal concern and love in many Latin American churches.... Roman Catholics who have learned something about spiritual sharing in the small Base Communities have said to Evangelicals who have been successfully capturing the crowds and erecting large buildings, "You seem to be going to where we have just come from" (Berg and Pretiz 1993, 126-27).

Whatever the case, Pentecostals now seem to be growing, at least partially, at the expense of the BECS. A recent study by a Brazilian ecumenical agency suggests that Catholic base community members are joining Pentecostal churches in mass (CEDI 1990, 3,6). Fr. José Comblin, a missiologist and BEC pastoral theologian, states categorically about the once burgeoning BEC movement in Northeastern Brazil: "It is obvious that the BECs multiplied much less than the Evangelical communities, at least during the past ten years." And this is because "we do not have enough pastors and we lack the missionary drive of the *crentes*" (Cook 1994).[2]

Historian Peter Winn suggests an alternative explanation for the flight of BEC Catholics to Pentecostal groups. To "conservatives... progressive base communities were part of the problem, not its solution, because they offered 'sociological support,' not the 'human support' that the Protestant sects provides. However, he concludes, "The problem was not the social concerns of the base community, but the character of its members and the burdens of its theology" (Winn 1992, 383).

The BECs, with their stress on Bible reading and the analysis of the written word, emphasized a literacy that many poor Brazilians did not posses (Winn 1992, 383). An illiterate woman who left a base community in a Rio shantytown to become a Pentecostal explained that:

> I used to be a Catholic. But when these Bible circles came, all they did was read, read, read. There was no more prayer. I felt they only liked those who could read. The Assembly of God is a place of prayer. They know that the Word kills, but the Spirit revives (Winn 1992, 383).

This testimony raises an interesting historical question. One of the sources of the Brazilian BECs was the MEB or Basic Education Movement, which an "intellectual, idealistic, and radical" young Catholic Action elite pioneered in the 1960s. "From a mere literacy program," it gradually developed into "a movement that had a growing stake in changing the basic socio-economic structures of Brazil." This literacy program "can be credited with laying the foundations for the BECs. This is probably one reason why the *comunidades* have proliferated more in Brazil than anywhere else in Latin America." The MEB leadership debated the wisdom of non-directive versus directive methodology and eventually chose the latter "more efficient" way of achieving their goals (Cook 1985, 65-67; see also De Kadt 1970, 102-21, 212-20). Today, a theologian who identified closely with those "young radicals" describes the result of this methodological decision.

> The priests are low-key: they listen, ask questions, show a lot of patience and kindness; they take part in meetings, and remain silent when they are in disagreement; people feel free to speak up. Priests practice every kind of dialogue; they have every intention of being dialogical. Nonetheless, there is generally not much dialogue, or dialogue does not come easily.... What this means is that no one learns to take initiatives, to accept risks, to debate and deliberate, and then to arrive at conclusions. No one learns how to be dialogical and fraternal in community. Everyone remains passive and expects

[2] *Crentes*, "believers," is a popular Brazilian term for Protestants.

> everything from the priest. He has solutions for every problem. This is a very profound malaise in Northeastern Brazil. Wherever the priest fails to take the initiative nothing happens. The laity have become accustomed to receiving everything on a platter, with bowing and scraping (Cook 1994).

In another Rio *favela*, Cecilia, a teacher who had no literacy problem, had also left a base community for an Evangelical congregation because of the difference in people. "Here I found peace and love and a community of help. Elsewhere there is a lot of egotism, but here people always help you with your problems." She went on to say that in her base community she "had been reluctant to discuss her family problems in front of neighbors who might gossip about her." But, in the "Universal Church," which was made up of people who, like herself, had come for help, she found people more supportive (Winn 1992, 384).

Catholics do not always leave the base communities for the sorts of reasons that Protestant observers can feel comfortable about. The spiritual dimension which many Protestants (perhaps mistakenly) have claimed to find lacking in the BECs, has become distorted in some of the fastest growing Pentecostal churches. For example, "Bishop" Macedo's Universal Church in Brazil teaches a gospel of "absolution from personal responsibility."

> "I learned that many of my problems were caused by evil spirits," Cecilia said. In the Catholic Church individuals are responsible for their sins. But in the Universal Church, if your husband left you or your child was unruly or you fell ill, evil spirits are to blame, and prayer, exorcism, or the laying on of hands could solve the problem (Winn 1992, 384).

In the mid 1980s I wrote that the Catholic base communities were a hope for renewal of the church (Cook 1985, 251). I did not foresee that the major beneficiaries of their vision of social transformation might turn out to be grassroots Protestant churches and a new breed of ecumenical base communities! The Catholic base communities seem to have a "short shelf life" compared to the continuity and numerical growth of Protestant congregations. When the BECs achieve the immediate goals of their struggle, or when the issues become fuzzy during periods of political pluralism, they often experience an identity crisis. Catholic grassroots communities, says Comblin, are searching for a new identity as they move "from the phase of being prophetic, spontaneous, and improvising to an institutional phase" (Cook 1994). Meanwhile, Latin American Protestants are defining their own identity increasingly in terms of their social and religious impact.

Dynamics of the Protestant Presence

Before we can assess the potential impact of Protestantism on its social environment, we must acknowledge two factors that constrain and complicate the movement's impact. First, superficial discipleship hinders the response of the Evangelical churches to the social crisis. Rapid growth often comes at the expense of responsible Christian discipleship. Large numbers of pastors and lay leaders are ill equipped to meet the challenges of today. As Protestants grow numerically, they are more susceptible to secular values. It is becoming less easy to distinguish Evangelical conduct from that of non-Evangelicals. The second factor that makes the future impact of Protestantism difficult to predict is the fact that Protestant upward mobility is slowing down. As the economic crisis makes it more difficult for Protestants to achieve economic and social progress, Evangelicals have begun making inroads among the very poor. The fact is, along with the main population, Evangelicals also seem to be slipping backward economically. Evangelicals may soon not be any more upwardly mobile than the general population. This unhappy fact is bringing about competing perceptions of the role of Christians in society.

These two factors help to explain why the Protestant presence is making itself felt in seemingly contradictory ways. In the early days of mission in Latin America, new life in Christ meant responsible citizenship and good works on behalf of fellow believers and of the needy with whom Protestants came in contact. Changed lives in time produced an upwardly mobile people who made an impact upon society through hospitals, schools, and orphanages, as well as in the significant number of well trained Protestant professionals. But over the years, as Evangelicals moved up in society through sobriety and hard work, they became more protective of their new status and thus more politically conservative. They preferred not to rock the boat.

Major changes are coming in the 1990s, as authoritarian leaders and politicians of every ideological persuasion begin to realize the political potential of Protestants and to court their votes. Protestantism, however, is neither politically nor ideologically homogenous. Martin comments that the transformational potential of the Pentecostals "social strike **from** society" (vs. the Marxist "strike **against** society") should not be underestimated. The security which comes from large numbers, greater maturity, and social improvement should make Pentecostals more aware of their civic responsibilities (Martin 1990, 235, 287).

There are indications that this is indeed begining to happen. (CLADE III) the Third Latin American Congress on Evangelization was convened in Quito, Ecuador, in August of 1992. More than 1000 Protestants attended, including conservatives and "progressives" from historical, independent, and Pentecostal churches. The CLADE III document is the most recent expression of a new social awareness among Latin Americans Evangelicals. In reference to its theme -- the proclamation of "the whole Gospel from Latin America to the whole world," -- the document states:

> The church must affirm and promote the life denied by all sin, by unjust structures and by avaricious interest groups. Within its community the different forms of discriminations predominant in society on the basis of sex, educational level, age, nationality, and race, must be ended. The church fulfills its mission as it follows Jesus' example and takes seriously God's question to Cain, "where is your brother?" We recognize that the Latin American church generally has not assumed this responsibility faithfully. It has confused the world, into which it was sent to serve, with worldliness and sin and has isolated itself from social and political processes. In some cases it even justified violent dictatorial regimes (Quito Document, 3).

David Stoll says that grassroots Protestant congregations may be going through the same slow process of consciousness raising that the Catholic base communities experienced in the '50s. As Protestant growth collides with increasing impoverishment, there are increasing opportunities for radicalization. But this process has its own peculiarly Protestant twist. Stoll suggests that Evangelical conversion may have become for the masses a more peaceful outlet for revolutionary fervor than the political message of liberation. Pentecostal churches and Protestant relief agencies are delivering more tangible material results without setting off unmanageable class and ethnic confrontations (Stoll 1990, 182, 310-314). All of the above factors must be taken into account as we turn now to the various agendas for social change which are dividing Protestantism in Latin America.

Protestants and Politics

Evangelicals are now at every level of society. Thrust into the mainstream of Latin American life, Protestants are becoming afflicted by the same social malaise as their non-Protestant neighbors. They now share with Catholics and others responsibility for the future of their nations. They are less and less a people unto themselves. Protestant responses reflect the major tensions in society rather than a coherent Evangelical position. Latin Americans -- the churches included -- are experiencing a crisis of ideology and of identity as they search for new utopias and role models. The "health and wealth gospel" competes with grassroots activism. Meanwhile, the poor have not lost their innate capacity for creative adaptation. They pick and chose from among available political and religious options those that best seem to meet their immediate needs, including Pentecostal churches and the more radical base communities.

It is not easy to categorize the involvement of Protestants in socio-political endeavors. Ideological, sociological, and religious variables complicate the issue. Some generalizations are possible however. The most significant division within the Protestant movement is that which separates a relatively small number of "Progressives" from a much larger group of "Conservatives." This distinction encompasses both theological and ideological issues.

Progressive Protestants

A tiny minority of Latin American Protestants established their own identity in relation to Catholic Liberation Theology during the 1960s and 1970s. They did so, it would seem, with insufficient reference to their own Reformed heritage. Unfortunately, Latin American Protestantism has produced very few "organic intellectuals" -- that is, theological exponents of the caliber and commitment of Catholic Liberation Theologians who actually leave their "ivory towers" to live and work among the poor. Paul Freston, a British political scientist who resides in Brazil, quotes the critique of Edin Abumanssur, a young sociologist associated with the Centro Ecumênico de Investigação (CEDI):

> The Ecumenical Movement of the 1960s and 1970s [in Brazil] looked toward society and politics... It was restricted to a small group of people... [in] a few autonomous organizations which survived on foreign financing... [It constituted] a tribe... the Movement was founded on politics... but was not very given to personal piety (Cook 1994).[3]

Freston documents the beginnings of this group in the Brazilian chapter of the Christian Student Movement in the 1950s and 1960s, and its gradual radicalization and removal from conversionist Christianity. He quotes Edin Abumanssur again: "The Ecumenical Movement... [is] a homogeneous group of Christians... ['Ecumenism' has become] a tribal term... which defines the insiders" (Freston 1992, 58). This "ecumenism" as Abumanssur describes it, fits neatly into a "sect" typology. In the same way that sects claim a

[3] Edin Abumanssur, "A Tribo Ecumênica: Um Estudo do Ecumenismo no Brasil nos Anos 60 e 90," pp. 8,9,58,85. Masters Thesis at The Pontifical University of Sao Paulo. Quoted in Paul Freston, "Church Growth and Politics: Para-church Organizations in Brazil," from his PhD. dissertation; forthcoming in Cook 1994.

monopoly on universal meaning, the young ecumenists in the 1960s and 1970s saw themselves as a sort of vanguard of the Christian proletariat.

> Paradoxically, this "tribe" gave to ecumenism the widest possible meaning: the unity of the churches would result from the political transformation of society and not vice-versa. "Religious discourse was just a working tool to explain reality." Following the theological fashion, the "tribe" spoke of Marxism, secularization, and the autonomy of the world. This discourse obviously distanced the "tribe" from the churches, but also reflected the estrangement that already existed.... In Brazilian Protestantism they were outsiders and their political concept of ecumenism was the only one in which they could find a role for themselves (Cook 1994).

Elitist Protestant ecumenists seem to have had little contact with their own grass roots. I have written elsewhere that "liberal institutions, stuck in their ivory towers, largely overlook the fact that the churches which they lionize in Latin America -- Protestant congregations that express their solidarity with the poor -- are mainly Evangelical in theology" (Cook 1990, 1177). Significantly the grassroots ecumenism is more evident in Central America and the Andean region -- where conservative Protestant churches are strong and the more liberal denominations are fairly inactive.

A less elitist, more socially and theologically "rooted" type of Progressive Protestantism made its appearance in Central America in the late 1970s when popular insurrections and violent repression prompted some Protestants in Guatemala, El Salvador, and Nicaragua to form their own versions of the Catholic base communities. These Protestant BECs were sustained by their faith in God and the Bible, and by the example of their own and Catholic martyrs. In a part of the world where Catholics and Protestants have been hostile to each other for generations, Archbishop Oscar Arnulfo Romero, became an inspiration to many ordinary Protestants.

> Noel Vargas was a young Pentecostal pastor and recent seminary graduate. In October of 1983, he was working as a school teacher on a farm cooperative in a Nicaraguan village near the Honduran border. Noel was murdered by a band of contras along with the coop director and the health worker, both of whom were members of the Church of the Nazarene. In Perú, lay Quechua Presbyterians were dragged out of their rural chapel and executed by a military patrol, on suspicion of being Shining Pathway cadres. This atrocity produced a sharply worded protest by the conservative Evangelical Confederation of Perú (CONEP) and galvanized Protestant involvement in defense of the native American population. Socioeconomic and military violence radicalized peasant Protestants along with their Catholic relatives and neighbors. One result of this process has been the base church communities (Cook 1991, 543-549).

In Nicaragua and El Salvador innocent civilians, some Evangelicals among them, suffered from armed violence. Protestants, along with Catholics, were forcibly conscripted, tortured, exiled or jailed, their women raped and their children savaged, on the merest suspicion of collaboration with the insurgents. Their response -- ecumenical solidarity with Progressive Catholics and principled opposition to the abuse of human rights by governments that claimed to be fighting communism -- is what prompts us to place them on the Progressive side of the Protestant communities.

For a time, something new seemed to be happening in Central America. A Protestant lay pastor summed it up in the following words:

> What God is doing amidst his people really escapes our theological comprehension... especially among the base of the Christian Community.... This eagerness for liberty, this enthusiasm for building a new society, this revolution, is evangelizing the church. This may seem like heresy, but today it is the truth. Never before have we seen how Evangelical Christians and Catholics can meet together in a village of the highlands to celebrate their faith, because there are no longer ministers nor priests in this zone (Fried *et al.* eds. 1983, 230, 231; see also Spykman *et al.* 1988, 222).

The anguish of violence was not the only factor that drew together the peasant peoples of Guatemala, El Salvador, Honduras, and Nicaragua into Protestant and Catholic base communities, in such numbers that it exceeded "the limits and technical capabilities" of the support groups. It was also hope that brought them together, a hope so great, the same layman testified, "that for the first time we can feel it profoundly. This people which... had been silent and bent over... [have] overcome this situation to rise up proudly amidst the pain, with hope." The situation, said he, "for those of us who have worked in the service of the Lord as Protestants... is a miracle... of God" (Fried *et al.* 1983, 230).

Small Protestant *comunidades* are still to be found throughout Central America. They are lead by prophetic churches and church leaders. The respected Iglesia Bautista Emmanuel in San Salvador, has its *grupos de solidaridad*, non-denominational rural cooperatives cum Biblical reflection centers. The courageous Lutheran Bishop, Medardo Gómez, has at great personal risk, stepped into Archbishop Romero's prophetic shoes. Lutherans and Baptists have suffered physical harm at the hands of government death squads. Despite the peace accord between government and guerrillas, the lives of local church leaders continue to be threatened. Better known, thought much misunderstood, was the support of numerous Baptist, Nazarene, Pentecostal and other leaders for many of the social changes that were set in motion by the Sandinista regime in Nicaragua during the 1980s

(Transformation 1992, 20-25). Over the years, Mennonites have promoted grassroots initiatives in Honduras. A handful of Baptists, Nazarenes, Church of God, and Independent Protestants still struggle to maintain a base community ethos in Costa Rica. Each of these expressions of the base community church has managed to hold on to its own distinctive liturgy, church discipline, and doctrine, alongside varying approaches to social involvement. But the tide of history seems to have turned against them -- at least for now.

Conservative Protestants

The majority of Latin American Protestants are conservative in theology and individualistic in their approach to social ethics. The Roman Catholic heritage of Latin America has deeply influenced Protestantism in the region. Conservative Evangelicals used to define their identity more in terms of their not being Catholic than of their own Reformation heritage. Yet even when Protestants defined themselves as non-Catholics (or anti-Catholic), they still clung to a magical worldview -- a legacy of 500 years of Catholicism. Baptist missionary Stanley Slade comments:

> ... listening to the prayers of Salvadoran Baptists, one hears the powerful echo of medieval spirituality.... One goes to the sanctuary not to meet with other believers, but to establish genuine contact with God.... This sacred character of the church building means that it cannot be profaned by non-religious activities (Slade 1992, 159-50).

Traditional Protestant piety also hinders the social involvement of Protestants. Kim Erno, a Lutheran pastor with ties to El Salvador, tells the following story. When Esperanza, a Catholic activist and the victim of an army bombing in 1990, sought refuge with her cousin, a member of a Fundamentalist church, the woman advised Esperanza to turn herself in to the army. "Esperanza protested, 'Why should I turn myself in? I've done nothing wrong!'" When the army began a house to house search for "guerrillas," Esperanza, "implored her cousin to protect her by claiming her as a daughter, but her cousin, refused saying that she had to obey God's law and therefore could not tell a lie. Esperanza countered, 'You are lying for a greater good!' Still the cousin refused" (Cook 1994). This kind of passive spirituality informs probably the majority of Latin American Protestants, who believe that a changed society will only come as a result of the accumulation of individual lives who have been transformed through the power of Jesus Christ.

Theologically conservative Protestants have traditionally avoided political controversy but recently some have become increasingly active in politics.

While there seemed to be an opportunity for social betterment as a fruit of the gospel, middle class Evangelicals saw no need to tamper with the existing social order. Their minority status also made such activism highly impractical. But Protestants now have high political visibility in several countries. René Padilla observes that "many Latin Americans continue to avoid politics for theological reasons. But times are clearly changing. The social engagement we are seeing today could not have been imagined just a few years ago" (Transformation 1992, 7). In October of 1991, some 60 Evangelical politicians, political scientists, and theologians met at the Kairos Center on the outskirts of Buenos Aires. The participants represented the entire ideological and political spectrum in Latin America -- from the far left to the extreme right. They organized a Union of Evangelical Politicians.

Undeterred by such recent setbacks as the Fujimori coup against his own Peruvian supporters and charges of corruption against several Evangelical lawmakers in Brazil, (Transformation 1992, 15-19) conservative Evangelicals have founded parties in Bolivia, El Salvador, Chile, and Panama. Moving beyond a fellowship of Evangelical politicians, they are calling for an Alianza Cristiana Internacional de Partidos y Movimientos Políticos. Sponsored by SEMILLA,[4] with headquarters in Regent University, this Latin American Evangelical coalition is developing a strategy that aims to promote a conservative political agenda. A "Meeting of Latin American leaders of Christian Political Parties and Movements" was to have taken place this year. The list of participants included both Protestant and charismatic Catholics who are actual or potential political leaders.[5] But the self-coup and subsequent ouster of Guatemalan president Jore Serrano Elías, (a leading "apostle" of a right-wing neo-Pentecostal church), who was to have been the honorary chair, caused considerable discomfort to right-wing Protestant activists. Nevertheless, the "kingdom" or "dominion" theology that undergirds this movement could, according to Stoll, "...conceivably encourage a new sense of moral responsibility" among the elites (Stoll 1990, 321).[6]

Such partisan Evangelical involvement is still a divisive issue among Evangelicals and not without dangers. Political involvement tends to be self-

[4] SEMILLA is an acronym which also means "seed." Besides this Evangelical Coalition related ministry, of recent vintage, there is also a Menonite continuing education program named SEMILLA that has been in existence for a number of years in Latin America.

[5] Documents and information were given to me by the Alianza interim coordinator, José L. González Souza March, 1993.

[6] "Dominion teaching" draws some of its theological rationale from Old Testament Reconstructionism (Theonomy). See "Democracy as Heresy," in *Christianity Today* (February 20, 1987), pp. 17-23.

serving, instead of promoting the general good of the people. Padilla points out that, like its counterpart in the U.S., "Latin American Evangelicalism... has a theological deficit which means that its movement runs the risk of investing its energies in fruitless and even destructive political activism" (Transformation 1992, 7). Is it too early to tell whether Stoll's optimism or Padilla's pessimism is the more appropriate response to the new wave of conservative political activism.

Conservative Theology -- Social Awareness

Pentecostalism and Evangelicalism have been in Latin America for many years. They have usually been associated with conservative theology and a conservative attitude toward society. Yet in recent years, some Pentecostals and a new breed of Evangelicals have been developing something new and unexpected: social awareness and involvement built upon a fairly conservative theology. Both religious movements span the "class barrier" -- intellectual elite and the popular masses -- but the "progressive Evangelicals," as I shall call them for want of a better name, are more identified with the intelligentsia, than the Pentecostals who, in two modalities, are represented at both the "top" and the "bottom" of the social pyramid.

Pentecostalism belies easy classification (Sepúlveda 1992). One can look at the movement chronologically and begin with the so-called "classical Pentecostals" who sprouted up in South America with very little outside encouragement in the early years of this century. Fifty years later, the "New Pentecostalism" exploded in Catholic and mainline Protestant churches in the U.S. (the Charismatic Renewal). It was soon exported to Latin America. Both kinds of Pentecostalism include both U.S.-related and indigenous churches. Over the years, classical U.S.-related Pentecostals have been moving up the social ladder. Currently, along with the New Pentecostals, they are the prime movers in the recent upsurge of conservative political activism. Meanwhile, some of the poorer, mostly indigenous Pentecostals became involved in the popular movements in Central America. Although their efforts did not involve the majority of Pentecostals, there has been a growing politicization of classic grassroots Pentecostals precisely at the point of their greatest numerical growth -- among the very poor and socially alienated.

Samuel Escobar quotes three Hispanic Catholic missiologists who are impressed with the growth of popular Protestantism. Fr. José Comblin, a Belgian missiologist who works in Northeastern Brazil, makes the point that the Pentecostal churches, while innately conservative, "are poor and of the poor. A large part of the poor are already there" (Cook 1994). A similar situation prevails as well in the sprawling urban areas of southern Brazil. According to a leading daily:

> The decline of the so-called historical churches -- both Catholic and Reformed -- and the growth of the Pentecostal sects can be seen as the consequence of the disillusionment of urban Brazilians who do not find in them where and how to spiritually compensate for the bitterness of their daily lives. Disillusionment largely explains why five churches from "new denominations" appear in Rio de Janeiro every week. This is a religious phenomenon of great consequences, if one pays attention to the recently converted mother who remarked: "We grab whatever religion is closest to us...." The more dehumanizing that life becomes in urban spaces it would seem that the less space there is for acceptance of historical religions.... The poorer the population of Rio becomes, the less Catholic it is (O Estado de Sao Paulo 1993; see also VEJA 1991, 32-38).

Extreme poverty and the gospel, both growing, now overlap. This has produced a new set of factors on the Latin American religious scene.[7] It has become very difficult for conservative Protestants to ignore the social ills of their countries. Christian compassion, enlightened self-interest, and pastoral expertise combine to mobilize Evangelicals socio-politically. And Pentecostals, who are closer to the masses of poor than any other Protestant movement, are uniquely situated to respond creatively. Their theology, which was once thought to be a drawback, can now become a driving force. It was a Brazilian Marxist sociologist, Carlos Rodrigues-Brandao, who in 1980 pointed out the latent revolutionary potential in "small sect" Pentecostalism. He suggested that this movement of "the poor of the earth" was perhaps more uniquely prepared than even the Catholic BECs to confront social ills because Pentecostals see themselves as engaged in a holy war; they are buoyed by a hope of "a final struggle that will re-create a social order." If Pentecostals ever became politically aware, they could become a potent force for change. "Their active belief in supernatural forces is not escapism, but a source of hope in their struggle to change their environment" (Brandao 1980, 317, 330; see also Cook 1985, 54-58, 251).

The union of Pentecostalism and political activism is not just a possibility for the future. During the 1970s and 1980s, *Brazil para Cristo*, a church headed by Manoel de Mello, was active in politics in ways that gave some evidence of a social conscience. The movement may be losing its social impact now that it has joined the political establishment. In depressed Northeastern Brazil, many of the best leaders of the *Ligas Camponesas* (Peasant Leagues), an agrarian reform movement in the 1960s, were Pentecostals (Cartaxo Rolim 1985, 249).

[7] This is my personal evaluation which I now find supported by Paul Freston, "Evangélicos en la Política Brasileña" in Padilla 1990. Also quoted by Brown 1992, p. 49.

> Soon after the Peasant Leagues were formed came the 1964 military takeover, and many believers associated with the *Ligas* were sentenced to jail. One of these leagues was in Maranhao, where owners of large amounts of land would permit their cattle to enter the smaller territories of local residents (*posseiros*). Most of the residents were Pentecostals who gathered to protect themselves. They formed a syndicate which was closed down during the military repression (Cartaxo Rolim 1985, 86, 87).

During the same period, more than half of the rural labor leaders in the Brazilian state of Rio de Janeiro were Pentecostal (Freston 1992, 81; see also Reyes Novaes 1985, 136). Recently, eighteen of the 33 Evangelical members of the Constituent Assembly were Pentecostal (Freston 1992, 81). A masters' thesis published in 1992 shows "the highly significant **positive** effect of being a publicly identified Pentecostal on pro-worker voting behavior, not only when compared to the 460 deputies who are not religiously identified," but even when compared to the 22 deputies with a high traditional Protestant and Catholic profile (Brown 1992, 63, 64, see also 39, 49, 56, 68).[8] Put differently, "Evangelicals in general were slightly less favorable to workers than the entire Constituent [Assembly] but Pentecostals were a little more favorable" (Freston 1992, 78).

The other side of the coin of the pro-labor stance of Pentecostal leaders (which is probably a function of their working class roots) is their political inexperience and theological naivete. In the recent past, Pentecostal office holders in Brazil have tended to apply inflexible churchly answers to complex social problems. For example, a leading Protestant federal deputy was quoted as saying: "President Sarney is not to blame for a bad administration. Everything that is happening is in the Bible and will get worse from now on" (Freston 1992, 74). In other instances the actions of Pentecostal politicians seemed too much like that of every other politician -- self-serving. In August of 1988, a leading newspaper exposed a vote selling scandal that involved "a goodly number of Evangelicals involved in preparing the new Constitution" (77-78). As a result, only 7 of the 13 congresspersons were voted back into office. One of those who were reelected was Benedita da Silva, an Assemblies of God woman who belongs to the Workers' Party. Meanwhile, a small but significant number of young Latin American theologians are reflecting holistically on the social implications of their Pentecostal

[8] Based on statistics published in *Quem é quem na Constituinte*, Leoncio Martins Rodrigues, ed. Sao Paulo: Jornal da Tarde, 1987, and *Quem foi quem na Constituinte*. Sao Paulo: DIAP, 1988 (Who is/was Who in the Constituent [Assembly]). DIAP is the Departamento Intersindical de Assesssoria Parlamentar, an organization with special interest in workers' rights and labor unions.

experience.[9] This brings us to the second Protestant movement which is contributing to the new political awareness of conservative Evangelicals in Latin America.

A new kind of Evangelical began to appear in the 1970s. Freston argues that, contrary to their conservative image in the U.S., "Latin American Evangelicals are linked to the renewal of world evangelicalism, especially in the socio-political area." Their nearness to poverty and injustice in a supposed Christian continent led some theologically conservative Protestants "to take up positions which were not on the horizons of First World Evangelicals." After the conflicts of the 1960s, a new Evangelical leadership developed in the 1970s and 1980s, heavily influenced by a few parachurch groups. In Brazil, during the late 1980s, as a subproduct of this trend, an Evangelical Progressive Movement, emerged in politics (Freston in Cook 1994). Freston quotes R. Cavalcanti a well-known Brazilian Evangelical and political scientist who supported the Workers' Party candidate for president in 1989:

> Pressured on the one hand by the Fundamentalist tradition, with its one-sided verticalism, and on the other hand by the liberal and liberationist tradition, with its one-sided horizontalism, we [Evangelicals] represent a commitment to sound doctrine and godliness, a commitment to those who suffer and a struggle against unjust structures (Cook 1994; see also Cavalcanti 1990, 35).

The parachurch organizations that Freston refers to are: the Aliança Bíblica Universitária (ABU) which is related to the International Fellowship of Evangelical Students (IFES); the Latin American Theological Fraternity (FTL); and the Brazilian Evangelical Association (AEVB). Freston comments that while the ABU was begun in the 1950s as an essentially conservative student alternative to the ecumenical (UCEB) Student Christian Movement, it developed a more radical social awareness after the latter folded up.

[9] Juan Sepúlveda, a young Chilean Pentecostal with ties to the ecumenical movement, has written extensively. A few of his articles have been published in English. "Pentecostal Theology in the Context of the Struggle for Life" in Dow Kirkpatrick, ed., *Faith Born in the Struggle for Life*. Grand Rapids: Eerdmans, 1988, pp.298-318; "Pentecostalism as Popular Religiosity," *International Review of Mission*, 78(309), (Jan. 1989), pp. 80-88; "Pentecostalism and Liberation Theology: Two Manifestations of the Work of the Holy Spirit for the Renovation of the Church," in Harold Hunter and Peter Hocking, eds. *Altogether in One Place*. Sheffield, Eng.: Academic Press, 1993, forthcoming; "The Pentecostal Movement in Latin America" in Cook, 1993. Two Pentecostal members of the Theological Fraternity, Norberto Saracco of Argentina and Roberto Gondim of Brazil, presented two of the most missiologically profound position papers at CLADE III (Quito, Aug-Sept, 1992).

"While maintaining internal political pluralism, ABU leaned to the left, filling the gap in Protestant ranks after the [military] purges of the 1960s." Freston also credits international IFES support and the repercussions in Brazil of the Lausanne Covenant[10] for the changes in ABU. It refused, however, to become politicized on the university campuses (Cook 1994). For this reason, it was viewed with suspicion by ecumenical and progressive Protestants.

Most of the founders of the FTL in Brazil and throughout Latin America were closely related to IFES. Its members cover a broad socio-political spectrum in between the extreme Fundamentalisms of the left and the right. The Fraternity began in 1970 as a by-product of the First Latin American Congress on Evangelization (CLADE I, Bogotá, 1969). It has sponsored both CLADE II (Lima, Perú, 1979) and CLADE III (Quito, Ecuador, 1992). The FTL is not an association of theologians, but a fraternity of Evangelical Christians, pastors, teachers, doctors, lawyers, social scientists, who meet in local chapters to reflect biblically on their faith and practice.

> Like Liberation Theologians, FTL's members defined sin in social as well as individual terms. They recognized that... one's reading of the Bible was shaped by history and culture... But they were also critical of liberation theology. Instead of "liberation" as a paradigm, the fraternity chose another term: "contextualization" (Stoll 1990, 131, 132).

Another term which the FTL increasingly emphasizes is "holism" in mission. But it was not always so. Freston, at one time an IFES staff person and now an active FTL member, is nonetheless critical of the FTL for having, in its early years, shunned "political protest against government oppression of non-Evangelicals, and practical support for exploited workers."[11] He suggests that this stance "contributed to the exodus from Protestantism of much of a generation of young leaders, and to the isolation of the Pentecostals." Only in the last few years has it been possible to partially overcome this qualitative loss (Cook 1994). Nonetheless, the FTL has begun to provide, in Brazil and in the rest of Latin America, the kind of theological reflection that Evangelicals have needed to move ahead with a more biblically holistic approach to evangelization and socio-political involvement.

[10] The Lausanne Covenant is the relatively progressive document that was produced by the Lausanne Congress on World Evangelization, 1974.

[11] Freston, in Cook, 1993, quotes Anthony Christopher Smith, "The Essentials of Missiology from the Evangelical Perspective of the 'Fraternidad Teológica Latinoamericana,'" doctoral thesis, Southern Baptist Theological Seminary, Lousville, Ky., 1983, p. 283.

The FTL has convened consultations on "The Theology and Practice of Power" -- in Santo Domingo, 1983 (Padilla 1990, 7), and on political involvement -- in Buenos Aires, 1991. Between these two events, a series of regional consultations were held on the issues of poverty, oppression, and marginalization leading up to the 20th Anniversary Consultation of the FTL in Quito (1990) in which the Fraternity spelled out its theological position on socio-political involvement. Commenting on CLADE III, Jorge Maldonado of the WCC/CME observes:

> The Evangelicals who in the past were considered -- and considered themselves -- as being on the fringes of the political and social life of the region and were accused of being "on social strike," seem to have become aware of their numerical growth, their electoral potential and their capacity to commit themselves to social and political action. Slowly and persistently, they are claiming their space in the society and articulating their thinking, thereby making clear their intention to move away from mere nominal participation in elections and political demagogy. A whole evening was devoted to the dialogue, "Evangelicals and Political Life," with the participation of well known Evangelical political figures, analysts and theologians (Maldonado 1992, 2).

In 1991, the Brazilian Evangelical Association stepped into an ecumenical vacuum that had existed in conservative Protestantism since 1960 with the demise of the CEB, the Brasilian Evangelical Council. Scandals involving Evangelical politicians dramatized the need for an entity that could speak credibly on behalf of the enormous Evangelical population in Brazil. The key figure in the AEVB and its first president is Caio Fábio de Araújo, a well-known charismatic Presbyterian TV evangelist who has his own home grown parachurch organization, the National Vision for Evangelization (VINDE). He is also a forceful speaker on socio-political issues as the following quote illustrates:

> We have been on the wrong side of history in the last few years.... I am fed up with Protestant politicians who worry about putting the name of God in the Constitution. Politics is something to do in the name of man, not in the name of God. We need a politics which is verbally atheistic but practically Christian (Cook 1994).

The founders of the AEVB "represented the political center and left of the theologically conservative Protestant world. The idealizers were young and modern clergy from the historical churches and leaders of some parachurch organizations" (Cook 1994). As the Association has continued to attract representatives of the Protestant mainstream, including prominent Pentecostals, AEVB has had to scale back on some of its more "radical" pretenses. However, it does provide an important meeting place and opportunity for theological reflection for Pentecostals and other Evangelicals as they move into the political arena. Freston points out a parallel between the Evangelical Progressive Movement and the Catholic BECs in Brazil (1992). Unlike the Catholic and Protestant left of the 1960s which were isolated from their respective confessions, both movements have managed to remain within their churches, and retain the potential to effect profound changes within them.

Conclusion

Can Evangelicals make a difference in Latin America? Despite problems, tensions and set-backs, Latin American Protestants maintain a reserve of goodwill among the general public. So they can still influence society in positive ways. Their growing political strength is not just a function of their numerical strength. Evangelicals are garnering votes because (with some unfortunate exceptions) they stand for the old fashioned Protestant values of honesty, frugality, and fairness. Even those radical Protestants and Catholics who decry the loss of base community members to Pentecostal churches speak approvingly of the resulting lifestyle changes. Broken marriages and divided communities are healed, violence is reduced and socially acceptable conduct becomes the norm.

Protestants can make a difference in Latin America from both ends of the social scale. Middle class Evangelicals dream of changing society from the vantage point of political power. It remains to be seen whether or not this can be achieved without their being seduced by greed and succumbing to the lust for power. Meanwhile, growing numbers of grassroots Christians are involved in creative new models of witness such as community development, health education, cholera prevention, care for drug addicts and AIDS victims, food cooperatives, justice and peace initiatives. These modest efforts may be more significant in the long run than the Protestant involvement in formal politics.

Stoll remarks on the "immense social power of those praying masses of believers" (Stoll 1990, 321). But Catholic charismatics and BECs believers also pray, so it would seem that more than prayer is needed if the Evangelical contribution to social change is to make a difference in Latin America. Instead of resisting change, Latin American Protestants must recognize the new challenges and prepare for them, as they enter a new century. They must take up the task of responsible discipleship based on the model of the Suffering Servant, and avoid self serving political involvements. Otherwise we are in danger of repeating the tragic mistakes of the first 500 years of evangelization in Latin America.

Reference List

Berg, M. and Pretiz, P. 1993. *The gospel people.* Monrovia: MARC and Miami: LAM.

Brandao, C. R. 1980. *Os deuses do povo.* Rio de Janeiro: Editora Brasilense. (For English summary, see *Missiology*, X(2), (April 1982)).

Brown, Eric. 1992. *Pentecostals in politics: Their effect on worker's issues in the Brazilian constitution of 1988.* MA Thesis, University of Wisconsin, Madison.

Cartaxo Rolim, F. 1985. *Pentecostais no Brasil.* Petropolis: Vozes.

Cavalcanti, R. 1990. Lausanne: Caminhos ou descaminhos do Evangelismo. *Boletim Teológico.* n.s. 12 (August). Sao Paulo: Fraternidade Teológica Latinoamericana.

CEDI. 1990. Pentecostalismo autônomo, uma inversao sedutora? *Aconteceu no mundo evangélico.* Suplemento especial no. 548 (December). Sao Paulo, Brazil: Centro Ecuménico de Documentacao e Informaçao.

Cook, G. 1985. *The expectation of the poor: Latin American base ecclesial communities in Protestant perspective.* Maryknoll: Orbis.

________. 1990. Evangelical groundswell in Latin America. *The Christian Century* (12 December): 1172-1179.

________. 1991. Entstehung un Praxi der Evangelischen Basisgemeniden in Mittelamerika. *Evangelisches Theologi: Latinoamerika 1492-1992.* no. 6-91. University of Tubingen.

________. 1992. Growing Pains. *Christianity Today.* 36(4) (6 April): 1172-1179.

________. 1994. *New face of the church in Latin America: Between tradition and change.* Maryknoll: Orbis.

CT Institute. 1992. Why is Latin America turning Protestant? *Christianity Today* 26 (6 April): 4.

De Kadt, E. 1970. *Catholic radicals in Brazil.* London: Oxford University Press.

Freston, P. 1992. *Fé Bíblica e crise Brasileira.* Sao Paulo: ABU Editora.

Fried, J. L., M. Gettlemen, D. T. Levenson and N. Peckenham, eds. 1983. *Guatemala in rebellion: Unfinished history.* New York: Grove Press.

Maldonado, J. 1992. A monthly letter on evangelism. no. 3 (October-December). Geneva: WCC/CWME.

Martin, D. 1990. *Tongues of fire: The explosion of Protestantism in Latin America.* Oxford: Basil Blackwell.

O ESTADO DE SAO PAULO. 1993. A religiao que passa. Sao Paulo, Brazil (21 February).

Padilla, R., ed. 1990. *De la marginación al compromiso.* Quito: Latin American Theological Fraternity.

Reyes Novaes, R. 1985. *Os Escolhidos de Deus: Pentecostais, trabalhadores e cidadania.* Rio de Janeiro: Marco Zero.

Sepúlveda, J. 1992. Die Pfingstbewegung und ihre Identität als Kirche. In *Jahrbuch Mission*, ed. K. Wells, 146-147. Hamburg: Evangelisches Missionswerk.

Slade, S. 1992. Popular spirituality as an oppressive reality. *American Baptist Quarterly*, 11(2), (June): 145-158.

Spykman, G., L. Grahn, G. Cook, S. Rooy, M. Dodson and J. Stam. 1988. *Let my people live: Faith and struggle in Central America.* Grand Rapids: Eerdmans.

Stoll, D. 1990. *Is Latin America turning Protestant? The politics of Evangelical growth.* Berkley: University of California Press.

Stoll, D. and V. Burnett. 1994. *Rethinking Protestantism in Latin America.* Philadelphia: Temple University Press.

Transformation. 1992. *An international dialogue on social ethics* (July-Sept.): 2-7.

Vallier, I. 1970. *Catholicism, social control and modernization in Latin America*. Englewood Cliffs: Prentice Hall.

VEJA. 1991. Fé em desencanto. Rio de Janeiro (25 December).

Winn, P. 1992. *Americas: The changing face of Latin America and the Caribbean*. New York: Pantheon Books.

Chapter 6

Protestantism, the State, and Society in Guatemala

Timothy J. Steigenga

This chapter represents an attempt to understand the role of the Protestantism in Guatemalan state-society relations from 1871 to the present. My analysis relies upon the theoretical framework presented in Joel S. Migdal's *Strong Societies and Weak States: State-Society Relations and State Capabilities in the Third World* (1988).

Essential to an understanding of the history of the Protestant church in Guatemala from 1871 to 1930 is the concept of state autonomy. Roughly, autonomy means that state officials can act on their own preferences by changing, ignoring, or circumventing the preferences of other strong societal actors (Nordlinger 1987). It is my thesis that Guatemala's Liberal governments (1871-1920) supported Protestantism as one method of gaining autonomy from a strong societal actor, the Catholic church. In order to gain a higher degree of autonomy, the Guatemalan state needed to achieve greater *social control* over its strongly Catholic rural areas. *Social control* requires the effective regulation of resources and services, as well as the use of symbols.[1]

I have divided my chapter into four sections, each of which correlates to a particular time period and represents a new stage in the evolution of Guatemalan Protestantism. The first section describes how the Protestant church was introduced into Guatemala in the 1870s as one aspect of state attempts to gain social control over areas traditionally under the influence of the Catholic church and indigenous leaders.

The second section of the chapter explores the rapid growth of Protestantism in Guatemala since the 1950's. From 1955 to 1989, Protestant church membership grew from less than five percent to more than twenty percent of the Guatemalan population, giving Guatemala the highest proportion of Protestants to Catholics of any Latin American country (Larmer 1989, 6). It is my thesis that Protestantism has been particularly successful in Guatemala because it has represented a new *survival strategy* for a large sector of Guatemala's rural poor whose traditional strategies of survival have become obsolete. According to Joel S. Migdal, *survival strategies* are

> blueprints for action and belief in a world that hovers on the brink of a Hobbesian state of nature. Such strategies provide not only a basis for personal survival but also a link for the individual from the realm of personal identity and self serving action (a personal political economy) to the sphere of group identity and collective action (a communal moral economy) (Migdal 1988, 27).

Examining Protestantism as a new survival strategy in Guatemala sheds light on the debate between those who accept a rational choice theory of personal motivation (such as Robert H. Bates in *Toward a Political Economy of Development: A Rational Choice Perspective*) and those who view peasant activity as motivated by concerns of moral economy (such as James Scott in *The Moral Economy of the Peasant: Rebellion and Subsistence in Southeast Asia*). Conversion to Protestantism among Guatemalan peasants cannot be explained *purely* in rational choice or moral economy terms. Rather, peasants convert to Protestantism *both* for reasons of political and economic security (rational actor considerations) and as part of a larger change in value systems (moral economy motivations).

[1] According to Joel S. Migdal, "social control rests on the organizational ability to deliver key components for individuals' strategies of survival." Social control requires the effective regulation of resources and services as well as the use of symbols. Social control may be measured in terms of compliance, participation, and legitimation (Migdal 1988, 27, 32 and 80).

In the third section of the paper I will use Migdal's conceptions of social control to explain the relationship between the Guatemalan state and the Protestant church during the past two decades. During the 1970s and 1980s, the Protestant church in Guatemala was criticized for being an ally of the repressive military regimes of General Lucas García and Efraín Rios Montt. This period represents an example of how the Protestant church may be used by an authoritarian state as a tool for gaining social control over a potentially rebellious population.

The final section of the paper examines the downfall of Rios Montt in 1983 as an example of the limits of Protestantism in Guatemalan politics. Rios Montt's devotion to charismatic Protestantism and his accompanying attitude of moral superiority exacerbated conflicts within his regime and eventually led to his loss of power.

The implications of this study reach beyond the role of Protestantism in Guatemala. As the Protestant church continues to grow throughout Latin America the Guatemalan case may be understood as a test case that can aid in future attempts to explain the role of Protestantism in state-society relations elswhere.

The Protestant Church and State Autonomy

In Guatemala during the nineteenth century, the battle lines for the control of the state were clearly drawn between the Conservatives, made up of a coalition of landowners, bureaucrats, and religious leaders, and the Liberals, made up of an export-oriented elite that was heavily influenced by an ideology compounded of "enlightened liberalism" and the French revolution. The Catholic church, firmly on the side of the Conservatives, had established itself as a powerful actor both in the Guatemalan state and in society by the late nineteenth century.

The Liberal revolution of 1871 marked the end of Conservative rule in Guatemala. With the rise of Liberal strongman Justo Rufino Barrios as supreme commander of the Republic in 1873, Liberals began to consolidate their rule. A key to their success would be their ability to undermine the authority of the Catholic church, which continued to be a competing base of social control and a threat to state autonomy. According to Douglass Sullivan-González, when the Liberals took power more than one-third of Guatemala's land remained in the hands of the Catholic church and the upper class (Sullivan-González 1989, 5). This control over land, along with Catholic control over education, helped to make the Catholic church an effective regulator of resources and services (according to Migdal 1988, 27, 32, 80 -- the key to social control) for most Guatemalans. Perhaps more important, however, was the church's ability to provide the symbols associated with many rural Guatemalans' strategies of survival. The "semi-theocratic" government structures of most Guatemalan villages were often intricately linked to a system of *cofradías* or religious brotherhoods (Handy 1984, 46; and Van Oss 1986, 109). *Cofradías* provided both a political-religious structure and a cultural-economic system for Indian villages. The political-religious system was formed by a hierarchy of religious and secular offices that were ranked in terms of prestige and social honor (Nash 1970, 177). The cultural-economic system provided a leveling mechanism that encouraged economic parity by forcing the wealthy to spend their time and money on religious rituals and by the break up of estates through bilateral inheritance (179). Together, these factors created an autonomous Indian social structure that was linked to the Catholic church and isolated from national society. According to Manning Nash, the only link between the Guatemalan countryside and the national government was through local chieftains who were loosely allied to the central regime. While the *cofradías* were not directly supported by the Catholic hierarchy, they had the strong support of parish priests, many of whom depended upon the *cofradías* for a portion of their income (178).

The fundamental goal of the Liberals under Barrios was to impose order on Guatemalan society in an effort to promote rapid development along the lines of the modern nations of the nineteenth century. In order to accomplish this goal, the Liberals felt that traditional cultural practices had to be changed, opening the way for an ideology of progress similar to that held in other developed nations, the United States in particular. Once again, the Catholic church, with its large landholdings and its links to local leadership through the *cofradías*, represented the largest obstacle to the Liberal program (Miller 1966, 254).

The Liberals took a number of steps in the early 1870s to undermine the strength of the Catholic church. Jesuit landholdings were nationalized, monasteries were abolished, and on March 15, 1873, Barrios declared freedom of worship for "any and all religions" (Burnett 1987, 27). For Barrios and the Liberals, this declaration represented an attempt to convince North American missionaries to enter Guatemala. Barrios was so concerned with the introduction of foreign missionaries into Guatemala that in 1882 he personally requested that the Presbyterian Board of Missions send a missionary to his country (Latourette 1961, 115-116; Millett 1973, 372).

While the declaration of freedom of religion was not the most important factor behind the waning strength of the Catholic church, it merits further attention as an example of how a relatively weak state may attempt to introduce a new societal actor in order to weaken a relatively strong actor in civil society. Like his Mexican counterpart, President Benito Juárez, Justo Rufino Barrios hoped to bring North American Protestant missionaries to Guatemala and thereby to undermine the traditional power of the Catholic church.

The introduction of Protestantism to Guatemala fit the Liberal agenda primarily in three ways. First, the Liberals hoped that by opening Guatemala to Protestants they could encourage both North Americans and Europeans to immigrate to Guatemala. Part of the declaration of freedom of worship stated "The right to freedom of religion in Guatemala should remove one of the principal obstacles which heretofore impeded foreign immigration to our country, for many do not wish to settle where they are not allowed to exercise their religion" (Burnett 1987, 28). The Liberals saw immigration as a key aspect in the transformation of traditional values into more modern, progress-oriented values. According to the Liberals, hardworking Protestants from developed countries would set an example for Guatemalan society. Perhaps, with luck, some Guatemalans would even convert to Protestantism and the "work ethic" of Protestantism would be spread even further. Also the Liberals believed that immigration would bring the foreign capital and advanced technology considered essential to Guatemalan development.

Second, the Liberals felt that the introduction of Protestantism could help to undermine the influence of the Catholic church on Guatemala's system of education. Beginning with Barrios, a system of *quid pro quo* was established between the Protestant church and the Guatemalan government in the area of education. After inviting Presbyterian missionary John Clark Hill to Guatemala in 1882, Barrios provided him with a building to open an English speaking school in downtown Guatemala City (Dekker 1984, 388). José María Reyna Barrios, Barrios' successor, continued this policy, providing Protestant missionaries with free transportation and the free use of government printing presses for the publishing of Protestant literature (Burnett 1987, 106). At the same time, the government set out to undermine the Catholic church and to secularize all other forms of education (Herring 1968, 437).

Under Liberal strongman Manuel Estrada Cabrera (1898-1920), the relationship between the Protestant church and the Guatemalan government grew even stronger. Estrada Cabrera provided Protestants with free mailing privileges, police protection, the right to preach in public schools, and tax exemptions on imported equipment (Burnett 1987, 106). In return, Estrada Cabrera was pleased to observe Protestant progress in both educational and linguistic programs (Burnett 1987, ch. 3 and 4).

Finally, and perhaps most importantly, the introduction of Protestantism into Guatemala helped the Liberals to create a form of societal conflict that facilitated greater state control over fiercely Catholic and traditionally more autonomous rural areas. Central to the Liberal's plan for order and progress in Guatemala was the need to break down the autonomy of villages in order to gain access both to land and to a larger labor force (Weeks 1986, 37). The introduction of the Protestant church into rural villages served as one aspect of the Liberal government's "divide and rule" strategy of gaining social control over traditional Catholic indigenous areas.[2] By sending Protestant missionaries into strongly Catholic Indian areas, the Liberals hoped to create religious factions that could further promote the disintegration of the traditional Catholic power structure (Stoll 1982, 40). The groups that sent missionaries into rural Guatemala around the turn of the century included the Presbyterians, the American Bible Society, the Central American Mission (CAM -- an interdenominational faith mission), the Nazarene church (Pentecostals), Quakers, Primitive Methodists, and the Foreign Bible Society (Zapata 1982, 43-110). In 1902, the four largest denominations agreed to split Guatemala into sectors of influence in order to avoid interchurch conflicts. Burnett outlines the divisions as follows:

> [T]o the Presbyterian Mission, it gave the departments of Guatemala, El Progreso, Quetzaltenango, and Suchitepéquez. To the CAM went the departments of Chimaltenango, Sacatepéquez, Sololá, San Marcos, Huehuetenango, Esquintla, Santa Rosa, Jalapa, and Jutiapa. The Nazarene Mission took the departments of the Alta and Baja Verapaz, and laid claim to the department of the Péten, although that region was not specifically included in the agreement. The Friends claimed the departments of Chiquimula, Zacapa, and Izabal (Burnett 1987, 50).

Figures documenting the exact numbers of Protestant missionaries and converts during the late 1800s and early 1900s are sketchy. According to one estimate, the Central American Mission (CAM) alone claimed at least 6,000 in its Evangelical community by 1915 (Zapata 1982, 73). By 1926, Cameron Townsend of CAM claimed to have counted 2,000 Protestants among the Indian population. (The majority of these Protestant Indians were Cakchiquel) (Stoll 1982, 55). Whether or not these figures are completely accurate, they do point to the fact that by the 1920s the missionaries had begun to take their message to the Guatemalan countryside.

While the first Protestant missionaries were not particularly successful in terms of converting large numbers of the indigenous population, they did manage to stir up a good deal of societal conflict. Conflicts between Catholics and Protestants arose mainly from the fact that the Protestants' self

[2] In this sense, the Liberal strategy may be considered a simplified version of what David D. Laitin has called a "divide and recombine strategy." I refer to it as simplified because it is concerned primarily with the creation of divisions in society and not with the conscious cooptation of elites with high legitimacy and declining resources. See David D. Laitin, "Hegemony and Religious Conflict: British Imperial Control and Political Cleavages in Yorubaland, " in *Bringing the State Back In,* Evans, Rueschemeyer, Skocpol, eds. (Cambridge: Cambridge University Press, 1985), p. 311.

image fit the Liberal leaders' image of them. According to one Presbyterian missionary:

> The Liberal Party in the country, who at first favored us mainly for the purposes of weakening the grip on the Church of Rome . . . are now waking up to the fact that they have imported a splendid public moralizing force that is powerfully cooperating with their noblest patriotic efforts (Burnett 1987, 111).

The inhabitants of local communities often resented the foreign values presented by Protestant missionaries. Furthermore, the early Protestants often attempted to win converts primarily by criticizing the weaknesses of Catholicism (Burnett 1987, 59). In some cases, confrontations between Protestants and Catholics reached the stage of violence. Virginia Garrard Burnett describes some of the myths created by indigenous people about the Protestants. According to one such myth in Chiquimula, Protestants turned children into soap, which accounted for their clean appearance in that dusty area (60-65).

> It was not unusual for angry mobs to storm prayer meetings and noisily disrupt worship services with fireworks, often with the tacit approval of their parish priests. In one extreme episode in 1903, a Bible agent in a village in the Cuchumatanes was attacked and horsewhipped fifty times before barely escaping with his life. In 1915 Nazarene missionaries in Baja Verapaz reported that local pranksters had tainted their entire food supply with crushed red ants and hot peppers (Burnett 1987, 131).

While the anti-Catholic rhetoric of the Protestant missionaries did not win them large numbers of converts during the years of Liberal rule in Guatemala (1871-1920), it did manage to create divisions between traditional village leaders and those associated with the Protestant missionaries. These divisions, while not extremely significant on their own, added to the effects of the land tenure laws, weakening the traditional relations and political structure of Indian villages. Although the Catholic church and *cofradías* remained important aspects of village life, political authority and social control began shifting toward local landowners and *jéfes politicos* who controlled the Indians through forced labor and debt bondage. As Jim Handy explains,

> The forced labour, the debt contracts, the forced sale of village common land and the confiscation of *tierras baldias* had the desired effect. In combination they broke down the autonomy of the highland villages, impoverished peasant agriculture and drove increasing numbers of peasants to labour on the developing coffee *fincas* (Handy 1984, 69).

By the end of Estrada Cabrera's regime in 1920, it became clear that the Guatemalan state had gained a large degree of social control over the traditionally Catholic indigenous areas that make up most of Guatemala. *Ladinos* with direct connections to the national government and the newly professionalized Guatemalan military exercised increased levels of influence at the local level (Handy 1984, 70). As the traditional Indian societal structure broke down, a new system arose under the leadership of the *ladinos* who controlled land and labor and had access to the coercive powers of the state. According to Handy:

> Thus it was during this period that the basic structure of highland village politics, which continued to exist through much of the twentieth century, was created. Power and influence percolated down from the government to local *caudillos*, landowners mostly, who maintained their control through favours and patronage passed out on the local level and through the brutal repression of any challenge to their authority (Handy 1984, 71-72).

The relationship of *quid pro quo* between the Protestant church and the Guatemalan state was actively continued with the Unionist government (1920) and succeeding governments in the 1920s. Having stripped the Catholic church of its traditional role in education and medicine, the Guatemalan state now saw the Protestant church as an acceptable substitute in these areas. As Virginia Garrard Burnett explains:

> The social expedience in supporting missionary expansion was clear, for by the mid-1920's, the Protestant missions had begun their many programs in education, medicine, and Indian dialects. Each project which the Protestants undertook relieved the overextended government of another responsibility (Burnett 1987, 118).

Liberal President José Orellana (1921-1926) was particularly impressed with the influence of the Protestants in the Guatemalan countryside. After visiting the mission of Cameron Townsend (of the Central American Mission), Orellana asked, "Why don't more missionaries come now that we want them, as I would like to see one in every town" (Stoll 1982, 31).

The revolution of 1944 and the subsequent elections of Juan José Arévalo in 1945 and Jacobo Arbenz in 1950 marked the beginning of a new era in relations between the Protestant church and the state in Guatemala. Under the constitution of 1945, freedom of religion was reaffirmed and Protestants continued to work in literacy and education programs during the Arévalo years. Arbenz, however, was strictly opposed to the "Americanized" brand of religion preached by most Protestant missionaries in Guatemala. Under Arbenz, visa requirements for foreign missionaries were tightened and legislation was begun that would take education out of the hands of missionary agencies and place it more firmly under state control (Burnett 1987, 149). The strong nationalist sentiments of the Arbenz administration effectively ended the mutually supportive relationship that had existed between the Protestant church and the Guatemalan state for the previous 75 years.

During this period, the Protestant church in Guatemala split into two tendencies. On one side, American missionaries began actively to oppose the Arbenz regime, charging that the revolutionary reforms proposed by the government represented the growth of communism in Guatemala. As Burnett explains, "[t]o the missionaries, the national sympathy for communism was a special source of sadness, for it represented a rejection of the package of American ways and Protestant beliefs that they had preached for so many years" (Burnett 1987, 150). On the other side, native converts to Protestantism began to disassociate themselves from their foreign pastors. These indigenous Protestants, often the beneficiaries of the Arbenz reforms, were very supportive of the government and actively participated in land reform programs.

As the Protestant church struggled with its internal divisions, the Catholic church began to reassert itself politically under the leadership of conservative Archbishop Mariano Rossell y Arellano. Deeming "communist" the land reform programs instituted under Arbenz, members of the clergy allied themselves with landowners and segments of the military in a coalition that posed a serous threat to the autonomy of the Guatemalan state. In 1951, 200,000 Catholics attended the closing ceremony of the First Eucharistic Congress, a demonstration that was considered to be a show of church power vis-a-vis the government (Berryman 1984, 7). Two years later, Archbishop Rossell y Arellano began an organized tour carrying the revered "Black Christ" of Esquipulas throughout the country. He stated that the Black Christ would not come to rest while communism existed in Guatemala (Melville 1983, 24). The actions of the archbishop and other members of the clergy played a key role in undermining the support of the Arbenz administration. Members of the clergy actively supported the June, 1954 coup that brought General Carlos Castillo Armas to power. Archbishop Rossell y Arellano met with CIA agents prior to the coup and gave them permission to drop thousands of copies of his pastoral letter, "On the Advance of Communism in Guatemala," from airplanes on the day of the coup. The letter read in part:

> The people of Guatemala must arise as one man to fight the enemy of God and of their country. Our fight against communism, therefore, must be based on a nationalistic and Catholic attitude . . . Catholics everywhere, by utilizing all means available to them as free human beings in a hemisphere not yet enslaved by the Soviet dictatorship, enjoying the sacred freedom that is theirs as sons of

> God, must fight and counterattack this doctrine that is opposed to God and to Guatemala (Pike 1964, 178).

Castillo Armas rewarded the Catholic church handsomely for aiding his rise to power in 1954. Archbishop Rossell y Arellano was awarded the *Order of Liberation*, priests were appointed to positions in the National Assembly, and restrictions were removed on church landholdings, educational responsibilities, and ceremonial duties (Berryman 1984, 9). As for relations with the Protestant church, Armas and his strongly Catholic *Movimiento Liberacíon Nacional* (MLN) ushered in a period of benign neglect that would last until the 1970s. While Armas did not actively persecute Protestants, he also did not restore the police protection, mailing privileges, and other marks of favored status that Protestants had enjoyed under his predecessors, some Protestants, particularly those who had been active in Arbenz revolutionary reforms, suffered repression during this period. The violence against Protestants, however, was generally at the local level, with little evidence of any state involvement (Burnett 1987, 167-169).

For the first time since 1871, Protestants were on their own in Guatemala. Ironically, during this period the Protestant church began the pattern of growth that has made Guatemala the only Latin American country with a population that is more than one quarter Protestant. In order to understand more recent relations between the Guatemalan state and the increasingly expanding Protestant church, it is necessary to examine the factors influencing this growth.

Protestant Church Growth: Conversion as an Alternative Survival Strategy

By 1982, the annual growth rate of Protestantism in Guatemala had reached 23.6%, the highest of any Latin American country. In this section, I explore some of the reasons for the success of Protestantism in Guatemala. First, I will briefly outline three external factors that have influenced the growth of Protestantism and then I will examine more closely the internal factors that have made Protestantism an alternative survival strategy for many Guatemalans.

Until the late 1950s, Protestants never made up more that five percent of the Guatemalan population (Huntinton and Dominguez 1983, 13). Keeping this in mind, one approach to the issue of growth in the Protestant church is to ask why the church did not see significant growth prior to the 1960s. The answer to this question lies in the fact that the very things that made the Protestant church appealing to the Liberal governments during the heyday of church-state relations made it unappealing to important segments of the Guatemalan population. The liberal, progress oriented, North American values preached by Protestant missionaries often fell on hostile ears. Protestant churches stressed democratic church government, traditional liturgies, and other North American customs and values that were completely foreign to the predominantly indigenous population of Guatemala (Millett 1980, 54). Conversion to Protestantism for a Guatemalan often meant a complete break with traditional culture and society. It is little wonder that in the early years, Protestants met with limited success in their attempts to win Guatemalan converts.

During the early 1960s, the character of Guatemalan Protestantism began to change dramatically. Three factors played the largest role in this change. First, divisions within the various Protestant denominations encouraged the emergence of a new set of indigenous Protestant leaders. Reasons for splits within the Protestant churches included differences between U.S. missionaries and indigenous Protestants over the Arbenz reforms, resentment by local church workers over the imposition of North American styles of worship, and personal battles between charismatic leaders in the church community (Burnett 1987, 180-183). The new generation of indigenous leaders began to break down many of the cultural barriers that had been constructed around Protestantism by North American missionaries. Charismatic leadership came to replace the externally imposed democratic forms of church government, and sermons were preached in the native languages of the various Guatemalan. A second reason for the accelerating growth of Protestantism was the arrival of charismatic Pentecostals who preached a premillennialist message, stressing the gifts of the Holy Spirit, faith healing, and personal testimony. This new strain of Protestantism provided both a sense of individual participation and an emotional outlet for Guatemalan Evangelicals. Third, a renewed emphasis on missions during the 1960s and 1970s helped encourage the growth of Protestantism. Both the closing of Asia to missionaries and the recent "battle with communism" in Guatemala brought the country to the attention of the North American public and led to a movement among many U.S. Evangelicals to push missions as an alternative to communism in Guatemala. A prime example of the new push for evangelization was the "Evangelism in Depth" program organized under the Latin American Mission (an interdenominational faith mission) in 1962. "Evangelism in Depth" employed media events, door-to-door proselytizing, crusades, and training seminars in an effort that eventually produced 15,000 converts to Protestantism (Huntington and Dominguez 1983, 15; Burnett 1987, 175).

While these external factors certainly made Protestantism more accessible to Guatemalans, a series of internal factors influenced Guatemalan society, making Guatemalans more receptive to the Protestant message. Beginning in the 1950s, political and economic forces began to undermine the foundations of the traditional village structures that had survived the Liberal reforms. As this occurred, the survival strategies of many rural Guatemalans became increasingly unworkable. Conversion to Protestantism represented an alternate survival strategy that gained acceptance among those whose traditional strategies of survival had become obsolete. In order to understand this process, it is necessary to examine the traditional system of agriculture around which the survival strategies of most rural Guatemalans had centered.

The dominant form of agriculture in Guatemala for the past two centuries has been the *milpa* system. The term, *milpa* refers to a small plot of corn which is usually interspersed with various other subsistence crops (Annis 1987, 31). While corn is certainly not the most profitable crop available to Guatemalan farmers, it has come to represent the foundation of their survival strategy because it provides a "least possible risk" strategy for those who live on the line between poverty and starvation. According to Sheldon Annis, "by planting corn a family might assure itself poverty, and possibly even hunger, but it will not face starvation" (33). Annis further points out that the *milpa* system provides the "physical and intellectual superstructure" for many Guatemalan villages:

> Its key characteristic is that it "produces" by absorbing the low-cash-value "spare inputs" that a poor family is likely to have in abundance and transforming them to higher value. Moreover, this occurs in a way that is socially stabilizing: by optimizing input rather than maximizing output, the *milpa* produces nothing that can be extracted; thus, it reinforces the internal sphere (village society) without increasing vulnerability to the extractive external sphere (the *ladino* overclass) (Annis 1987, 34).

A key aspect of the *milpa* system is that if a surplus is produced, it is reinvested into the community in the form of symbolic acts and celebrations designed to solidify the basis of village society. Annis explains the logic of this process: "Since Indians could not realistically translate wealth into economic and political power in the *ladino* sphere, the accumulation of wealth was morally rejected in favor of reinvestment in a kind of social currency negotiable only at the village level" (Annis 1987, 61). The religious celebrations, offerings to the saints, and the ritual consumption of alcohol that constitutes Indian "social currency" have created a Catholic "cultural tax" for rural Guatemalans. While this tradition stems from participation in the *cofradía* system, it has been carried over into modern Catholic ceremonial life (90-91). Thus, participation in the *milpa* system provides for both the physical and the spiritual (or communal) needs of rural Guatemalans.

Following the downfall of the Jacobo Arbenz administration in 1954, the traditional system of Guatemalan *milpa* agriculture and village life has been steadily undermined by two sets of forces (Annis 1987, 73). The first is linked to the increasing shortage of land available to small farmers. The small percentage of Guatemala's land that was left to small farmers after the Liberal reforms has come under extreme environmental pressure due to population growth and the ravages of government counterinsurgency campaigns (Annis 1987, 63). In 1964, 87.4 percent of Guatemalan landholders had access to only 18.6 per cent of Guatemala's land. Since that time, land has become even more scarce, with 88.4 percent of Indians farming only 14.3 per cent of the available land. To make matters worse, the number of people depending on agriculture for their living more than doubled between 1950 and 1980 in Guatemala (Handy 1984, 208). Unable to produce enough corn on their increasingly small plots, many *milpa* farmers have been forced to use their meager surplus earnings to rent land from large landowners. At the same time, surpluses have become smaller as farmers are forced to pay higher prices for agricultural inputs due to rising levels of inflation. Without any surplus, growing numbers of dispossessed *milpa* farmers have not been able to meet survival needs or to reinvest in the communal rituals that solidify the basis of village society (Annis 1987, 63). With each year, more *milpa* farmers are forced to sell their land and find themselves marginalized socially as well as economically.

A second set of forces is linked more directly to the increasing modernization of Guatemala's rural communities. Rural villages have become less isolated as improvements in communication and transportation have linked them to larger cities. Annis describes how electoral reforms have undermined the *cofradía* structure by establishing a clear juridical separation between religious and civil office. At the same time, agricultural extension programs have created what he calls "a kind of local meritocracy that has further undercut the religious gerontocracy" (Annis 1970, 62). More importantly, however, the level of education has risen in rural Guatemala, raising the expectations of the sons and daughters of *milpa* farmers. As expectations have risen and traditional agricultural practices have become unworkable, increasing numbers of the poorest rural families have turned toward alternative strategies for survival. Conversion to Protestantism has come to provide one such strategy.

The motivation for Guatemalan peasants to convert to Protestantism cannot be explained in rational actor terms or in purely moral economy terms. Rather, the decision to convert to Protestantism is both an economic necessity (rational actor) and part of a larger change in value systems (moral economy) for most Guatemalan converts. In practice, these two sets of motivations are intertwined to such a degree that they can hardly be unravelled. For conceptual purposes, however, I will treat each set of factors separately, beginning with the rational actor aspects of conversion to Protestantism.

The most obvious physical or rational choice reason for conversion to Protestantism among Guatemalans is the fact that it is cheaper to be Protestant than it is to be Catholic. Protestant converts exempt themselves from the "cultural tax" of participating in village celebrations, religious festivals, and ritual alcoholism. Furthermore, Protestants are more likely to receive material aid from their church than are their Catholic counterparts (Denton 1971, 26). Particularly following the 1976 earthquake, Protestant church organizations provided relief and shelter for Guatemalans whose entire systems of survival had been shattered. Witnessing the rapid growth of Protestantism following the earthquake, some Catholic observers accused Protestant converts of trading *"anima por lámina"* (a word play inferring that converts trade their souls for tin roofing).[3] Protestant churches also provide one of the few voluntary organizations open to peasants who leave their villages and seek work in the capitol. Bryan R. Roberts explains: "In this respect, joining a Protestant group aids an individual in maintaining himself in the city and slowly improving his social and economic situation until new opportunities and non-religious relationships gradually become available through his work or chance contacts" (Roberts 1967, 765).

In many cases, conversion to Protestantism represents increased physical security as well as economic security for potential converts. While Protestants have been far from immune to the political repression that has characterized life in the Guatemalan countryside since the late 1960s, their apolitical nature has made them less likely targets for state sponsored violence. James C. Dekker outlines the roots of this Protestant aversion to political involvement:

> Not willing to lose the privileges of freedom of worship granted after much suffering, Protestant leaders accept or court government blessing. To outside observers, overt political involvement as church institutions seems a spurious application of Romans 13:1 and an inconsistent turnabout. Many Protestant churches long preached that politics was of the devil; when Jesus returns *only* He will clean up that realm. Thus involvement in *la política* was taboo (Dekker 1984, 391).

While the majority of Protestants remain withdrawn from politics, increasing numbers of Guatemala's Catholics have embraced the messages of liberation and an option for the poor as expressed in the 1968 Medellín and 1979 Puebla Bishops conferences (Beeson and Pearce 1984, 26-27). Recently, Catholics who are active politically or preach a social gospel have come under direct attack by death squads and government security forces. Under the government of General Lucas García in particular, Catholic priests, layworkers, and church members became the focus of a systematic campaign

[3] The fact that churches have growth even where little material aid was available seems to point to deeper reasons for conversion. (See Simons 1982, 47.)

to silence those who called for social justice (Berryman 1984, 49-56). While some Protestants who work at the grassroots level and preach a social gospel have faced this repression as well, the Evangelical doctrines stressing obedience to authority have made them a less likely target for repression.

Reinforcing the physical and economic benefits associated with conversion to Protestantism is a second set of factors: the spiritual or moral economy aspects of Protestantism. A gospel of "health and wealth" is commonly preached by charismatic Evangelicals. According to this teaching, economic advancement is a sign of spiritual wealth. Closely tied to this message is the Protestant emphasis on a personal God and personal salvation. For charismatic Evangelicals, the world is a battleground for good and evil and each person must internalize this battle by gaining control over their own life. Personal piety is emphasized as a primary responsibility of the Protestant convert. According to Sheldon Annis, many rural Guatemalans actually define Protestantism in terms of not drinking, gambling, or smoking (Annis 1987, 80). Thus, as Protestants "win" on their personal battlegrounds by giving up ritual alcoholism and other "vices thought to be in the Catholic church" they also become more productive economically. As David Stoll explains:

> Infused with the kind of spiritual power generated by collective religious enthusiasm, Evangelicals regularly ritualize their refusal to allow social traditions like ritual alcoholism to hold sway over the body. Freed from these constraints, at least in the heat of collective religious experience, they cultivate a new discipline, the abstinence and thrift necessary to attain the good life advertised by North American Evangelists (Stoll 1988, 18).

The scenario described by Stoll has been repeated by recently converted Protestants numerous times and has come to be known as moving "*del suelo al cielo*," literally, from "the floor to the heaven" (Annis 1987, 86-87). Sheldon Annis documents a number of these cases in San Antonio Aguas Calientes, a small town near Antigua, Guatemala. According to Annis, Protestants perform better economically than Catholics both in terms of agriculture and textile entrepreneurship (Annis 1987, 141). While country-wide data on this phenomena is not available, various area specific studies seem to verify Annis' conclusions (Sexton 1978; Stoll 1988, 18; Denton 1971).

As part of a new survival strategy, Protestantism also provides a spiritual shelter and an emotional outlet for recent converts. For charismatic Evangelicals, personal testimonies, religious retreats, and emotionally charged nightly church services have come to replace the ceremonies and fiestas of folk Catholicism. In the face of deteriorating economic conditions and increasingly repressive military regimes, the premillennialist message presented by charismatic Evangelicals has allowed converts to turn away from the troubles of their daily lives and focus on the imminent return of Christ. Protestants isolate themselves from the surrounding social turmoil by focusing on their own spiritual battles. By turning inward, Protestants gain both a physical shelter, as their apolitical nature makes them less likely targets for state sponsored repression, and a spiritual shelter, as they gain power over their own lives in terms of personal piety and self-discipline. Exempt from the cultural tax of folk Catholicism, freed from traditional vices through an intense focus on personal piety, and imbued with a new worldview that emphasizes personal salvation and individual achievement as signs of spiritual wealth, Guatemalan Protestants have accepted a new survival strategy that provides a new set of economic possibilities (rational actor motivations) and a new value system that reinforces these possibilities (moral economy motivations). I will now turn to examine how Protestantism as a large scale survival strategy has come to effect the relationship between the Protestant church and the Guatemalan state.

Protestantism as Social Control

According to Joel S. Migdal, state incorporation of social organizations that provide survival strategies for large sectors of the population has been a particularly effective tool in state attempts to increase levels of social control (Migdal 1988, 229-234). Under the leadership of General Romeo Lucas García, the Guatemalan state attempted to use such a strategy by improving its relations with the Protestant church. While the state did not "incorporate" the Protestant church, it did consciously attempt to reestablish the traditional relationship of *quid pro quo* between Protestants and the Guatemalan government. The ability of Protestant churches to provide a survival strategy for Guatemalans in areas of conflict (between government troops and guerrillas), along with the fact that this survival strategy often included a large dose of apoliticism and anti-communism, added to the attraction of using Protestantism as a method for expanding the social control of the state.

During the 1960s and 1970s, the Protestant church experienced its highest growth rates in the rural areas of Northeastern Guatemala ("Las Sectas" 6). It was in these areas, the departments of Zacapa (34.9% Protestant), Péten (37.7%), Izabal (29.5%), and El Progreso (29.5%) in particular, that the guerrillas were first active and that large scale counterinsurgency programs were first applied under Colonel Carlos Arana Osorio and General Romeo Lucas García ("Las Sectas" 6). Not surprisingly, Pentecostal churches, with their traditional emphasis on obedience to authority (Romans 13:1) and anti-communism, were the most successful in these areas.[4] For many of those caught in the fighting, Pentecostal Protestantism provided both a political refuge, because of its apolitical stance, and a spiritual refuge through a personal relationship with God (Burnett 1987, 216). As Protestants turned inward, the likelihood of their mobilization for social goals decreased. It was not long before the Lucas García government began to see Protestantism as a tool for demobilizing the potentially radical population of northeastern Guatemala. As Virginia Garrard Burnett explains:

> The growth of the Evangelical church in the areas of conflict was not lost of the officers of the Guatemalan army, who saw in the Protestant church an opportunity to create a new base of support to replace the old alliance they had previously enjoyed with the Roman Catholic Church (Burnett 1987, 216).

The actions of the Lucas García regime were consciously designed to improve relations between Protestants and the Guatemalan state. In 1980, the General's Minister of Education made a widely publicized conversion to Protestantism and García himself began to open many public functions with a prayer from a Protestant minister (Burnett 1987, 216). In the countryside, the military encouraged Protestants to settle in areas of conflict (217). Soon Lucas García's strategy began to pay off as some Protestants became informants for the army. The testimony of one mission staff person is particularly telling:

> It is interesting to note that many Evangelicals are in favor of the repression being undertaken by the government [of Lucas García]. Some have even stated that the only way to really solve the [communist] problem is to eliminate many people. We have actual accounts of pastors guiding and assisting death squads and the government. This situation is very confusing and very complex (Renner 1985, 5).

Penny Lernoux has documented one case in the village of Semuy where residents were forced to leave their village because they were denounced as "communist" by an Evangelical after he was unsuccessful in his attempts to convert them (Lenoux 1988, 52). According to Burnett, one observer

[4] The anti-communist rhetoric that came to Guatemala intermingled with Pentecostal Protestantism has carried over into the more indigenous churches, leading many Guatemalan Protestants to believe that all social unrest in their country is the result of invading communism. In Quiché, 99.5% of Protestants are Evangelicals (generally Pentecostal); in Petén, 95%; in San Marcos, 94%; in Huehuetenango, 98.5%; and in Chimaltenango, 100%. "Las Sectas. . .," pp. 7-8.

estimated that almost 50% of the Evangelicals in army-controlled zones either passively supported the military or were active informers (Burnett 1987, 217).

While Lucas García's strategy of using the Protestant church as a tool for gaining social control was effective, it is important to point out that not all Protestants remained apolitical or became active supporters of the government during the Lucas García years. Among the much-divided Protestant church in Guatemala were a number of Protestants who either accepted the invitation of the rebel *Ejercito Guerrillero de Los Pobres* (EGP) for religious workers to join them or who openly opposed the government, as did the predominantly Indian presbyteries of the Presbyterian church. Evangelicals as well as Catholics made up the *Cristianos Revolucionarios Vicente Mechu*, a revolutionary group that took up arms against the government (Burnett 1987, 218-223). While these groups certainly represented only a minority of Guatemalan Protestants, they are a significant reminder that the Protestant church in Guatemala is not a single, conservative body. This idea is further highlighted by the fact that many Protestants also fell victim to the repressive tactics of the Lucas García regime (Berryman 1984, 62-65). While the majority of Protestants either passively or actively aided government attempts to increase social control, a small but important minority supported the guerrillas in their fight to gain control of the Guatemalan state.

The significance of Protestantism in Guatemalan politics was again highlighted in the presidential elections of 1982. General Aníbal Guevera, Lucas García's Minister of Defense, ran against three civilian candidates in an election that many saw as a transparent attempt by the government to gain legitimacy in the face of a mounting threat from Guatemala's guerrilla movement. Aníbal Guevera went out of his way to influence the vote of Protestants, who, at that time, made up almost 19% of the Guatemalan population (Renner 1985, 6). During his campaign, Aníbal Guevera's wife gave donations to various Protestant organizations and publicly announced that she was considering becoming a Protestant. The General himself promised special consideration to Protestants under his administration before a crowd of 50,000 during a "healing campaign" headed by Puerto Rican evangelist Yiye Avíla (6). While many Protestants were offended by Aníbal Guevera's blatant attempts to win their approval, others lent passive support to both the General and the government.

Aníbal Guevera was the official winner of the March 1982 elections. As in earlier Guatemalan elections, charges of fraud were numerous, leading the three civilian candidates to join forces in protest (Berryman 1984, 69). In the midst of this potentially explosive situation, a group of young officers in the Guatemalan military decided to take matters into their own hands. Upset with corruption at all levels of government service and inefficiency in the face of an increasing guerrilla threat, these officers staged a coup on March 23 that brought General Efraín Rios Montt to power. Rios Montt, a devoted member of a Pentecostal sect called the Church of the Word, was chosen to head the ruling junta because he provided a degree of legitimacy (he had been popularly elected in 1974 with 56% of the vote but was not allowed to take office) and because he was both anti-corruption and pro-military. Also, many of the young officers involved in the coup had studied under Rios Montt at the military academy (Renner 1985, 10). According to some accounts, the officers who led the coup originally intended to have new, "clean" elections in which the civilian candidates could participate without the fear of repression. They were hoping to improve Guatemala's image in an effort to gain more military aid from the United States (Berryman 1984, 69). Soon, however, it became clear that Rios Montt did not believe that Guatemala was ready for another election. He consolidated his power and within three weeks of the coup declared himself President.

Under Rios Montt, the use of the Protestant church as a tool for social control expanded, and relations between Protestants and the government continued to improve. At the same time, Rios Montt's own Protestantism and the outpouring of support he received from previously "apolitical" church members began to be perceived as a threat to the traditional sources of power within the state (the military and the bureaucracy). This led to a unique situation in which the Guatemalan Protestant church acted as both a tool, used to increase levels of social control, and a threat to the regime's stability, as Protestant values expressed through the policies of Rios Montt clashed with the interests of certain sectors of the military and bureaucracy. I will focus, first of all, on the Protestant church as a tool for social control and secondly on how Protestantism exacerbated conflicts within the Rios Montt regime.

Despite the fact that the military officers who brought Rios Montt to power were ignorant of his religious convictions, they did believe that his leadership would provide legitimacy for the government as it attempted to address the problem of the Guatemalan insurgency (Burnett 1987, 229). Soon after the March 1982 coup, the military circulated a copy of the "National Plan for Security and Development," a comprehensive counterinsurgency strategy emphasizing civic action and population control through the creation of strategic hamlets and model villages in the Guatemalan countryside (Davis 1983b, 34). In May, Rios Montt declared that during the month of June there would be a general amnesty. On July 1, however, he instituted a state of siege under which military powers were expanded to an alarming degree. Under the state of siege the military is empowered to arrest and hold suspects without charge, to take over private homes and offices at night, to force all former soldiers under the age of 30 to register at military bases, and to sentence suspected guerrillas to death before military courts (Davis 1983b, 34). During this period, Rios Montt's counterinsurgency program known as *fusiles y frijoles* (rifles and beans), went into effect in the Ixil triangle. This plan combined counterinsurgency with civic action in an attempt to win the allegiance of Indians living in zones where the guerrillas were active.

Protestant groups played an important role on the civic action side of Rios Montt's *fusiles y frijoles* program. One such group, the Foundation for the Support of Indian Peoples (FUNDAPI) was formed by Gospel Outreach (the California-based counterpart to Rios Montt's Church of the Word), the Behrhorst Foundation (a rural health program run by Protestants), and the Institute of Linguistics/Wycliffe Bible Translators. While the *fusiles y frijoles* program was carried out, FUNDAPI raised money in the United States under the name International Love Lift. It also organized food, health, and housing programs in the Ixil triangle of northern El Quiché. FUNDAPI workers received the full support of the military during this period, making use of army escorts and free transportation into zones of conflict (Westropp 1983, 30). Other groups also expanded their operations in areas of conflict during Rios Montt's tenure in office. The Central American Mission (CAM) helped distribute government relief supplies and the Nazarene church recorded high growth rates after declaring its "Campaign of Sanctity" in the Transversal del Norte near the Mexican border (Burnett 1987, 235-236).

There is also evidence of increased collusion between Protestants and the military during the Rios Montt years. In the Ixil town of Cotzal, a Mayan Evangelical pastor helped to organized the first "civilian militia" in the Ixil area (Davis 1983a, 8). In the nearby town of Salquil, another Evangelical pastor (of the Pentecostal Church of God) led more than 1,700 townspeople and refugees out of their village and into army protection (8). These stories are not simply isolated incidents. According to Deborah Huntington:

> In the newly established "strategic Hamlets" they [the Protestants] became the preferred liaison between the army and the local community, leading civil defense patrols and weeding out guerrilla sympathizers. Army commanders in turn rewarded this cooperation by appointing Evangelicals to posts of authority (Huntington and Dominguez 1983, 26).

Virginia Garrard Burnett relates another incident in which an indigenous Protestant pastor played a prominent role in a military sponsored rally. The pastor's message included the statement that "He who lacks God in his heart is the one who is unable to love the authorities" (Burnett 1987, 238). While this message may seem a complete misrepresentation of Romans 13:1, its impact provided what has been called a moral "high ground" for the military and for the Rios Montt government. As Sheldon Annis explains:

> The new high ground allowed those villagers who were nominally neutral but afraid (the majority probably who wished only for an end to violence) to rationalize their support for the perceived winners. Thus, while the army and the paramilitary burned and scourged, evangelism helped to further alienate the

guerrillas from popular sympathy, that is, "to separate the fish from the water" (Annis 1987, 8).

Thus, Protestants aided the state in its quest for social control by providing for the physical needs of potentially revolutionary groups, demobilizing these groups through symbolic appeals to a higher authority, and actively collaborating with the military by denouncing suspected subversives.

Protestantism's Limitations as a Means of Social Control

While the Protestant church under Rios Montt was certainly a valuable ally for the state in its attempts to gain social control in the Guatemalan countryside, it was also becoming a source of conflict between Rios Montt and traditional power centers within the state. The coup coalition that brought Rios Montt to power was delicately balanced between a group of conservative and traditional military officers linked to the National Liberation Movement (MLN) and a group of younger military technocrats associated with the Institutional Democratic Party (PID). To a large degree, Rios Montt's position depended on his ability to cautiously carry out the reforms desired by the junior officers without completely antagonizing the more conservative senior officers (Handy 1984, 273). Rios Montt's moral posturing and the vocal support that he received from the Evangelical population severely undermined his ability to complete this task.

Rios Montt *was* deeply committed to his newfound faith, a faith that led him to believe that evil was in the hearts of individuals and that therefore, in order to change society, individuals' hearts must be changed (Rios Montt 1987). Each Sunday, Rios Montt made an appearance on national television to preach on issues from personal morality to civic duty, leading some to dub him "Dios Montt" (Berryman 1984, 70). Rios Montt also appointed two of his church elders to positions within his government. Francisco Bianchi, Secretary of the President of the Republic, and Alvaro Contreras, Secretary to the Private Affairs of the President, were considered to be the most powerful men (outside of the military) in the President's cabinet (Simons 1982, 117). According to a Guatemalan pastor, numerous local Evangelicals gained positions of authority in Rios Montt's regime, including two American members of the Church of the Word whom he named "Counselors to the President" (Renner 1985, 14-16). Many Catholic observers were convinced that Rios Montt took his orders directly from his superiors in the church hierarchy (Renner 1985, 11).

Whether or not Rios Montt made his decisions based on direct orders from his ecclesiastical superiors, his policies did reflect his church's emphasis on law, order, and authority. Immediately after assuming office, Rios Montt took steps that effectively cut violence in Guatemala's largest urban centers.

Under Rios Montt's supervision, more that 265 national policemen and 50 members of the armed forces were arrested and tried for various abuses (Burnett 1987, 245). In December, 1982, Rios Montt initiated a plan to cut corruption by public officials called "Project David" (Anfuso and Sczepanski 1984). Under the plan, signs were posted in all public offices proclaiming *"No robo, no miento, no abuso"* (I don't steal, lie, or abuse) and all public officials were forced to take a pledge of anti-corruption (Burnett 1987, 151-153). Rios Montt's anti-corruption campaign was very popular among the citizens of Guatemala City and other urban centers. On November 28, 1983, hundreds of thousands of Evangelicals rallied at the *Campo de Marte* in Guatemala City to celebrate 100 years of Protestantism in Guatemala and to show their support for Rios Montt.

While Rios Montt's popularity soared with Evangelical (and many non-Evangelical) citizens of Guatemala, he came under increasing suspicion in the eyes of some military leaders and members of the state bureaucracy, as well as the Catholic church. The split within the military that had brought Rios Montt to power persisted, making Rios Montt's tenure somewhat precarious. Traditional elements within the military and the bureaucracy resented Rios Montt's moralistic sermons and his campaign of anti-corruption. At one point, General Oscar Humberto Mejía Víctores stated that what Guatemala needed was more executions--not prayers. Rios Montt's economic policy and rumors of agrarian reform also eroded his support within the military and the bureaucracy (Handy 1984, 271). Acting together, these groups organized the coup that forced Rios Montt from office on August 8, 1983. After taking power, the new government lead by General Mejía Víctores issued a press release calling Rios Montt and his advisors:

> [A] fanatical and aggressive religious group which took advantage of their positions of power as the highest members of government for their benefit, ignoring the fundamental principle of the separation of church and state (Burnett 1987, 248).

The Catholic church, while not in alliance with the coalition that ousted Rios Montt, was increasingly critical of the Rios Montt administration. Pope John Paul II's visit to Guatemala in 1983 highlighted this situation. Rios Montt ignored the Pope's appeal for clemency for six suspected guerrillas and had them executed days before the Pope arrived, drawing severe criticism from the Vatican (Berryman 1984, 73). The Guatemalan clergy slowly followed step, becoming increasingly open in their criticism of Rios Montt's policies. The Bishop of Verapaces, Gerardo Flores, openly called Rios Montt and his Protestant supporters "the North American State Department's answer to the options taken by the Catholic church" (Handy 1984, 271).

The overthrow of Rios Montt in 1983 demonstrated, in one sense, the limits of charismatic Protestantism in Guatemalan politics. Rios Montt's moralistic sermons and his favoritism towards Protestants alienated the very sectors of the military and bureaucracy whose support he needed. While it is true that Rios Montt might have lost his position even if he had not been Protestant, his open devotion to charismatic Protestantism certainly added to the tensions existing within his regime. Perhaps more consequentical than Rios Montt's overthrow was the retreat of his Evangelical supporters following his downfall. Without their charismatic leader, most Evangelicals withdrew from overt political involvement. The same qualities that made Protestants such valuable allies of Guatemala's military regimes--apoliticism, passivity, and a heavy emphasis on law and order, made them shy away from any direct political conflict (Burnett 1987, 247).

The close relationship between charismatic Evangelicals and the military in Guatemala's areas of conflict has continued from the downfall of Rios Montt in 1983 through the election of another Evangelical president, Jorge Serrano Elias, in 1990. The rapid growth of Evangelical sects in conflictive zones has continued as well. According to a 1988 report by Servicio Evangelizador Para America Latina (SEPAL), Protestant growth in Guatemala's Northeastern departments continues to be particularly impressive (See Table 6.1).

While the relationship between the Protestant church and the Guatemalan state has generally entailed mutual cooperation (and even blatant collaboration on the part of some charismatic Evangelicals), it is necessary to point out that not all Guatemalan Protestants are apolitical, anti-communist, or Fundamentalist. According to Guillermo Cook, an expert on grassroots religious movements in Latin America, there are an estimated 200 Protestant Base Communities among the Indian population of Guatemala. These ecumenical community-based religious organizations stress social action as an

Table 6.1 Protestant Church Growth

Department	**Number of Churches per Inhabitants**	
	1980	1986
Quiché	1 per 1600 (or more)	1 per 500-800
Alta Verapaz	1 per 1200-1600	1 per 500-800
Petén	1 per less than 500	1 per less than 500
Huehuetenango	1 per 1200-1600	1 per 500-800
San Marcos	1 per 800-1200	1 per 500-800

outgrowth of reflection on the Bible and their environment. Severely repressed in the late seventies and early eighties, the BECs have recently begun to reorganize under the banner of the institutional Protestant church in an effort to build a network of protection against further attacks by the government.

Aside from the BECs, a group of mainline Protestants has recently steeped forward to play a more overt political role in Guatemala. In 1989, Protestants and Catholics joined to form the Permanent Assembly of Christian groups, an organization that was recognized by Guatemala's National Reconciliation Commission as an official participant in the National Dialogue set up under the Esquipulas II agreement. The Permanent Assembly has been accredited to six commissions in the initial stages of the dialogue: Ethnic Affairs, Human Rights, Peace and Security, Victims of Violence, Labor Relations, and Stimulation of Production (a euphemism for the land issue). While progress on the National Dialogue has been slow, Evangelicals are hopeful that they will be able to make a positive contribution to a solution to Guatemala's ongoing civil war (Smith 1989).

Conclusion

The history of the Protestant church in Guatemala provides evidence to support Joel S. Migdal's analysis of state-society relations throughout the developing world. Migdal's conception of third world states as relatively weak actors locked in a struggle to gain social control over their societies is particularly relevant to Guatemala. Beginning with Justo Rufino Barrios' gifts to Guatemala's first Presbyterian missionary, John Clark Hill, a symbiotic relationship was established between the Protestant church and the Guatemalan state. This relationship was actively pursued by the state as one aspect of a broader strategy to gain social control over areas traditionally under the influence of the Catholic church and indigenous leaders. The introduction of Protestantism into autonomous rural areas created conflicts that added to the effects of the "Liberal reforms," undermining Guatemala's traditional village system of political and religious authority.

Under the administrations of Jacobo Arbenz and Carlos Castillo Armas, the established ties between the Protestant church and the Guatemalan state were cut. However, Guatemala's traditional village structure continued to be undermined by political and economic factors that made the survival strategies of Indian farmers increasingly unworkable. The Protestant church has grown to include more than thirty percent of the Guatemalan population because it represents an alternative survival strategy for the poorest Indian farmers. In the Protestant church, the rural poor have found both a new set of economic possibilities and a new value system that reinforces those possibilities.

As the Protestant church has increased in numbers, its potential as a source of social control for the state has also increased. Under the authoritarian governments of General Romeo Lucas García and Efraín Rios Montt, Protestants were actively encouraged to settle in areas of conflict between the guerrillas and the government. In these areas, Protestantism became a demobilizing force as Protestant pastors preached a message of obedience to authority and anti-communism. In some cases, Protestants openly collaborated with the government, becoming informers for the military and aiding in the formation of civil patrols and model villages.

While the history of Protestantism in Guatemala does provide evidence to support Migdal's hypotheses about the relationship between state and society in the developing world, it does not support the commonly-held notion that Latin American Protestantism is necessarily conservative or apolitical. Evangelical support for the 1944 revolution and the continued existence of Protestant BECs in Guatemala demonstrate the heterogeneity within Protestantism in the Guatemalan context. Further generalizations about the political effects of the growth of Protestantism in Latin America must be critically analyzed, considering the independent effects of religious affiliation, religious beliefs, and political context on political attitudes and outcomes. The following represents a rough model to guide further research on Protestantism and politics in Latin America.

First, political orientation is likely to vary with denominational affiliation and religious beliefs. Preliminary research indicates that Mainline Protestants (such as Presbyterians and Methodists) tend to be more politically active and less politically conservative than their Pentecostal counterparts. While this is not always the case, it points to the need to differentiate between Protestant denominations and the beliefs (such as millenialism and doctrinal orthodoxy) that may influence political attitudes and actions.[5]

Second, the political context in which a Protestant community is located will effect the political orientations and actions of Protestants. Applying the Guatemalan experience elsewhere, we may assume that the tendency toward pietism and withdrawal, particularly apparent among Pentecostals, is likely to become more prevalent in a social and political context that discourages overt political activity. On the other hand, recent research on Protestantism in Chile suggests that under a democratic regime that encourages widespread participation, the Protestant church may become a vehicle for political mobilization and the articulation of class interests. Throughout Latin America, conversion to Protestantism represents a survival strategy for many

[5] See Ted G. Jelen *The Political Mobilization of Religious Beliefs*, (New York: Praeger, 1991), for an example of how doctrinal orthodoxy may have a conservatizing effect on political attitudes.

individuals of the lower classes who can meet both spiritual and material needs through membership in a tightly-knit community of believers. Depending on the degree of political openness within a society, this community of believers may become inward looking (avoiding the political realm and focusing directly on solutions available for individuals within the community) or more outward oriented (using the skills, resources, and mobilization abilities of the religious community to channel demands through the political system). Thus, Protestant communities may move in and out of the political arena over time and Protestants with very similar religious beliefs may display very different political orientations in different contexts.

Finally, it must be noted that involvement in a Protestant church represents an interaction structure that, over time, may affect the personal traits that individuals bring to political life. Various authors assert that Protestantism often promotes the spread of literacy and education among marginalized groups (Stoll 1990; Martin 1991). The Evangelical emphasis on Bible study gives converts a reason to pursue additional education as adults. This focus on education can be particularly important for women within Protestant churches. In many churches women act as elders and educational organizers--positions previously closed to them (Brusco 1986).

Protestants can also learn leadership skills, organizational skills, and self-discipline within Evangelical communities. The Evangelical experience may work to replace ascribed with acquired status, thereby leading to a demystification of authority and perhaps even to more egalitarian practices (Lalive d'Epinay 1983, 42-54). For many individuals, membership in a Protestant congregation may represent their first experience with any sort of voluntary organization. Church-going may provide skills essential to citizen demand-making as church members gain, in a more protected and intimate setting, the skills and confidence necessary for articulating their needs to political authorities in a wider arena. Also, conversion to Protestantism is often associated with a rise in economic status (Annis 1987; Stoll 1990). As converts experience upward social mobility it is plausible to assume that they will perceive both needs for state action and channels of demand making to meet their needs.

The history of Protestantism in Guatemala can serve as an important reminder for Evangelicals who do not wish to become the unwitting partners of authoritarian regimes struggling to gain greater autonomy in Latin America. At the same time, the heterogeneity within Guatemalan Protestantism should give pause to academics who tend to assume that all Latin American Protestants are either conservative or apolitical. The political effects of the growth of Protestantism in Latin America are likely to be as varied as the political contexts in which Protestant communities are located.

Reference List

Anfuso, J. and D. Sczepanski. 1984. *He gives or he takes away: The true story of Guatemala's former president Efrain Rios Montt.* New York: Radiance Press.

Annis, S. 1987. *God and production in a Guatemalan town.* Austin: University of Texas Press.

Bates, R. H., ed. 1988. *Toward a political economy of development: A rational choice perspective.* California Series on Social Choice and Political Economy, 14. Berkley: University of California Press.

Beeson, T. and J. Pearce. 1984. *A vision of hope: The church and change in Latin America.* Philadelphia: Fortress Press.

Berryman, P. 1984. *Christians in Guatemala's struggle.* Nottingham, England: Russell Press Ltd.

Brusco, E. 1986. The household basis of Evangelical religion and the reformation of *machismo* in Colombia. Ph.D. Diss. City University of New York.

Burnett, V. G. 1987. *A history of Protestantism in Guatemala.* Ph.D. Diss., Tulane University.

________. 1989. Protestantism in rural Guatemala, 1872-1954. *Latin American Research Review* 24(2): 127-140.

Davis, S. 1983a. Guatemala: The Evangelical holy war in El Quche. *The Global Reporter* 1(1), (March): 8.

________. 1983b. The social consequences of "development" aid in Guatemala. *Cultural Survival Quarterly* 7(1), (Spring): 32-35.

Dekker, J. C. 1984. North American Protestant theology: Impact on Central America. *The Mennonite Quarterly Review* 58 (August Supplement): 378-393.

Denton, C. F. 1971. Protestantism and the Latin American middle class. *Practical Anthropology* 18(1), (Jan/Feb): 24-28.

Handy, J. 1984. *Gift of the devil: A history of Guatemala*. Boston: South End Press.

Herring, H. 1968. *A history of Latin America*. (Third Edition) New York: Alfred A. Knopf.

Huntington, D. and E. Dominguez. 1983. The salvation brokers: Conservative Evangelicals in Central America. *NACLA: Report on the Americas* (Jan/Feb): 2-37.

Jelen, T. G. 1991. *The political mobilization of religious beliefs*. New York: Praeger.

Larmer, B. 1989. Religious row endangers Guatemala. *Christian Science Monitor* (10 March), 6.

Laitin, D. D. 1985. Hegemony and religious conflict: British imperial control and political cleavages in Yorubaland. In *Bringing the State Back In*, eds. P. S. Evans, D. Rueschemeyer, and T. Scalpol, 285-316. Cambridge: Cambridge University Press.

Las sectas Fundamentalistas y la contrainsurgencia en Guatemala. 1987. *Guatemala Ceri-Gua* (March): 6-8.

Latourette, K. S. 1961. *Christianity in a revolutionary age: The nineteenth century outside Europe*. New York: Harper and Brothers.

Lenoux, P. 1988. The Fundamentalist surge in Latin America. *The Christian Century*, (20 January): 51-54.

Melville, T. P. 1983. The Catholic church in Guatemala, 1944-1982. *Cultural Survival Quarterly* 7 (Spring): 23-27.

Migdal, J. S. 1988. *Strong societies and weak states: State-Society relations and state capabilities in the third world*. Princeton: Princeton University Press.

Miller, H. J. 1966. Positivism and educational reform in Guatemala, 1871-1885. *Journal of Church and State* (Spring): 251-263.

Millett, R. 1973. The Protestant role in twentieth century Latin America church-state relations. *Journal of Church and State* (Autumn): 366-380.

________. 1980. The perils of success: Post-World War II Latin American Protestantism. In *Religion in Latin American life and literature*, eds. L. C. Brown and W. F. Cooper, 52-66. Waco: Markham Press Fund.

Montt, R. 1987. Interview with Rios Montt by the Calvin Center for Christian Scholarship Scholars of 1987-88 at *Iglesia El Verbo*, 5 January.

Nash, M. 1970. The impact of mid-nineteenth century economic change upon the Indians of Middle America. In *Race and class relations in Middle America*, ed. M. Mörner, 170-183. New York and London: Columbia University Press.

Nordlinger, E. A. 1987. Taking the state seriously. In *Understanding political development*, eds. M. Weiner and S. P. Huntington, 353-390. Boston: Little, Brown.

Pike, F. B. 1964. *The conflict between church and state in Latin America*. New York: Alfred A. Kropf.

Renner, G. 1985. Central America: The church in conflict. Unpublished manuscript.

Retrato De Guatemala. 1988. *Equipo SEPAL* (15 December): n.p.

Roberts, B. R. 1967. Protestant groups and coping with urban life in Guatemala City. *American Journal of Sociology* 73 (May): 753-767.

Scott, J. 1976. *The moral economy of the peasant: Rebellion and subsistence in Southeast Asia*. New Haven: Yale University Press.

Sexton, J. O. 1978. Protestantism and modernization in two Guatemalan towns. *American Ethnologist* ns. 284 (5 May): 251-263.

Simons, M. 1982. Latin America's new gospel. *New York Times Magazine* (7 November): 47, 112-120.

Smith, D. 1989. Personal interview with author, Alajuela, Costa Rica, 21 March.

Stoll, D. 1982. *Fishers of men or founders of empire: The Wycliffe Bible translators in Latin America*. London: Zed Press.

________. 1988. Religious reformation in Latin America. Unpublished manuscript.

________. 1990. *Is Latin America turning Protestant? The politics of Evangelical growth.* Berkeley: University of California Press.

Sullivan-Gonzalez, D. 1989. Piety, power, and politics: A cultural analysis of religious discourse in Guatemala, 1839-1871. Unpublished manuscript.

Van Oss, A. C. 1986. *Catholic colonialism: A parish history of Guatemala: 1524-1821.* New York: Cambridge University Press.

Weeks, J. 1986. An interpretation of the Central American crisis. *Latin America Research Review* 21(3): 37.

Westrop, M. 1983. Christian couterinsurgency. *Cultural Survival Quaterly* 7(3) (Fall): 28-31.

Zapata, V. 1982. *Historia de la Iglesia Evangélica en Guatemala.* Guatemala City: Genesis Publicidad, S.A.

PROTESTANT AND CATHOLIC

VIEWPOINTS

Chapter 7

Protestant Mission Activity in Latin America

Roger S. Greenway

Before addressing the subject of Protestant mission activity in Latin America, I need to acknowledge my biases. To start with, I cannot help but view the subject through the eyes of a North American Protestant in the Reformed tradition. During most of my adult life I have been involved in the mission enterprise, a good deal of it in Latin America. Being who I am, I have some right to critique the Protestant mission enterprise, but much less right to judge the Latin American church and its activities. In view of this, I choose to focus mainly on the mission activity originating from outside Latin America, that is, the work of Protestant Churches, boards, and agencies that send and support mission work in the region.

As a missiologist, I approach the subject of Protestant mission work in Latin America with three assumptions. First, I believe that the church is by nature a missionary institution. Whenever there is religious vitality in one place while in other places there is ignorance, superstition, or out-and-out paganism, the Spirit of God creates a mission impulse that compels believers to initiate mission activity. The church's response to this impulse always falls short of what it should be. Both the workers and the work are vulnerable to criticism. Mission activity is often opposed from within and without.

Sometimes it is snuffed out. But the principle continues to operate that the Spirit of Christ wants the world filled with the gospel, and wherever there are vacuums the impulse to mission bursts forth anew. This is clearly illustrated in the history of Latin America, from both Catholic and Protestant sides.

A second assumption is that environmental factors such as social conditions, government attitudes, and the religious background of the population, affect the progress or decline of mission activity. Once the new faith has taken hold, it in turn begins to make changes in its new environment. The history of Catholic missions clearly illustrates this and as Protestantism expands in Latin America, it too can be expected to bring about changes of many kinds throughout the region.

A third assumption is that the strength of a religious movement can be accurately gauged by three things: (1) the degree to which the faith is contextualized in words and visible expressions that local people embrace as their own; (2) enlists the participation of its members in its own propagation; and (3) raises up and supports its own leadership. If this gauge is accurate, it suggests the kind of questions that need to be asked when the history of Protestant mission activity is examined. It also helps determine when the goal has been reached and mission activities from the outside can cease.

The focus of this study is on Protestant mission work beginning in the early nineteenth century and conducted in those countries that for three centuries were controlled by the two great colonial Catholic powers, Spain and Portugal. Protestant work prior to the nineteenth century lies outside the purview of this study, but for the sake of completeness the following should be noted. In the 1550s, French Huguenots had established a base in Brazil, which had it been successful might have served as a base for the evangelization of the Indians. In the mid-1600s, the Dutch, who were largely Protestants, controlled northern Brazil for over thirty years. But in 1661, like the French Huguenots before, the Dutch were driven out by the Portuguese.

By the late 1700s, Moravian missionaries had begun work among West Indian slaves. Two Guianas were in British and Dutch control, and Moravian missionaries arrived in these areas about 1738. In the early 1800s, Congregationalist and Methodist missionary societies conducted work in the Guianas. For many years, a high percentage of the Protestants known to be in Latin America were located in the Caribbean area and in the two Guianas that were colonies of Protestant countries (Read, Monterroso and Johnson 1969, 36-37). An important difference between Protestantism as it originated in Europe and the Protestantism of Latin America lies in the fact that in Europe the Reformation sprang up spontaneously and was sustained from the start by its own members and their resources. In Latin America, Protestantism entered from the outside and for many years depended on help from abroad (Kessler 1992a, 46).

Seven "Waves" of Protestant Mission Activity

Since the beginning of the nineteenth century there have been seven waves of Protestant mission activity in Latin America. Each has had its own particular evangelistic strategy and produced its own kinds of results (Pretiz 1985,[1] Stoll 1990a). Each successive wave has reached more people and made a greater impact than its predecessors (see table 7.1).

Table 7.1
Seven Waves of Protestant Mission Activity in Latin America

1800	1850	1900	1950	2000
1. Bible distribution and translation				
	2. Missions to the Indians			
	3. Protestant immigrants			
		4. Mainline Protestant churches		
		5. Faith missions		
			6. Pentecostalism	
			7. Electronic media	

Bible Distribution and Translation

In the nineteenth century, Bible distribution in Latin America was a high-risk undertaking. Placing the Bible in the hands of common people was a pillar of the Protestant Reformation in Europe, but for three hundred years after Europeans began settling in the New World the Bible was virtually an unknown book in the region. Its distribution was forbidden by decree of Pope and king. Having seen in Europe what the Bible in the hands of common people could do, the Catholic Church was determined to keep the Bible out of Latin America, and it used the awesome powers of the Inquisition to enforce the prohibition.

[1] Paul Pretiz, in a workshop presentation at the Overseas Ministries Study Center, New Haven, CT, October 16, 1985, identified five "waves," omitting 19th century missions among the Indians and the electronic media of the last four decades, and observed that each wave produced its own kind of results. Also David Stoll refers to the "waves," in *Is Latin America Turning Protestant? The Politics of Evangelical Growth* (Berkeley, CA: University of California Press, 1990), pp. 101-ff.

As it turned out, Bible distribution became the first and most persistently carried out means by which Protestant ideas were spread in Latin America. British Evangelicals were the first to introduce Bible sales in Catholic regions. Between 1820 and 1850, the British and Foreign Bible Society (BFMS) distributed thousands of Bibles. The prominent figure of that period was James Thomson, a Scott, who served as an agent of the BFMS and the Lancastrian Educational Society. Thomson travelled from Argentina up the entire Western coast of South America, into Central America and Mexico. He sold Bibles, set up local Bible Society depots, and in some places established schools that used the Bible as a textbook. At first Thomson met with overwhelming success. He established about a hundred schools in Argentina and was made an honorary citizen in both Argentina and Chile. In Columbia and Mexico he even received help from a number of sympathetic priests (Latourette 1943, 109-110).

During this period, revolution was in the air in Latin America, and Protestant Bibles and schools were viewed by liberal-minded priests and politicians as signs of freedom and forerunners of progress. The liberal movement had three main goals: first, to bring education to the general population, free from the control of the Catholic Church; second, to remove government restrictions on the immigration of talented and educated Europeans, many of them Protestants whom Latin America needed for its own cultural and economic development; and third, to put an end to the intervention of the clergy in the politics of the Latin American nations (Kessler 1992a, 43-44). Latin American liberals supported Bible distribution and the introduction of Protestantism because they considered these to be means of modernizing their countries.

With the arrival of immigrants from Protestant lands, liberals, masons, and Protestants joined forces for a time because their goals appeared to be similar. Before long, however, the alliance broke down in most places, though in Mexico the Revolution of 1910, viewed as a liberal achievement, saw the active participation of many Protestants (Baldwin 1990, 176-181). Liberals were mostly from the middle class, the more educated segment of society, and after they distanced themselves from Protestantism, Protestant mission work focused more on the poorer classes.[2]

In the second part of the nineteenth century there were conservative reactions in a number of places. Priests opposed the sale of Scriptures and warned the people not to read them. As a result, some of the gains that

[2] Baldwin 1990, p. xi, citing Brown, *Latin America: The Pagans, the Papists, the Patriots, the Protestants and the Present Problem* (New York: Fleming H. Revell, 1901), npn. Hubert Brown noted that masons, liberals and Protestants were lumped together in the minds of many Latin Americans.

Protestantism had made were temporarily lost. Despite opposition, however, the number of Bibles in Latin American hands continued to grow. The American Bible Society entered the work and replaced the British Society in Mexico and parts of Central America. Bible distributors were called "colporteurs." They travelled on foot or horseback from town to town selling Bibles, giving personal testimonies of their faith and preaching wherever they could. Often they alerted missionaries to likely locations for new churches (Brown 1901, xii). Sometimes it happened that years after colporteurs had passed by, small churches spontaneously appeared as a result of people reading the Scriptures (Kessler 1992a, 48).

To this day, distributing the Bible and teaching its content is the most widely used method of evangelization among Protestants. Every Latin American country has its Bible distribution offices, usually linked to international Bible publishers. Protestants generally use versions prepared by Protestant translators. Occasionally they distribute Catholic versions to avoid arguments over "approved" translations. Only in the latter half of the twentieth century has Catholic opposition to Bible distribution been relaxed. In recent years, Protestants have made great efforts to translate and distribute the Scriptures in the many hundreds of indigenous Indian languages of Latin America. The foremost organization in this endeavor is the Wycliffe Bible Translators, known in Latin America as the Summer Institute of Linguistics.

Missions to the Indian Population

As Latin American countries gained independence from Spain and Portugal in the early nineteenth century, restrictions were relaxed that had prevented the entrance of Protestantism during the colonial period. Protestant mission endeavor was in full swing throughout the world, and Latin America did not escape attention. Scattered in many places throughout Latin America were Indian populations that had remained largely unreached by Christianity in either its Catholic or Protestant forms. As early as 1833-34, the American Board of Commissioners for Foreign Missions, in response to reports brought home by sea captains about the aboriginal people of South America, sent two men to look into the possibility of beginning mission work among the Indians of the Patagonia in southern Argentina (Latourette 1943, 102).[3]

According to Kenneth Scott Latourette, the most extensive of the early Protestant mission efforts among the unreached Indians was led by an Englishman, Allen Francis Gardiner. After seeking in vain to interest the (Anglican) Church Missionary Society in starting work in southern Argentina,

[3] After hearing the report the Board decided not to pursue the venture.

Gardiner and his friends organized a new mission, called the Patagonian Missionary Society, in 1844.

They confronted enormous difficulties, and in 1851 the entire missionary party died of exposure and starvation in the inhospitable region of Tierra del Fuego (Brown 1901, 102-103). The loss of these missionary lives inspired other English Protestants to take up the work, and a mission headquarters was established in the Falkland Islands where new missionaries were trained for work on the mainland. Another disaster occurred in 1859 when, on an island off Tierra del Fuego, a missionary party of eight was killed by the aborigines they were trying to evangelize (103).

Nevertheless, efforts to reach the unevangelized native population of South America continued. The Patagonian Missionary Society eventually was taken over by the Church of England and its name was changed to the South American Missionary Society. The society's work expanded to include Indian people in Argentina, Chile, and Bolivia. The aim of the mission was not only to win the Indians to the Christian faith, but also to improve their lives in all respects through education, medical work, and economic development. Indian languages were reduced to writing, grammars and dictionaries were produced, and the Bible was published in the native languages (Brown 1901, 103-104).[4]

Besides these efforts in the southern part of South America, there were other mission groups in the nineteenth century that established work among isolated Indian people. Of special note is the work done by the Moravians among the mixed Indian, African, and white population of the Miskito Coast in Central America. This territory was for a considerable time British controlled. In 1849, the Moravians established a mission on the coast which later expanded inland and included work among people of mixed lineage and also pure-blooded Indians. A religious awakening occurred in 1881, and a high percentage of both groups became Protestant Christians. Today in Nicaragua and Honduras, when you meet people from the Miskito Coast you may assume they are Protestants or at least favorably disposed to the Protestant faith. During the recent Contra war, the Miskitos suffered greatly from both sides in the conflict (Brown 1901, 104-105).

From the beginning of Protestant mission work in the Patagonia down to the present time, serious efforts have been made to bring the gospel to unevangelized Indian groups which number in the thousands in Latin America. Among the organizations dedicated to work among Indians are the

[4] In regard to this mission work Latourette states that "Charles Darwin was so impressed with the achievements registered among peoples whom he had regarded as hopelessly degraded that he became a regular contributor to the funds of the society," p. 104.

Wycliffe Bible Translators, the Andes Evangelical Mission, and the Seventh Day Adventists.

The tradition of martyrdom has not ended, as the death of the five American missionaries killed by the Auca Indians in Ecuador in 1957 reminded us. In more recent years, missionaries have suffered harassment and even death at the hands of both government soldiers and guerrilla groups because they defended the cause of the Indians against the efforts of outsiders to control or exploit them.

Protestant Immigrants

Latin American liberals pressured their governments during the nineteenth century to allow skilled and educated Europeans and North Americans, most of whom were Protestants, to immigrate. They did this not so much because they wanted to see Protestantism gain a following, but because they believed the influx of Europeans would benefit their countries. Even before permanent immigrants arrived, British merchants and sailors were prominent in Latin American port cities and Anglican chaplains sent from England ministered to their spiritual needs. The first Protestant church building in nineteenth century Latin America was an Anglican chapel erected in 1819 in Rio de Janeiro, Brazil (Latourette 1943, 105).

A colony of Scottish Presbyterians settled near Buenos Aires in 1825 and an ordained Presbyterian minister was sent to minister among them a year later. This minister remained in charge of the Presbyterian church and school until 1850. There were Presbyterian and Independent congregations, with clergymen, in other parts of Argentina as well. Outside of Argentina, there were Protestant congregations in Chile, Peru, Uruguay, and several in Brazil. Eventually there were European and North American Protestants in almost all parts of Latin America. Besides Presbyterians, there were German and Swedish Lutherans, Dutch and South African Reformed, Waldenses from Italy, and Baptists, Methodists and Seventh Day Adventists from England and North America. After the American Civil War, large numbers of Southerners, refusing to live any longer in the United States, migrated to Brazil, carrying their Protestant faith with them. Something similar occurred after the Boer War in South Africa, when a number of Boers of Reformed persuasion resettled in South America (Brown 1901, 107-108). It happened again after World War II when some Europeans, fearful that the Cold War would erupt into a shooting war, moved to South America to be out of danger.

Protestants in most places had initially to meet for worship in private quarters. Not until the liberal Constitution of 1857 was Protestant worship legal in Mexico. Protestants of foreign origin conducted their worship services in English, Dutch, German or Italian, and made little or no effort to win converts from the Catholic population. But the Protestant faith could not be kept private for very long, and soon the immigrants added Spanish and Portuguese services. Inquirers from the Catholic population were welcomed to the services and those who were interested in the message of the Bible were instructed. Some Protestant congregations were started as a result of mission outreach (Brown 1901, 108).

Those Protestant churches that were composed mostly of European and North American immigrants and their descendants did not, in general, play a very active role in the spread of the Protestant faith in Latin America. They did, however, serve as an important link with the next wave of mission effort. As the Protestant residents of Latin America became acquainted with the religious situation among professing Catholics and native Indians, they were shocked. They perceived gross ignorance of the essentials of biblical Christianity, widespread superstition, and lax moral standards. The reaction of the Protestant immigrants to this state of affairs in Latin America was to call for missionaries from abroad to come and plant Protestant Christianity. This set the stage for the next wave of Protestant mission activity. During the second half of the nineteenth century, country after country opened its doors to Protestants, and the Catholic clergy no longer had the power to stop it. For the Catholic Church it was not an easy time. Morale among the clergy neared an all time low as traditional power structures tottered on the verge of collapse and liberalism grew in influence, often accompanied by bitter anti-clericalism.

Mainline Protestant Churches

The latter half of the nineteenth century saw a tremendous influx of Protestant activity throughout Latin America. Mainline Protestant churches sponsored work intended to win Catholics to the Protestant faith and build up strong Protestant communities. From the outset they placed heavy emphasis on schools and education. They opened bookstores and distributed Bibles and Protestant literature. In some places they built hospitals and established health programs. The approach they followed was comprehensive, addressing the physical and social as well as the spiritual needs of the people (Read, Monterroso and Johnson 1969, 40).

The emphasis that mainline Protestant missions placed on schools and education can be readily understood. In 1900, three-fourths of the population in most Latin American countries was illiterate. Although Protestant schools could only hope to educate a fraction of the population, they were the best schools available. In many instances they became models for the national education systems that came later (Read, Monterroso and Johnson 1969, 40). "Such a vacuum existed in the field of education that it would have been impossible for the missionary enterprise not to help correct the fault that had existed under colonial rule for more than three hundred years" (Read, Monterroso and Johnson 1969, 40).

To illustrate the kind of work carried on during this time, Latourette tells of an Englishman, William Case Morris, of Buenos Aires, Argentina. Morris himself was left motherless as a child and in adult life he developed a strong interest in helping orphans. While working as a clerk, he began a school for the children of the poor. Eventually he was ordained by the Episcopal church and dedicated his life to helping children gain an education. Thousands of children passed through Morris' schools. Besides his work with children, Morris sought to bring the Christian message to adults and translated a number of Protestant books into Spanish. He died around 1914 (Brown 1901, 109-111).

Protestants from the British Isles were initially at the forefront of the work. This is not surprising because Great Britain was the leading Western power and its churches the most active in the missionary enterprise. In the second half of the nineteenth century, however, the United States emerged as the principal source of missionary energy in Latin America and other parts of the world.

Mission agencies representing nearly all the North American mainline denominations had established mission programs in Latin America before the end of the nineteenth century. In addition to the denominational mission boards there were many agencies supported jointly by mainline and undenominational congregations. In most cases there were missionaries of some kind working in the various Latin American countries before the new agencies' work started. These forerunners provided the contacts and in many cases arranged the invitation for the new wave of mission activity to begin.

The story of David Trumbull was somewhat typical of the missionary pioneers of that period. Trumball went to Chile in 1845 under the auspices of the Evangelical Foreign Missionary Society of New York. Protestant mission activity was against the law at that time, so Trumbull began working in Valparaiso with foreign sailors and English-speaking residents of the city. Despite severe opposition, Trumbull began publishing Evangelical magazines in the Spanish language. When the authorities caught on to what he was doing they announced that his magazines were not to be circulated or read. They made the mistake, however, of using the exact titles of Trumbull's material in their proclamation. Trumbull promptly changed the titles and continued publishing. In 1861 he ventured to begin a Bible society in Valparaiso and soon afterwards opened a Protestant bookstore (Kessler 1992a, 51). In 1863, a prolonged drought in Chile provided Trumbull with a unique opportunity to make his religious convictions known to a wider audience. As the drought grew more severe, local residents of Valparaiso took a statue of Saint Isidro, the patron saint of rain, and led it through the streets with its hands tied and its feet in chains. They went on to beat the image for not sending rain. At last, a heavy rain fell and the Catholic population attributed it to the saint's intervention on their behalf.

The editor of a liberal newspaper, however, wrote that the rain was not caused by the saint's intercessions but by atmospheric conditions. A heated debate ensued, and the Catholic bishop Mariano Casanova became involved in the controversy. For some reason, the writer who had provoked the commotion invited Trumbull to respond to the bishop in the public press (Brown 1901, 52). Seizing the opportunity, Trumbull based his response on the Scriptures, particularly Zechariah 10:1-2:

> Ask the Lord for rain in the springtime; it is the Lord who makes the storm clouds. He gives showers of rain to men, and plants of the field to everyone.
>
> The idols speak deceit, diviners see visions that lie; they tell dreams that are false, they give comfort in vain. Therefore the people wander like sheep oppressed for lack of a shepherd.

Trumbull's reply avoided both popular superstition and secular materialism. He affirmed that God, not a saint or an image, nor merely atmospheric conditions, had brought the rain. By so doing, Trumbull placed before the public a strong case for Protestantism and its approach to Christianity based on the Scriptures. In fact, Trumbull's address made such an impact on the Chilean people that on July 27, 1865, the legislature changed the article in the constitution that prohibited non-Catholic worship services.

This was the signal Trumbull was waiting for. He immediately requested that his New York-based mission society send additional workers to Chile, but the society was not in a position to do so. Trumbull then turned to the Presbyterians, and even though he himself was a Congregationalist he supported the offer of the Presbyterians to send missionaries. He put himself under the Presbyterian Board of Missions and in that way became the founder of the Presbyterian Church in Chile.[5]

Presbyterians took an early interest in Latin America. In 1817 the United Foreign Missionary Society was organized as a joint effort of the Presbyterians, the Dutch Reformed, and the Associate Reformed Church, including among its long term objectives mission work in Mexico and South America. Presbyterian mission activity in Brazil began in 1859 and in Argentina and Venezuela about the same time.

In 1882 a North American living in Guatemala suggested to the country's liberal president, Justo Rufino Barrios, that Protestantism would be good for

[5] Brown 1901, 53. Kessler's source is his own earlier work, *A Study of the Older Protestant Missions and Churches in Peru and Chile* (Goes: 1967), citing the *Record*, Valparaiso, Dec. 21, 1877.

Guatemala. He urged the president to invite a Protestant missionary to come to Guatemala to help him with his reform program while also distracting the Catholic clergy who were opposing reforms (Brown 1901, 53). President Barrios acted on the idea. During a visit to Washington and New York he met with the Presbyterian board of missions and asked them to send a missionary to Guatemala. As a result of this invitation, John Clark Hill accompanied President Barrios back to Guatemala to establish a Presbyterian school and the first Guatemalan Presbyterian churches.

The story of a woman missionary, Melinda Rankin, is yet another illustration of the way mission operations began for many of the North American boards and agencies. In 1852 Rankin, on her own initiative, went to Brownsville on the Texas side of the Rio Grande. Mexico was still closed to Protestant mission activity but Brownsville was close enough that the school which Rankin began for Mexican children was able to exert an influence across the border (Latourette 1943, 114).

With the growth of liberalism in Mexican political circles, traditional resistance to the entrance of Protestantism was breaking down. Latourette records that the first Protestant communion service in Mexico was celebrated in 1859. In 1860, the American Bible Society sent an agent into Mexico and the following year two Mexicans joined a Protestant Church in Brownsville. By 1865, Rankin was able to move to the city of Monterrey, well inside the borders of Mexico, where she set up headquarters for the spread of Protestantism. She purchased property and began subsidizing Mexican converts to serve as missionaries among their own people.

Due to his Union sympathies in the Civil War that was raging in the United States, James Hickey, an Irish convert from Catholicism, was forced to flee to Mexico. He arrived in Monterrey where he gathered a group of converts soon after he began to evangelize. In the 1860s the State of Zacatecas was opened to Protestants and in 1872 Northern Presbyterians from the United States placed a missionary in the area. The Northern Baptists began work in Monterrey in 1870. In 1873 Melinda Rankin's mission, which for a time had been helped by the American and Foreign Christian Union, was taken over by the American Board of Commissioners for Foreign Missions. Between 1870 and 1880 the Northern Methodists, the Southern Presbyterians, the Southern Methodists, the Society of Friends, and the Associate Reformed Presbyterian Church all established missions in Mexico. The Seventh Day Adventists followed soon afterwards (Brown 1901, 114-115).

The early missionaries all suffered some persecution, in some cases they met violence and even death. Their arrival was viewed by many Catholics as a threat to the community and to the Catholic faith which held it together. By the end of the nineteenth century, legal rights were granted to Protestants by many Latin American countries. But these rights were constantly infringed upon by local authorities and the Catholic clergy. During the period, a meeting was reportedly held in Rome, attended by Catholic leaders from various parts of Latin America, to devise a plan to hold in check the spread of Protestant missionary activity. As a result of the meeting, waves of persecution struck Protestant churches throughout the region (Read, Monterroso and Johnson 1969, 37). Because Protestants were few in number and the missionary challenge was so large, mission leaders early on felt the need for cooperation. In 1913, the Foreign Missions Conference of North America, convened in New York, appointed a continuing committee that became known as the Committee on Cooperation in Latin America. This committee planned an interdenominational congress in Panama in 1916 (339-340).

The Panama Congress was significant for the growth of Protestantism in Latin America. Missionaries, and missionary concerns, dominated the Panama meetings, and the language used was English. But after Panama came seven other meetings, held in specific regions -- San Juan, Puerto Rico; Santiago, Chile; Rio de Janeiro, Brazil; Barranquilla, Columbia; and Buenos Aires, Argentina. At these meetings the language used was Spanish (Portuguese in Rio) and the issues discussed were mostly relevant to the Latin Americans of the region. These regional meetings set forth the guidelines for cooperation that mission organizations would follow for decades ahead (Brown 1901, 340).

In addition to the Panama Congress of 1916, the Committee on Cooperation in Latin America sponsored two other large congresses, one in Montevideo in 1925 and another in Havana in 1929. These meetings were landmarks of cooperation and strategy formation for Protestant work in Latin America. At each gathering it become more evident that the Protestant movement was growing. Though Protestants remained a small minority of the overall population, by mid-century its base in Latin America was firm and its seminaries were supplying an increasing number of well qualified pastors and teachers. Besides cooperation between mission organizations, efforts were also made to divide up the areas where the various mission organizations might work. These understandings were known as "comity" agreements, their purpose was to avoid conflict between missionizing bodies and reach out as efficiently as possible to all parts of the Latin America.

The best known comity plan was the "Cincinnati Plan" drawn up by North American mission leaders in Cincinnati, Ohio in 1917. It was designed for Mexico, a country emerging from the ravages of its Revolution. Included were plans for cooperation in literature production and distribution, a union seminary, and the dividing up of Mexican territory between the various mission organizations and their related churches.

The Cincinnati Plan was, by in large, a failure. It is still remembered with negative feelings by older Mexican Protestants. While the missionaries felt the plan was needed, it was viewed by Mexican Protestants as a foreign import, drawn up by foreign missionaries without consulting Mexicans, and foisted upon Mexico from the outside. Mexicans also perceived it as a money-saving device that really did not take into account the needs and wants of Mexicans. It brought division between those Protestants who cooperated with it and those who refused. As urbanization increased, the plan broke down in the cities where people were coming together from all different parts of the country. With the burgeoning growth of newer mission groups that had never participated in the Cincinnati Plan, the whole thing fell apart. Comity agreements were also drawn up in Peru and Venezuela, but nowhere do they play any significant role today. "As Latin American society has become more complex, and as the Evangelical church has grown and matured, the fortunes of all Evangelicals have become so intertwined that no mere geographical division is an adequate base for cooperation" (Read, Monterroso and Johnson, 1969, 346).

In keeping with the mission theory prevailing at that time, the goals of the mainline missions were to gain converts, establish growing churches, and influence the overall community for good. Schools were a forté of mainline Protestant mission activity, but in the long run they proved difficult to staff and finance. Yet, the school strategy was successful in part. Schools helped make Protestantism respectable; many of Latin America's leaders are the products of these schools. Gradually, however, for the sake of convenience or economy, or due to an erosion of conviction, the schools began to hire non-Christian staff and their spiritual standards dropped. As the schools became secularized their distinctive Protestant influence waned and churches lost interest in supporting them. In one instance, MacKenzie University in Sao Paulo, Brazil, a major Presbyterian school, was turned over to the government and remained there until it was recovered through litigation some fifty years later.

One of the effects of the mainline emphasis on education was that it tended to produce middle and upper class churches that were not in a good position to enfold Latin America's masses when their hour of receptivity to the gospel arrived. Today, some fine old church buildings belong to mainline denominations, and sizeable congregations of Protestants worship in them each week. But the masses that are now turning to Evangelical faith gather for worship elsewhere. Despite their early start and solid foundations, the mainliners did not reap so large a harvest as many of the Protestant groups that came later (Pretiz 1985).

Faith Missions and Independent Churches

"Faith mission" means a mission program that does not pay fixed salaries to its workers, but expects missionaries to present their appeals, or at least their reports, to a circle of supporters who pray for them and supply their financial needs. The main source of support for faith missions has been among the conservative Evangelical churches. Their social base is generally in the upper end of the working class and the middle strata of society. They are known for their religious fervor and missionary zeal.

The faith mission movement can be traced back to the late nineteenth century, but its greatest impact came after World War II. By the time the faith missions arrived on the scene it was obvious that the schools that were a key element in the mainline strategy were losing their effectiveness. They were sapping resources without producing much evangelistic growth. Hence, most faith missions avoided the general education emphasis of the mainline churches and concentrated instead on direct evangelism, church planting, Bible institutes, and in some cases, popular-level seminaries, to train leaders for the churches the missions were planting. In many ways the strategies used by the faith missions and those of the Pentecostals who came after them were similar. They concentrated on teaching the Bible. They emphasized a basic gospel message of sin, grace, and salvation by faith. Neither group had a strong ecclesiology or a deep understanding of the church's historic development.

The faith missions religious commitment and vigorous evangelism bore results and the number of independent, non-historic Protestant churches in Latin America increased dramatically. They soon outdistanced the mainline churches in gaining converts. The independents introduced a variety of methods including correspondence courses, evangelistic campaigns, tent meetings, and stadium-side crusades which captured public attention and helped the churches grow. They were the first to use radio. They opened bookstores, set up printing presses, and everywhere promoted an Evangelical (some call it "fundamentalist") approach to Christian faith and life. They generally stayed away from political controversies. The independent Evangelicals usually aimed their mission at the middle class where they found the greatest response. In the course of time, many of their members rose socially and economically and today are a main source of Protestant strength and leadership.

The Central American Mission (commonly called CAM) is an example of a well organized faith mission in Latin America. Established in 1890 through the initiative of Rev. C.I. Scofield (of "Scofield Bible" fame), CAM soon spread its operation throughout the Central American republics (Latourette 1943, 116). It established a pastor training school, the Central American Seminary, in Guatemala City. Dispensational in theology in the "Dallas" (Seminary) mold, this school became one of the largest Protestant seminaries in Latin America. CAM's emphases from the start were gospel proclamation, church planting, training of local leaders, and dependence on God and his people to supply the resources.

The faith system made a great impact on Protestant mission endeavor. It proved effective in raising large amounts of money to support mission activity. It bonded supporters and missionaries. But it also created among some missionaries an unhealthy individualism and freedom from accountability. When they began, faith missions were largely non-denominational or inter-denominational, but that is no longer the case. Some denominational boards now use the faith support approach also.

Before moving on to the sixth wave of Protestant mission activity in Latin America, it must be acknowledged that Protestant mission activity largely failed to convey to Latin American Evangelicals the importance of identifying with the church's long history and essential unity. This is a regrettable aspect of Protestant mission endeavor in Latin America. While it transferred to the region the biblical gospel and many of the strengths of the Protestant Reformation, it also imported most of the church divisions of Europe and North America, plus an assortment of unique traits formed by highly individualistic missionaries. Many of the imports made little or no sense in the Latin American context, but the missionaries brought them and now they are firmly entrenched. Like the Catholicism brought by earlier missionaries from Spain and Portugal, Latin American Protestantism bears the strengths and weaknesses of its missionary origins. Despite such imperfections, discerning eyes could identify the growing strength of Latin American Protestantism even before the Pentecostal explosion. Decades ago, Stephen Neill made this prophetic statement about the Protestant churches of Latin America:

> It is hardly possible to take part in the life and worship of these Churches without realizing that here is something potentially different from anything that has been produced by the Christian Churches in other parts of the world. South America, so long regarded as the backward continent, may yet come to be the continent of hope for the whole Church of Christ (Neill 1964, 509).

Pentecostalism

In considering the sixth wave of Protestant mission activity it is necessary to distinguish between the Pentecostal movement that was introduced to Latin America by foreign missionaries, and the autochthonous, "grass roots" Pentecostal churches that have few if any ties to foreign bodies and spring up spontaneously almost anywhere. The latter group are sometimes called "neo-Pentecostals," to distinguish them from traditional Pentecostals. The Assemblies of God is the leading representative of traditional Pentecostalism; and they are the largest of all Protestant groups in Latin America. Both streams of Pentecostalism are growing rapidly. One of the difficulties in gathering data about the autochthonous churches stems from the fact that they have few if any ties with the outside church world. But it is largely this autochthonous character that explains their strength and growth.

A number of factors worked together to make Pentecostal mission endeavor especially effective. First, Pentecostals contextualized their methods to a greater extent than their predecessors. Their emphasis on the spontaneity of the Holy Spirit, while making them vulnerable to aberrations and excesses, at the same time freed them from following foreign liturgical traditions. Church traditions were at best a mixed blessing to mainline and Evangelical missions, and often they proved a hindrance. But from the start, Pentecostal churches were free to express their praise and worship in ways that fit the tastes and disposition of Latin Americans. If they preferred lively church services, they could have them (Latourette 1943, 148-149).

Pentecostals also concentrated their evangelistic efforts on the lower classes that made up the bulk of the population (Latourette 1943, 149). By the time the Pentecostals moved in, the mainliners and Evangelicals had moved up the social ladder, leaving the masses to be reached by the Pentecostals. Pentecostal mission strategy targeted the impoverished masses in Latin America's mushrooming cities. Millions of rural-to-urban immigrants, their village life left behind forever, were ripe for new ideas, including religious teaching. The Pentecostals provided them the opportunity to hear the gospel free of intimidation from relatives or neighbors, to experience warm Christian fellowship in the impersonal city, and be treated with dignity as children of God (149).

Third, the growth of Pentecostalism had to do with leadership. From the start, Pentecostal pastors were nearly all Latin Americans. They were ordinary people who had personally undergone a profound spiritual change, and had received from their mission just enough training to be able to evangelize, teach, and nurture common people. The Assemblies of God in Brazil with a membership of more than six million are reported to have more than 27,000 lay workers and some 30,000 credentialed ministers. This is nearly twice the number of Catholic priests in the entire country (Martin 1990, 50-51). Brazil's Assemblies have only about twenty foreign missionaries serving with them. The Brazilian pastors and workers support themselves through secular employment or are supported by their congregations. They never learned the habit of depending on income subsidies from overseas.

A fourth reason had to do with some of the more well known characteristics of Pentecostalism, i.e. the teachings and practices associated with tongues, healings and exorcisms, and with the theology behind them. In a society looking for tangible evidence that God hears prayer and still does powerful things, Pentecostals offered tangible evidence. To people who feared evil spirits and believed that they could become possessed by demons, Pentecostals showed that the Bible addressed these very things and that the

God of the Bible could deliver them from Satan's power. To the poor who could not go to doctors or afford expensive medicines, Pentecostals came with healing prayer and simple faith that God was so good that he listened to the poor when they prayed. And to the despised, uneducated and oppressed, the experience of tongues testified with overwhelming effect to the Spirit's indwelling and the reality of grace. Regardless of the world's low opinion of them, these tongues-speakers knew deep down inside that God esteemed them highly, so highly that he filled them with his Spirit and made them his sons and daughters.

Related to this is a fifth cause of Pentecostal growth, their contagious zeal for Christ and their aggressive and persistent evangelism. Pentecostals enlist everyone in evangelism: pastors and lay persons, men, women, and youth. As one exasperated Mexican Presbyterian exclaimed: "They out-preach us, out-pray us, out-work us, and out-grow us." The other side of the phenomenon was summed up by a Pentecostal pastor, also a Mexican, who told me, "Presbyterians take their young people on outings to entertain them, while we Pentecostals take our young people to the streets to evangelize."

In support of these observations I recall a Saturday a few years ago in Mexico when I accompanied my Pentecostal son-in-law, Francisco Domínguez and the evangelism team from the church he had started. Never in all my years as a missionary had I participated in such fearless and aggressive evangelism. Several times that day I wondered if I would get home alive, but I stopped wondering what made their church grow so fast. These people took seriously Jesus' words about going to the highways and byways and compelling folks to come in. Furthermore, they depended on local pastors and evangelists like my son-in-law, whose level of training did not alienate them from the common people. Whatever they lacked in theological sophistication was made up for in other ways.

Today, approximately 75% of Latin America's fifty million Protestants are affiliated with Pentecostal churches. In addition to Pentecostal church membership, Pentecostal ideas, styles of worship, and music have made their way into all the historic Protestant churches, the independent and fundamentalist churches, and the Catholic church itself. It is impossible to discuss Latin American Christianity without talking about Pentecostalism. Its influence has spread far beyond Latin America; and there is hardly a part of the world that its impact is not felt.

Electronic Media Evangelism

The seventh wave of Protestant mission activity in Latin America rolled in soon after World War II in the form of radio and television broadcasting. American missionaries were the first to introduce Protestant broadcasting in the region. Since the first Christian radio stations were begun in Latin

America, the use of electronic media has grown immensely. Looking back from the vantage point of the 1990s, it is impossible to explain the growth of Protestantism in Latin America without factoring in the creative and dynamic use of the electronic media by Protestant Evangelists.

Guatemala is a case in point. Susan Rose and Quentin Schultze researched the phenomenal growth of Protestantism in Guatemala, and they evaluated the media's role as follows:

> Fundamentalist broadcasting did not cause the rapid proliferation of Pentecostal and neo-Pentecostal churches in the country.... There were numerous other factors in the rise and spread of Latin American Evangelicalism. Nevertheless, radio and television were important conduits for the transmission of fundamentalist values, beliefs, and practices throughout the country, especially in the Spanish-speaking cities and regions. More than anything else the electronic media legitimized Protestant fundamentalism and helped make it socially acceptable for Roman Catholics to jump over to Evangelicalism (Rose and Schultze 1993, 433).

Throughout Latin America, mainline Protestant churches continue to fill large auditoriums on Sunday, and traditional Pentecostals have shown that on special occasions they can fill large tents and stadiums. But media evangelists using satellite hookups reach more people than all the tents, stadiums and church auditoriums combined. In terms of the number of listeners and the potential impact on all branches of the Christian church, electronic media evangelism is the largest of the seven waves of Protestant mission activity to reach Latin America. It is no exaggeration to say that radio and television have shaped the form and content of almost all areas of Protestant life (Brown 1901).

Jimmy Swaggert was the most popular radio and television evangelist in Latin America, before the scandal that destroyed his ministry. At the height of his career, Swaggert's weekly broadcast was carried on more than 500 Latin American television stations (Lattin 1988). Swaggert's popularity helped make the Assemblies of God the fastest growing Protestant denomination in Latin America. Following Swaggert in popularity among Evangelicals are Luis Palau, Hermano Pablo (Paul Fikkenbinder), and the PTL Club.

The woman evangelist most listened to in Latin America at this time is probably María Miranda. Her radio program, "Para ti, mujer," is sponsored jointly by the Brethren Church of Ashland, Ohio, and the Fuller Evangelistic Association of Los Angeles, California. Carried over 537 stations, her program is heard by an estimated one hundred million people every day, in twenty-two countries (Piecuch 1987). In her broadcasts, Miranda deals with the unique cultural problems faced by Latin American women. Her programs come in two forms, a five-minute program Monday through Friday, and a fifteen minute program on weekends. Her messages convey biblical light on problems that women know well: loneliness, widowhood, alcoholic husbands, and youth drug use. The broadcasts generate an enormous amount of mail, which is answered by staff members in the USA, Bolivia, Spain, and Argentina.[6]

A change is taking place in Protestant broadcasting as sponsors realize that today's listeners prefer broadcasts produced locally to programs heard by short-wave and produced in the United States. Though local programming generally lacks the professionalism of foreign broadcasts, broadcasters recognize that there is a "growing tendency in Latin America to listen to stations that even though low-powered, are broadcasting from the same area and give a feeling of identification and ownership to the residents of a given place" (Serrano 1993, 9).[7]

Hundreds of locally produced Protestant radio broadcasts are now heard daily throughout Latin America. Because of the cost factor, radio is more often used than television. Rose and Schultze described the programming they heard in Guatemala as follows:

> Clearly the most important aspect of Evangelical radio in Guatemala is the live, local character of so many of the broadcasts. Latino Evangelicals have naturally moved beyond the rather dull, pedantic, and literary styles of North American religious radio stations to entertaining and dramatic programs that are typically broadcast live. Eighty-seven percent of Evangelical radio is aired live in the studio, compared with only sixty-six percent of Catholic programming.
>
> Moreover, nearly all Evangelical broadcasts are produced in Guatemala, even those made by North American mission organizations. On the air Evangelicals preach, sermonize, persuade, cajole, interpret, and encourage. In short, fundamentalists enthusiastically and committedly witness to their faith via the spoken work to a culture that loves conversation and discussion, with the apparent authority of the voice of a real person presenting the word of God (Rose and Schultze 1993, 434).

Some independent Pentecostal churches in Latin America are making extensive use of radio stations and TV networks to evangelize and train their leaders. An example of this is the Universal Church of the Kingdom of God

[6] Both Mária Miranda and her husband Dr. Juan Carlos Miranda serve as missionaries of the Brethren church. Dr. Miranda has served on the Executive Committee of the National Association of Evangelicals (Piecuch 1987).

[7] Guillermo Serrano is a Spanish Broadcast minister of the Back to God Hour (Hora de la Reforma), a missionary broadcast of the Christian Reformed Church in North America.

in Brazil. It was started fifteen years ago by Edir Macedo de Bezerra with just a small group of people. It now has two million worshippers meeting in eight hundred locations throughout Latin America, Portugal, Angola and the United States. Macedo makes strategic use of the electronic media to nurture his far flung membership and instruct the 2,000 pastors connected with the movement (Tapia 1992).

While there are obvious advantages to locally produced religious broadcasts, it must be acknowledged that there are serious drawbacks as well. Many programs present a kind of "Christ the Magician," who will solve everyone's problems if they will only believe. Some programs spend more time promoting the sponsoring institution than proclaiming the gospel. Like some of their North American counterparts, some programs place heavy emphasis on fund-raising.

Many Protestant broadcasts are aired over Christian stations, and hundreds more are aired on commercial, secular stations. Juan Boonstra, who for many years was the Spanish broadcaster of the *Hora de la Reforma*, preferred to air his programs on commercial stations because his chief purpose was to reach the non-Christian audience that was more likely to be tuned in to a secular station (Boonstra 1993). In some instances commercial stations are so eager to find quality programming that they will air Protestant programs without charge. This is the case with hundreds of María Miranda's programs that are aired without charge because station managers like Miranda's material (Piecuch 1987).

The seventh wave of Protestant mission activity has unquestionably made a major impact in Latin America. At a time when Protestants were struggling to win acceptance, media broadcasting helped them to look good. Broadcasting gave Evangelicalism legitimacy. It won converts, helped build churches, and contributed to the shaping of beliefs and values among listeners. The fact that most Evangelical broadcasting is now being taken over by local broadcasters testifies to the value Latin Americans put on the use of media. They regard it as important enough to shoulder responsibility for carrying it on. The financial costs are high, but the response from listeners is enormous. Letters pour in. When broadcasters make personal appearances, stadiums and auditoriums are jammed.

The popularity of certain Protestant radio and television preachers is so great that it raises the question whether something may be wrong, or at least missing, in ordinary Protestant churches. It may be that an absence of good teaching in the average local church explains why Protestant radio and television broadcasts are so popular. The speed at which many Protestant churches have grown has produced a situation in which a majority of pastors lack sufficient training, time, and resources to prepare carefully for preaching. Their weekly sermons often offer meager fare. Sensing they need more than their pastors can give, members look to the electronic media to supplement the instruction received locally.

Two personal recollections reinforce to this point. The first is that of a warm and energetic embrace I received from a Venezuelan woman in the city of Maracay. She was an active member of a Venezuelan church, yet she became very excited when she learned that radio preacher Luis Pellecer of the *Palabras de Vida* broadcast of the Reformed Church in America, was one of the pastors of my local church in Grand Rapids, Michigan. "He is MY pastor!" she exclaimed several times. During an extended conversation I heard her speak with great affection about her local pastor. Yet I received the clear impression that while she appreciated her pastor as a man of prayer and godliness, most of her biblical instruction came not from him but from the radio broadcast of Luis Pellecer.

My second recollection is that of a group of Evangelical believers sitting in a circle, their pastor in the middle, in a small village in the Dominican Republic. The pastor was the only literate person in the group, and he had learned to read on his own. He had not received any formal training to be a pastor or teacher. In the center of the circle was a radio, and with intense interest they were listening to radio preacher Juan Boonstra, of *La Hora de la Reforma*. After the broadcast was over, the pastor led the believers in an hour-long discussion of what they had heard. This pastor was handling the situation well. He recognized his personal limitations as a Bible teacher, and to avoid depriving his congregation of spiritual nourishment he made use of Boonstra's radio broadcasts to instruct the people. Until such time as local pastors receive better training for the ministry of the Word, I believe the electronic media will continue to play an important role in the spiritual renewal of Latin America.

An Assessment of Protestant Mission Activity

The basic goal of Protestant mission activity in Latin America apparently has been achieved. Though Latin America remains a Catholic region, Protestantism is firmly established with fifty million adherents, growing churches, and national leadership. Across the region, on an average Sunday there are probably more Protestants than Catholics involved in worship and church fellowship (Martin 1990, 50).

The goals of most mission organizations were to win converts in sizable number and to establish churches that could carry on their own ministries, pastored by their own clergy. In addition, through schools and benevolent institutions such as hospitals and clinics, Protestant missions hoped to demonstrate that Protestants were not "traitors" for having left the Catholic church. They were concerned about the welfare of their fellow citizens and wanted to build up their countries. For a major part of Latin America, these goals have been achieved. This is not to say that every part of Latin America has a vital and growing Protestant church or that everything a mission endeavor may hope to achieve has been accomplished. Countries like Columbia, Cuba, Uruguay, and Venezuela are weak in terms of Protestant populations. There are Indian tribes with no church at all, and towns and villages with no resident Protestant witness. There are huge sections of Latin American cities without an Evangelical church of any kind. In megacities like Mexico City, there are sectors containing twenty to thirty thousand people each that have no Protestant churches of any kind.[8] As long as such conditions continue, it cannot be argued that the Protestant missionary task is finished.

Nevertheless, in terms of the essential missionary goal of establishing a viable Protestant base in Latin America, the story of Protestant mission activity in Latin America is a success story. The Evangelical base is now established. A great number of pastors are in place. The decadal growth of the Protestant movement stands at about ten percent. As it expands in size and influence it will broaden the application of the gospel beyond individuals and families, to issues of work and community, and as is already happening in some places, to national politics. The day when Protestantism leavens Latin America lies directly ahead (See Table 7.2 below).

A Sending Base of Mission

Of great significance is the fact that parts of Latin America are now a sending base for mission activity in other parts of the world. Protestant churches in countries such as Brazil, Guatemala, Costa Rica and Mexico are sending out their own missionaries. Some of these missionaries go across national borders within Latin America, some go to remote Indian tribes, while others cross oceans, master difficult languages and adapt to new cultures just as missionaries from Europe and North America have done.

These Latin American missionaries, coming as they do from churches that are the product of two centuries of outside mission endeavor, are the clearest evidence that the Protestant faith has indeed taken root in Latin America. As Latin American Christians act upon the compulsion of the Holy Spirit to carry the gospel to places where the gospel is scarcely heard, the Protestant mission achieves "full circle" status. Latin Americans now add fresh resources to the global Christian enterprise.

[8] *México, Hoy y Mañana*. Documento No. 1. Directorio Evangélico de la gran ciudad de México. Mexico, 1987. In the case of Mexico, government restrictions against religious programs on radio and television severely limit the effects of media on religious faith and community life.

Table 7.2
Estimated Evangelical Growth Factors in Latin America from 1960 to 1985 with Extrapolation to 2010

	Evangelical Percentage of Total Population 1960	1985	Growth Factor Percentage From 1960 to 1985	Extrapolated Evangelical % Population in 2010
Argen.	1.63	4.69	2.9	13.6
Bolivia	1.27	6.51	5.1	33.2
Brazil	4.40	15.95	3.6	57.4
Chile	11.71	21.57	1.8	38.8
Colom.	.39	2.43	6.2	15.1
Costa Rica	1.30	6.48	5.0	32.4
Cuba	2.41	2.11	-.9	1.9
Dom. Rep.	1.73	5.17	3.0	15.5
Ecuador	.48	2.75	5.7	15.7
El Salvador	2.45	12.78	5.2	66.5
Guatemala	2.81	18.92	6.7	126.8
Haiti	6.09	14.18	2.3	32.6
Hond.	1.51	8.75	5.8	50.8
Mexico	2.21	3.08	1.4	4.3
Nicar.	2.26	6.32	2.8	17.7
Panama	4.40	9.72	2.2	21.4
Paragy.	1.05	2.47	2.4	5.9
Peru	.63	2.98	4.7	14.0
Puerto Rico	5.87	20.85	3.6	75.1
Urugua	1.19	1.91	1.6	3.1
Venezuela	.82	1.95	2.4	4.7

Figures in first two columns are courtesy of Patrick Johnstone, WEC (Worldwide Evangelization Crusade) International, Gerrards Cross, England. (*The Christian Century*)

The Latin American Missionary Congress (COMIBAM), held in Sao Paulo, Brazil, November 23-29, 1987, was a momentous event for Protestant mission activity in Latin America. Three thousand Evangelical leaders, representing all Latin American countries, were present. For the first time in modern mission history, the Protestant leadership of an entire continent declared that

Christ was leading them to assume responsibility for the unreached peoples within their region and beyond, and to move from being a mission field area to being a sending force for mission everywhere.

The aftermath of COMIBAM has been a flurry of activities from Latin American youth seeking mission training to follow-up meetings for the purpose of laying concrete plans to missionize unreached people groups in Latin America and elsewhere. COMIBAM's spirit and goals find expression in the organization called COMIBAM International, which has set as its goal the evangelization of 3,000 unreached peoples groups. By "unreached people group" is meant an identifiable ethnic community where a viable Evangelical church has not yet been established (Bogosian 1993, 22). (See Table 7.3.).

Plainly the impulse of the Spirit that first sent missionaries to spread the gospel in Latin America is now moving Christians from within the region to finish the tasks that remain and to join with fellow believers around the world in global mission. It is further evidence of a universal principle, that where vital Christian faith is found amid spiritual ignorance and need, faith invariably reaches out in mission activity.

A Matter of Concern

Having addressed the optimistic side of the Protestant story in Latin America, something must be said about a matter of serious concern to Protestants. The issue is that of desertion from the Protestant church, and in some cases from the Christian faith altogether. John Kessler, a missionary of many years in Latin America, has studied in depth the phenomenon of desertion, particularly with reference to Costa Rica. He has documented his findings in the book *500 Años de Evangelización en América Latina*. Kessler found that identifying the causes of Protestant desertion was not an easy matter, "because many people are not willing to talk openly about this subject," which may explain why few people seem aware of the extent of the problem (Kessler 1993).

Because he was curious as to the accuracy of the claim made by both Protestant and Catholic sources that twenty percent of the Costa Rican population was Evangelical, Kessler urged an independent research organization to conduct a religious survey. That survey was carried out in 1989. It consisted of five basic questions:

1) What is your religion?
2) Into what religion were you born?
3) How often do you attend a worship service?
4) Were you ever a Protestant, without being one now?
5) Have you attended a large evangelistic campaign?

Interviewers added a number of explanatory and follow-up questions, but these five were the basic areas of investigation (Kessler 1992a, 18).[9]

As far as the size of the Protestant population was concerned, the results of the 1989 survey were not surprising. Just under twenty percent declared they were Protestants. There was also sprinkling of Jews, Mormons and Jehovah's Witnesses (Kessler 1992a, 19). In 1991, the same research organization repeated the survey, with the first four questions unchanged. A change was made in the fifth question, the question dealing with large evangelistic campaigns, because a Luis Palau campaign had been conducted close to the time of the survey.

Two surprises came to light when the results of the two surveys were compared. First, the surveys showed that big evangelistic campaigns were not winning the large numbers of converts that many people had assumed. Second, the rate of Protestant desertion was much higher than anyone realized.

According to the 1989 survey, 8.1 percent of the adult population indicated that it had been Protestant at one time, but was not Protestant any longer. Sixty-two percent of those who had abandoned Protestantism went over to the Catholic Church while thirty-one percent stopped professing religion altogether. Six percent became Mormon or Jehovah's Witness, and one percent converted to the Jewish faith (Kessler 1992a, 20).

In the 1991 survey, the number of respondents who said that they had abandoned the Protestant faith rose to 12.1 percent, while the number of desertions from the Catholic Church diminished. In the 1989 survey, 6.1 percent of the Catholics said that at one time in their lives they had been Protestants. In 1991, that figure rose to 12.9 percent. In 1989, 32.3 percent of those who professed some other religion said they had been Protestants at one time, but in 1991 the figure was down to 23.5 percent. The conclusion seems inescapable that there has been in recent years in Costa Rica a massive desertion in favor of the Catholic Church. The surveys also suggested that church attendance among present day Catholics may be better than Protestants generally assume (Kessler 1992a, 21).

After studying results of the first survey, Dr. Carlos Denton, director of CID, the research organization, told Kessler:

> Don Juan, if you were a business man, I would say to you, based on this information, that you ought to call with great urgency a high level meeting of all your sales personnel, for the purpose of finding out why so many of your clients try out your product but afterward let it go. (Kessler 1992a, 19)

[9] The organization that conducted the survey was the Consultoria Interdisciplinaria en Desarrollo S.A (CID). Possibility of error, ±3 percent.

Table 7.3[*]
Proportional Distribution of 3,000 Unreached People Groups

COUNTRY	TOTAL POPULATION	TOTAL EVANGELICALS	PERCENT EVANG.	% OF all IEs[**]	UNREACHED PEOPLE GPS
Brazil	180,000,000	35,000,000	19.44	53.85	1615
Mexico	90,000,000	6,750,000	7.50	10.38	312
U. S.	30,000,000	5,400,000	18.00	8.31	249
Chile	13,000,000	3,990,000	30.69	6.14	184
Guatemala	9,500,000	2,400,000	25.26	3.69	111
Argentina	33,000,000	1,700,000	5.15	2.62	78
El Salvador	6,000,000	1,500,000	25.00	2.31	69
Puerto Rico	3,500,000	1,200,000	34.29	1.85	55
Columbia	34,000,000	1,100,000	3.24	1.69	51
Venezuela	20,000,000	1,000,000	5.00	1.54	46
Nicaragua	3,800,000	800,000	21.05	1.23	37
Peru	24,000,000	800,000	3.33	1.23	37
Dom. Rep.	7,600,000	700,000	9.21	1.08	32
Honduras	5,200,000	550,000	10.58	0.85	25
Bolivia	7,200,000	500,000	6.94	0.77	23
Costa Rica	3,500,000	350,000	10.00	0.54	16
Ecuador	11,000,000	330,000	3.00	0.51	15
Panama	2,500,000	300,000	12.00	0.46	14
Cuba	11,000,000	200,000	1.82	0.31	9
Paraguay	5,000,000	150,000	3.00	0.23	7
Portugal	11,000,000	100,000	0.91	0.15	5
Uruguay	3,200,000	70,000	2.19	0.11	3
Spain	42,000,000	60,000	0.14	0.09	3
Canada	1,000,000	30,000	3.00	0.05	1
Belize	200,000	20,000	10.00	0.03	1
TOTAL	557,200,000	65,000,000	11.67 (ave.)	100.00	3000

[*]COMIBAM
[**]Percentage of all Iberoamerican Evangelicals (including Spain and Portugal) who live in this country.

Commented Kessler: "If he said that to me after examining the 1989 figures, I don't even want to think about what he would say after seeing the 1991 results!" (Kessler 1992a, 19). Protestant growth was so great in the 1970s and 1980s that churches ignored the leakage. Records were kept of baptisms and new members, but not of those who departed. The 1991 investigation showed that at that time the Protestant desertion rate in Costa Rica was so serious that within a few years the Protestant movement could stagnate or even diminish (Kessler 1992a, 19). More disturbing to Protestant observers is evidence that in some parts of Latin America, pre-Columbian Indian religions are in resurgence, in some cases attracting more followers than Protestantism.

Causes And Solutions

Kessler's findings demand serious attention and further research. Was there something about the way Protestant churches were planted and developed that now produces such high desertion rates? Are the Costa Rica findings symptomatic of trends in other parts of Latin America? After participating in a number of seminars on the subject, Kessler believes that he can identify at least four main causes of desertion in the Costa Rica setting.

The number one cause of Protestant desertion has to do with money, and it stems from resentment caused by wrong handling of funds. Especially among certain Pentecostals there are customs regarding the handling of funds that appear suspicious. These customs were first introduced by missionaries for the purpose of stimulating the local support of pastors. But if the system is not replaced, desertions will increase. The number two cause relates to sexual misconduct. There are an alarming number of scandals among pastors and other church leaders. Though it probably would be impossible to prove any direct connection, some link seems to exist between the preaching of a "prosperity gospel," a leadership style that surrounds the pastor with an "in-group" of spiritual elites, and vulnerability to moral lapses. The third reason for Protestant desertion appears to be the legalistic impositions that some pastors place on their members, especially upon women. The fourth factor has to do with the poor quality of much of the preaching and teaching. The messages are shallow and repetitive, which is to be expected given the low level of instruction most Protestant pastors have received (Kessler 1993).

Kessler points out that the Protestant movement in general is experiencing a number of crises, partly due to its own growth and success and partly because Protestants are not immune to the changes and moral stresses occurring in society as a whole. Whereas in the past Protestants were known for their piety, their solid family relationships, their high moral standards and hard work, it is becoming increasingly difficult to distinguish Protestants from non-Protestants in these areas. The vices common in society are now found regularly among Protestants as well (Kessler 1992b, 91). "How sad it is," laments Kessler, "that at the moment of greatest opportunity, in some countries more while in other countries less, the breakdown of moral values occurring in society at large has found its way into the Evangelical church too" (Kessler 1992b, 91). Maybe it has become too easy to be a Protestant. Years ago, when society disapproved of Protestants, it was costly to respond to an evangelistic message and convert to the Protestant faith. But now it is as easy to go forward at an "altar call" in a Protestant evangelistic service as it is to go forward to the altar to receive the host in a Catholic mass. In both cases, uninstructed people think they get the benefits of Christ automatically, without a change of heart or life (93-94).

It is common among Protestants, observes Kessler, to charge that Catholic mission work was so superficial that it did not deserve to be called evangelization. But Protestant work may be vulnerable to similar charges. There is evidence of marvelous spiritual vitality in Latin American Protestantism. There is missionary zeal, and in many places remarkable growth. But too often the worst aspects of radical Pentecostalism dominate the Protestant scene, and there is hard evidence of a desertion factor that Protestants have not cared to recognize. The value of good education, religious instruction, service to others, and personal piety that characterized Latin American Protestantism in years past are eroding, and increasingly the Protestant religion appears to be valued for the emotional highs and material benefits it is reputed to bring its adherents (Kessler 1992b, 93).

The history of Protestant mission activity in Latin America is a story of religious commitment, sacrifice and, today, a large measure of success. But there is no room for Protestant triumphalism. A sober assessment of the present situation produces concern as well as joy and gratitude. There is a sense in which both Protestants and Catholics, coming though they do from different points in the Christian spectrum, confront similar challenges in Latin America. Neither can say that its mission is over.

Reference List

Baldwin, D. J. 1990. *Protestants and the Mexican revolution: Missionaries, ministers, and social change.* Chicago: University of Illinois Press.

Bogosian, Phil. 1993. The meeting of the century -- Number three. *Mission Frontiers Bulletin* (Jan.- Feb.): 176-181.

Boonstra, Juan. 1993. Personal interview with author. April.

Brown, H. 1901. *Latin America: The pagans, the papists, the patriots, the Protestants and the present problem.* New York: Fleming H. Revell.

Kessler, J. 1993. Personal letter to the author, 17 March.

________. 1992a. *500 Anos de evangelización en America Latina desde una perspectiva evangélica.* San Jose, Costa Rica: Departamento de Publicaciones del Instituto Internacional de Evangelización a Fondo.

________. 1992b. La realidad acerca del crecimiento evangélico en Costa Rica. *Maranata*: 18.

Latourette, K. S. 1943. *A history of the expansion of Christianity.* Vol. 5, *The great century in the Americas, Australia and Africa, A.D. 1800-A.D. 1914.* New York: Harper & Brothers.

Lattin, D. 1988. U.S. Evangelists. *San Francisco Examiner*, 1 February, p. 18.

Martin, D. 1990. *Tongues of fire: The explosion of Protestantism in Latin America.* Cambridge, MA: Basil Blackwell.

Mexico, hoy y mañana. 1987. Documento No. 1. Directorio Evangelico de la gran ciudad de Mexico.

Neill, S. 1964. *A history of Christian missions.* Pelican History of the Church, vol. 6. Harmondsworth, Middlesex: Penguin Books Ltd.

Piecuch, K. 1987. Miranda Heard by 100 Million. *Action*, (November/December): 15.

Pretiz, P. 1985. Workshop presentation at the Overseas Ministries Study Center: New Haven, CT., 16 October.

Read, W., V. M. Monterroso and H. A. Johnson. 1969. *Latin American church growth*. Grand Rapids: Eerdmans Publishing Co.

Rose, S., and Q. Schultze. 1993. Evangelical awakening in Guatemala: Fundamentalist impact on education and media. In *Fundamentalisms and society*, eds. M. E. Marty and R. S. Appleby, 415-451. Chicago: University of Chicago Press.

Serrano, G. 1993. Latin America, continent of hope. *Communique* (April): 8-9.

Stoll, D. 1990a. *Is Latin America turning Protestant? The politics of Evangelical growth*. Berkeley: University of California Press.

________. 1990b. A Protestant reformation in Latin America? *Christian Century* (17 January): 44-48.

Tapia, A. 1992. Why is Latin America turning Protestant? *Christianity Today*, 6 April, 28-29.

Chapter 8

Protestants and Catholics: Rivals or Siblings

Edward L. Cleary

Thus far the emphasis of this volume has been on the Protestant church. We now turn more directly to the Catholic Church. Accounts of Protestant growth often take for granted a Catholic decline while theories of modernization generally presume a gradual loss of belief in God. To avoid such one-sided views, a larger perspective on the religious situation in Latin America is needed.

Protestant Growth in Perspective

All but the smallest percentage of Latin Americans have a belief in God and a deeply religious sense.[1] Unlike the United States where religion tends toward private expression, religion in Latin America is an experience of encountering God and expressing that encounter as part of daily life (Hortal 1992, 74-76). Even in Brazil, a modernizing country with the world's tenth largest economy, the director of a recent survey has noted: "It is practically

[1] Uruguay and some urban areas of Argentina and Venezuela are exceptions and have higher percentages of non-believers.

impossible, outside of very restricted intellectual circles, to find in Brazil some one who proclaims themselves [sic] atheist. And, more, society as a whole, rejects that kind of declaration, as evident in a recent electoral dispute in the prefecture of Sao Paulo" (Hortal 1992, 68).

Protestant growth should be seen first as part of a larger religious revival in Latin America. Afro-American and spiritist religion flourishes in several countries. In Brazil some 20-30 percent of the population has contact with this religion (Piepke 1992, 180). In six geographic areas, ranging from Central Mexico to southern Argentina, the Indian movement and interest in Indian religion have been gaining strength.

Second, the Catholic Church has itself experienced an awakening in many countries. The most notable sign of this is the increase in the number of enrollment at major seminaries, increases of 300-700 percent in twenty years. Religious sisters currently number some 120,000 and their ranks are growing modestly (unlike the situation in the United States and Europe), thereby enabling them to replace retiring missionaries and deceased members. Among the laity, probably some 20 million or more can be counted as having gone through a deeper conversion process and having become committed, rather than merely observant, members.

Third, Pentecostal growth has often meant recruitment from older, historic Protestant churches rather than from the ranks of Catholics. Virginia Burnett noted whole congregations of Presbyterians and others joining neo-Pentecostal groups in Guatemala (Burnett 1986, 190-191). Very likely this has occurred elsewhere, making problematic the equation of Protestant growth with Catholic decline.

Consequently, the question of numbers is vexing. This will be considered at the end when addressing the question of competition, of winning and losing. Here I will follow Samuel Escobar and others who use 40 million *evangélicos* in Latin America. Rather than argue about the numbers, a word about the new conditions in which both Catholics and Protestants live is more helpful. Modernization and rationality were supposed to lead to the demise of religion. But urbanization, industrialization, and the reorganization of working life have not worked in that fashion. Rather a reorganization of religion has taken place (Cleary 1992a, 167-195). In response to massive social forces, persons have been freed from previous family and religious ties. They are cast into a world in which new relations can be chosen: new friends, new (surrogate) families, and new religious ties.

Catholic Responses

What does all this mean for Catholics? After years of making first hand observations, conducting systematic interviews, and reading countless journal articles and pastoral statements, I have noted a great range of responses on the part of Catholics to the challenge of Protestantism. Let me summarize two common, instinctual responses before taking up the more thoughtful and nuanced ones.

Many priests and bishops are so busy with pastoral duties that they can barely glance at what Protestants and others religious groups are doing. The increased fervor of lay Catholics who have been socialized into the idea that they are "the church" puts increased pressure on parish ministers, retreat house directors, and adult educators to take on new tasks and to do their traditional ones in greater depth and with more studied sophistication. As a consequence, many pastoral agents respond to the religious competition by simply working harder at what they are already doing.

A second response, often found in print and heard frequently in interviews with bishops in Latin America, is to denounce Protestantism as an alien religion that is undermining the Catholic soul and the Catholic culture (*una alma católica y una cultura católica*) of Latin Americans. (A Protestant counterpart can be seen in Sweden where non-Protestant outsiders were severely restricted for much of this century). The key idea, often implicit, goes like this: Protestantism in general and sectarian non-Catholics in particular have no right to establish themselves in Latin America. These religions do not fit in with Latin America's cultures which are fundamentally Catholic. Their proliferation is not a "normal" process but occurs because of insidious tactics and reflects hidden motives. Many *denuncias* of Protestants center on two issues: their tendency to proselytize and their alleged imperialist connection to the United States.

More reflective Catholic responses begin by recognizing that use of the term *sectas* is inappropriate for a complex phenomenon and is offensive to some of the groups to which it has been applied.[2] For example, the bishops of Panama in 1984 issued a document, called by Pablo Richard a benchmark document, which clearly distinguished between historic mainline Protestant churches, the Pentecostal movements, and non-Christian sects (Cleary 1989, 100-109).

Second, the appeal of Protestantism offers a challenge to Catholic theologians, inviting reflection. In a profound theological sense, Pentecostal and other non-Catholic religious growth is a "sign of the times," to be taken as part of the condition of God's people, a starting point for theological reflection. Antonio González Dorado, a distinguished Spanish theologian with long years of experience in Latin America, believes that the multiplication of

[2] For a discussion of John Paul II and the bishops and sects at the Santo Domingo CELAM IV Conference, see: Cleary, "Report from Santo Domingo," *Commonweal* Nov. 20, 1992, pp. 7-8. A Spanish version appeared in *Pastoral Popular*, 226 (March 1993), pp. 15-17.

churches and movements can be seen as a search for a new religiosity or a new spirituality in a fragmented world (González Dorado 1992, 50-54). Protestantism appeals to Latin Americans who are searching for new expressions of religion but who do not want to reject the Gospel.

Third, an examination of Catholic deficiencies helps explain the drain from the Catholic Church. John Paul II carefully called attention to these at Santo Domingo. Cecil Robeck, of Fuller Theological Seminary, commented that he "was very much heartened by... [the Pope's]... the clear admission that many are the Roman Catholic sheep in Latin America who are not receiving adequate feeding in the Roman Catholic Church" (Robeck 1992, 30-31). John Paul II cited shortage of priests and the lack of personal spiritual formation, and also observed that at times: "the faithful do not find in pastoral agents that strong sense of God that such agents should be transmitting in their lives" (Opening Address 1992, Section 12).

Protestant-Catholic Relations: Abrupt Change

Most observers of religion in Latin America during the last thirty years have tales to tell of the high walls between the Protestants and Catholics. Kenneth Strachan and W. Dayton Roberts describe the situation in this way:

> Any aggressive movement [public Evangelistic campaigns] of this sort -- especially in those days of unchallenged R.C. supremacy -- would inevitably draw down the fire and vehement opposition of the established church. The history of Catholic-Protestant polemics in Latin America is not a particularly happy or impressive one. Much to be lamented is the bigotry and intolerance on either side by which it has been characterized (Strachan and Roberts 1981, 90).

At times it seemed as though this hostility would continue forever. Emilio Nuñez described how he imagined the Catholic Church as a huge granite block that could not be moved or changed (Nuñez 1982, 4).

Three Protestant leaders especially stand out for the conversion they underwent to greater openness to Catholics and for the mediating role they played: John MacKay, former president of Princeton Theological Seminary; Kenneth Strachan of the Latin American Mission; and José Míguez Bonino. All are deeply embedded in the Protestant tradition. Míguez Bonino acted as a key interpreter of Latin America's historic Protestants to the Catholic Church. He was the single Latin American Protestant observer at the only Catholic Church council in this century -- Vatican II -- and his interpretations, signalled by *Concilio Abierto*, opened the doors to new relationships.

A symbol of this new openness could be seen in the Protestant organization Church and Society in Latin America (ISAL) which opened to

Catholic members to the extent that by 1970, ISAL had more Catholic participants than Protestants in Bolivia and some other places. An unusual ecumenical and theological insight began growing in response to the turmoil and repression that afflicted Latin America in the 1970s and 1980s. Catholics and Protestants began to band together authentic Christian living-out of peace and justice. In Bolivia, these efforts were especially aimed at the defense of human rights and were led in part by Mortimer Arias, bishop of the Methodist Church. Catholic priests were sponsored through the Methodist peace and justice center. Their ecumenical efforts were matched in the United States by the founding of the Washington Office on Latin America.

Jaime Wright, moderator of the Presbyterian Church in Brazil, recounts vividly the results of his collaboration with Cardinal Evaristo Arns and others in documenting human rights abuses in Brazil (Wright 1990, 94-98). Many other life-threatening collaborations occurred in Chile, El Salvador, and elsewhere. But more was involved than ecumenical resistance to tyranny. Latin American theologians, Protestant and Catholic, reflecting on these experiences in the light of the Old and New Testaments, developed the concept of *orthopraxis*. In contrast (not opposition) to the orthodoxy which had so characterized Latin American religion, orthopraxis meant especially fidelity (practice matching belief) and efficacious love.

Protestants and Catholics believed they shared the same vision at the point of action. This led to a practical ecumenism in Latin America, one not dependent on Catholic bishops or Protestant church administrators. The Seminario Bíblico Latinoamericano in Costa Rica, with roots in the Strachan tradition, routinely admits Catholic students. The dean of the Seminario Evangélico de Puerto Rico is Catholic. Catholics and Protestants collaborate in biblical journals, theological enterprises, and the writing of church history. Some observers, such as David Barrett, editor of *World Christian Encyclopedia*, notes a recent cooling of Catholic-Protestant relations in several regions of the world, including Latin America (1990). Robert McAfee Brown, writing about the Puebla Conference in 1979, noted almost no ecumenical concern at the conference (Brown 1979, 333). Instead of looking to bishops, Brown, Guillermo Cook, and others focused on grassroots ecumenism, as in base Christian communities.

Nonetheless, cooperation between churches continues in a notable fashion in the Caribbean Council of Churches. The Antilles Episcopal Conference of the Catholic Church was a founding member in 1973. CCC has accomplished virtually the only regionwide ecclesical linkage of any kind in the Caribbean which is fragmented by various languages and interests. CCC's monthly newspaper, *Caribbean Contact*, is rightly prized for its critical analysis of the social, economic, political, and religious issues of the region. The *Dictionary of the Ecumenical Movement* comments that "this publication has not infrequently been the cause for uneasy concern on the part of the political powers in the Caribbean" (Davis 1991, 125). It is reported to have caused unease in Washington, as well.

Two reservations should be expressed at this point about relations between Catholics and Protestants. Even where leaders -- bishops, official representatives for ecumenism, or local ministers -- may wish greater cooperation or understanding, the grassroots followers drag behind, at least in some places. In 1993, Dennis Smith, a Presbyterian working for CELEP, expressed the belief that: "110 years of backbiting between Catholics and Protestants, as in Guatemala, have taken a toll and [it] will take years of education before ordinary people are ready to follow ecumenical leadership."

Recently, the presence of five non-Catholic observers at CELAM IV (Santo Domingo 1992), represented a degree of cooperation with Protestant and Orthodox churches in Latin America. But the five observers did not represent well the dominant group of Protestants in Latin America, the Pentecostals. To them we turn next.

Dialogue between Pentecostals and Catholics

More than twenty years of dialogue between Pentecostals and the Catholic church provides a vivid insight into the two major religious forces in Latin America and their possible future. Almost no one in Latin America knows about this dialogue and for many reasons, including the hostility of Pentecostals to Catholics, it is extraordinary that it took place at all. No other dialogue like this exists. The Catholic Church, like most mainline churches, only sponsors sustained conversations about Christian unity with **churches** and not with **movements**. But the Vatican agency responsible for such conversations, the Pontifical Commission on Christian Unity, made an exception and opened a formal dialogue with the Pentecostal movement. The Pentecostals involved are "classical" Pentecostals, heirs of the first wave of experiences of the Holy Spirit that occurred early in the twentieth century. Later movements of neo-Pentecostals or charismatics, from the 1960s and after, have not as yet been included.

Obstacles to the Dialogue

The obstacles within the Catholic Church included the relatively "junior," or latecomer, status of the department of Christian Unity within the Vatican and the opposition of members of other departments who had been trained before Vatican II in a theology that was antithetical to that of many non-Catholic churches. Further, the practice of the Catholic Church has been to wait until a movement changed historically from a sect or movement phase to an established church before entering into dialogue with it. The last group to be accepted into formal dialogue was the Disciples of Christ, founded in the 1820s. So the officials in this department were breaking with tradition to deal with a "newcomer."

One wonders why so little is known of this dialogue since it began systematically in 1972 and has implications for Latin America and for much of the world.[3] Participants to the dialogue have said this is due to the sensitive nature of the interchange. How tender the sensibilities were became apparent early. Virtually all major Pentecostal groups (denominations, not "sects,") had shown hostility to any dialogue with Rome. When David du Plessis, a major figure in worldwide Pentecostalism, became the Pentecostal co-chair for the meetings, the Assemblies of God "disfellowshipped" him. The Assemblies of God, the largest denomination in classical Pentecostalism, also raised objections which resulted several times in cancellation of attendance at meetings of the dialogue by individual members who did not wish to antagonize their denominational leaders.

Jerry Sandidge was an Assembly of God missionary from the United States to Europe who got caught in the middle. Like a small but growing number of Pentecostals from the early tradition, Sandidge sought a higher degree in theology, in his case at the Catholic University of Louvain. As his dissertation, he wrote almost a thousand pages describing the second five years of the dialogue (Sandidge 1987). His involvement with the dialogue cost him his status (and financial support) as a missionary, though not as an Assembly of God minister. The turbulence he endured in his personal life was intensified by cancer which led to his death.

Styles and Themes

In most theological interchanges, discussants get down to differences and similarities centering on specific topics that rankle and divide. Something deeper divided the Catholic and Pentecostal participants; their manner of thinking about God, church, and self differed radically. The Catholic participants were trained in academic theology; the Pentecostals generally were not. The highly rational, systematic theology to which Catholics and historical Protestants had grown accustomed in European and mainline American schools of theology were foreign to the Pentecostals. Pentecostal theology which "communicated in stories, prophecy, spiritual impressions, and biblical utterances" (Sandidge vol. 1, 351), confused the Catholic participants. Sandidge characterized the two sides: "Like two ships passing

[3] Arnold Bittlinger shows the history of the first five years of the dialogue and makes an assessment in: *Papst und Pfingstler: Der römisch katholisch-pfingstlich Dialog und sein ökumenische Relevanz. Studies in the Intercultural History of Christianity*. vol. 16. (Frankfurt und Main: Verlag Peter Lang, 1978).

in the night -- both knowing where they were going and what they meant by what they said, but not aware that the other 'ship' was left in the dark" (Sandidge vol. 1, 327).

The great religions of Europe (Catholic, Protestant, and Jewish) have established a traditional way to enter into dialogue, a way which favors Catholic theologians over Pentecostal ones, Sandidge argued. Dialogue proceeds along a discursive, scientific, and intellectual path leaving little room for oral or narrative theology and spiritual experience to validate truth. The intellectual slant favors the First over the Third World as well (Hocken 1988, 210-211). One of the lessons being learned is that room has to be made in dialogue for what Sandidge calls the nonrational or preliterary elements of religion that are central to Pentecostalism. These "cultural" differences, of faith as science and faith as experience, underlie the dialogue taking place in the discussion. Formally, the agenda of the dialogue began with characteristic questions associated with both religions (more obvious and easier issues, too), such as the so-called "baptism in the Holy Spirit," the path to full membership, the nature of the gifts or talents received from God, and the role of scripture and tradition. More difficult questions came up as mutual confidence among the partners grew, questions such as why Pentecostals place such great emphasis on speaking in tongues. Discussion of this question brought a convergence:

> A personal relationship with Jesus Christ belongs to the definition of a Christian. Classical Pentecostals have never accepted the position or taught that this relationship must necessarily be expressed through speaking in tongues in the sense that one could not be a Christian without speaking in tongues.... The manifestation of tongues was never entirely absent in the history of the Church, and is found in a notable way among Roman Catholics and other Christians involved in Charismatic Renewal, as well as among other classical Pentecostals (Ronado 1992, 29).

Problem themes for Pentecostals also entered the discussion. Probably nothing has troubled them more than Catholic popular religion and devotion to Mary. Discussions resulted in this convergence:

> Both Pentecostals and Catholics teach that Mary in no way substitutes for, or replaces the one true Savior and Mediator Jesus Christ. Both believe in direct immediate contact between the believer and God. Both pray to God the Father, through the Son, in the Holy Spirit.

But differences remained:

> Catholics believe that intercessory prayers directed to Mary do not end in Mary but in God Himself. Pentecostals would not invoke the intercession of

Mary or other saints in heaven, because they do not consider it a valid biblical practice (Ronado 1992, 66).

A break of three years was taken before the third five-year period of meetings began again in 1985. Churches from or with large groups in Latin America lent further weight to future meetings. The Apostolic Church of Mexico; the Church of God, Cleveland, Tennessee; the International Church of the Foursquare Gospel, USA; and Visión de Futuro (Argentina) sent official representatives or observers.

During this third period, Catholic representatives pointed out that they recognize Pentecostal baptism and, "in consequence, that Roman Catholics believe that they share with Pentecostals a certain, though imperfect, *koinonia* (Christian community and identity)." For their part Pentecostals agreed "that to the extent that Pentecostals recognize that Roman Catholics have this common faith in and experience of Jesus as Lord, they share a real though imperfect *koinonia* with them" (Ronado 1992, 30).

This recognition, as elementary as it sounds, jumps light years beyond the typical experience of Catholics and Pentecostals in Latin America. Many Pentecostals believe that the Catholic Church is the "Whore of Babylon" and have said so, loudly. Or they hold their tongues but believe that Catholics are really pagans masquerading as Christians. Further, many Pentecostals, and Evangelicals generally, define spiritual progress by how far a convert has come from his or her Catholic ways. Thus, the admission that Catholics and Pentecostals share a common identity, albeit imperfect, is a major step.

Catholic Charismatics as Bridges

The dialogue of Catholics with Pentecostals could not have taken place for decades, perhaps a century, had it not been for "Pentecostal" persons within the Catholic Church. They belong to a second wave of Spirit experiences, this time occurring within mainline Christian churches. This expansion, called charismatic, not Pentecostal, to distinguish the two (Burgess *et al.* 1988, 130-160), began largely in the 1960s, spreading quickly from one denomination to the other, and, like wildfire, breaking out in unlikely places and times, as at a student-faculty retreat at Duquesne University in Pittsburgh (Mansfield 1992) or through a Catholic professor of preaching, Francis MacNutt, attending a Protestant workshop. In 1970, MacNutt accepted the invitation of a few of the Dominicans in Bolivia to come to Cochabamba, where U.S. missionary priests and sisters and English-speaking Bolivians were gathered for a retreat week. With the help of Tommy Tyson and others from the United States, MacNutt made a significant step in bringing the Catholic Charismatic Renewal to Latin America (Burgess *et al.* 1988, 152-155).

From the charismatic movement, a different style of being Catholic in Latin America began to emerge. Personal experiences and broadly expressed emotions began to supplant what had been a dominant reliance on academic theological schemata and tightly constrained expressions in preaching and celebrations of the Mass. Chrysotom Geraets, a North American priest serving in Santa Cruz, Bolivia, attended the Cochabamba meeting. Shortly before, on a mission leave to the U.S., Geraets reluctantly responded to his mother's desire "to look in on his younger brother," a Benedictine priest who was doing "unusual" (charismatic) liturgies at Benet Lake, Wisconsin. When he returned to Santa Cruz, Chrysotom Geraets also experimented with charismatic liturgies at a chapel largely for university students in Santa Cruz. From a Sunday group of about 150 persons, the congregation at La Mansión, about a mile and a half from Santa Cruz's central plaza, grew to a typical Sunday attendance of 4,000.

Seven thousand come nightly for special occasions, such as the days leading up to Pentecost, with some attendees travelling from other countries. Services for the Saturday evening liturgy for Pentecost Sunday began at 7:00 p.m. with most attendees present for the beginning, an atypical practice in the Hispanic subtropics. All were dressed for something special. Like the population of Santa Cruz, as a whole, the group inside was mostly young, parents in their 20s and 30s with many children, but adults in their 40s and older were also there. The evening began with full-throated singing even though many had no books. Geraets believed that the younger ones knew sixty songs by heart: "a lot better than they know the top 40 from radio." When the first prayers began, a variety of people prayed and Geraets and other priests kept minimal control so that a large measure of spontaneity would result. When selected readers stepped out of the congregation, many of those seated drew out their Bibles and followed along. Catholics reading the Bible seemed the most ordinary of events.

In the slight pause which followed the readings, everyone leaned forward to see who would give testimony. The entertainment value was great. In an culture where speech dominates, nothing surpasses a good story, especially one revelatory about the man or woman down the street. Hearing even the embarrassed and whispered personal histories was not a problem; charismatics are masters of sound systems. For more than an hour, men and women came forward. Some offered stories rehearsed a dozen times in their hearts; others gave rambling descriptions of emotional reactions to problems with no clear resolution, much like the lives of many in the congregation. Hardly anyone's attention wavered -- no one over five years old fell asleep even in the warm evening; the patience of charismatics is legendary.

The service continued for four hours. Only afterward did people remember that the essential parts of the Catholic Mass had been fitted, seamlessly, into the middle of the service after the testimonies and before the intercessory prayers which again got down to the troubles that were on the minds of the attendees. Speaking in tongues followed and attempts to interpret what being said in a language unknown to most. Speaking in tongues, interpreting, singing as one wished, all going on at the same time, served as a break from full attention to something more trancelike, like the state of marathon runners in the last miles.

When the service ended at 11:00 p.m., eyes glistened in the bright lights. All turned to focus on a centerpiece, a mammoth cake, being carried in along with many smaller cakes and lemonade from a tented area outside the church arena. Children pushed forward to join in celebrating the coming of the Holy Spirit to the faithful as the birthday of the church. After eating, disintegration of attention began to set in quickly. Parents and grandparents gathered up children and made their way home around midnight. The next day, many children and some adults reported that they had had dreams like Stephen Spielberg movies in which they were able to soar and to explore unusual universes.

From the time of the first retreat at Cochabamba, MacNutt typically included Protestants as part of his team. They were presented as equals and sorted themselves for preaching and other tasks on the basis of gifts and talents which one or the other had in greater abundance. For three years MacNutt and his team returned to Latin America to conduct start-up or follow-up retreat weeks in Bolivia, Peru, Chile, and Costa Rica. MacNutt, Ralph Rogawski, Helen Raycraft, and others also reached Colombia and Venezuela. By 1973, regional meetings of charismatics were being held in Puerto Rico. Thousands of Latin American Catholics began showing a preference for the charismatic way of expressing religion. MacNutt's heritage includes the ecumenical emphasis with which he began and which fifteen years later may be most evident in Costa Rica where Catholics and Protestants are joint members of several groups (Pretiz 1993).

The Catholic Charismatic Renewal touched the classical Pentecostals, too. Peter Hocken, secretary of the Society for Pentecostal Studies stated: "It was only through the emergence of Charismatic Renewal among Catholics that most [Pentecostals] had come to acknowledge that Catholics could be Christians" (Hocken 1988, 207). The Pentecostal reliance on experience as a guide to religious truth helped. Prominent Pentecostals such as Vinson Synan of India could not deny what they witnessed. After participating with 10,000 Catholics in a prayer meeting at Notre Dame, Synan wrote: "I found myself praying and worshipping with people against whom I had once harbored much prejudice and suspicion. I began to see these Bible-carrying, scripture-quoting, Christ-exalting Catholic Pentecostals as brothers and sisters in Christ" (Synan 1974, 207-208). As Hocken comments: "The process of winning the support of Pentecostal denominations for this dialogue involves a massive change of heart. In almost every case, this change of heart has begun through Pentecostals being confronted with the Charismatic Renewal among Catholics" (Synan 1974, 325).

The Catholic charismatic movement began two years after Vatican Council II closed, just as a leading edge within Catholicism was attempting to absorb the spirit John XXIII described as *aggiornamento*, a transforming spirit. Thousands of lay persons and priests joined the charismatic movement, especially in its birthplace, the United States, from which it spread rapidly to other places where English could be easily understood. Pentecostalism and Charismatic Renewal disrupted, aggravated, and brought turbulence. The history of these movements is full of tales of outbreaks of the Spirit, conflicts with authorities, and church divisions.

For charismatic Catholics as for Pentecostals, styles of thought (discourse) and culture (emotional creations to express thought) conflicted with established patterns of thought and culture. Some within the Vatican and some theologians had grave reservations about the unusual, "un-Catholic," ways in which this religion expressed itself. The charismatics' enthusiastic ceremonies and vigorous testimonies seemed emotionally unbalanced and fulfilled all the criteria of what a Catholic chaplain at Oxford had warned about years earlier in *Enthusiasm* (Knox 1950). Charismatics spoke another language, one which was nonrational in theological terms and which was based on personal experience. Thus it was unsystematic (unscientific) and not worthy of serious, adult attention.

Had it not been for the early presence of bishops in the movement, the tide of opinion within the Catholic Church might have swung against the movement. No presence was more important than Cardinal Leon Joseph Suenens. This bishop of Belgium, a hero to progressives, was one of the presidents of the Vatican Council, and a major figure in the European church. He and others pleaded the cause of the movement to Rome and helped to shape formal sponsorship for the movement within the Catholic Church. Through his command of English and other languages, Cardinal Suenens also acted as a bridge for the movement to non-English speaking countries. (See Burgess 1988, 125).

After MacNutt and others brought the original impulse, the Catholic Charismatic Renewal spread quickly in Latin America. Thousands filled the soccer stadium at Barquisimeto, Venezuela, and elsewhere for Charismatic Renewal services with Spanish-speaking preachers, matching what MacNutt was doing at Yankee Stadium and the Meadowlands. In the United States in the 1980s, the Charismatic Renewal began to decline, remaining nonetheless an important movement (Bord and Faulkner 1983, 149-152). In Latin

America the movement continues to grow, although varying from country to country.[4]

The Catholic Charismatic Renewal has been important for exposing grassroots Latin American Pentecostals to a kind of Catholic with whom they could identify, one who "might be" Christian. This perception of Catholics as Christian has been far from unanimous. Given the popular religious practices of Latin Americans Catholics which confirm the worst suspicions of Pentecostal and Evangelicals there still remains much needed dialogue before widespread cooperation can be expected.

Character of Catholic Charismatic Renewal in Latin America

The Catholic movement in Latin America differed considerably from its North American and European cousins in its class beginnings. The first participants in the MacNutt retreats were mostly priests and sisters working among the poor and they continued their work with lower classes. Further, by this time Liberation Theology's "preferential option for the poor" had became a special emphasis among grassroots workers. So the Latin American movement took on a different class complexion and a different theological emphasis from those of the North Atlantic groups. In Latin America, the basic cohort was poor, and many were committed to the goals of Liberation Theology.

The movement spread like fire through a dry field. Many Catholics in the early 1970s were awaiting change, as the church was in flux at this time and its numbers were invited "to be open." In 1973, twenty-three representatives from nine countries attended the first regional meeting of charismatics which was held at Bogotá. The next year, 250 leaders attended and by the late 1970s, thousands attended Interamerican meetings, especially those held in Puerto Rico.

The meeting in 1973 was crucial in setting the tone for the Latin American Catholic Charismatic Renewal at that time. Typical of the attendees was Father Carlos Talavera from Mexico, later bishop in the Veracruz region, who had been involved for a long time in the Mexican Bishops' Social Action Office. Silvio Carrillo, Missionary of Holy Spirit, a professor of Scripture in Rome, also attended. So did a highly influential Colombian priest, Rafael García Herreros, founder of "Minuto de Dios" television program. Two younger collaborators of García, Ricardo Jorge Jiménez and Diego Jaramillo took part. "Minuto de Dios" eventually expanded to include a community of

[4] Projections for the movement given in David Barrett, ed., *World Christian encyclopedia* (Nairobi: Oxford University Press, 1982) are impressive but are in need of revision.

committed charismatic Catholics in Bogotá within a larger Colombian charismatic community of an estimated 300-400 thousand.

The participants at Bogotá struggled to fit the ideas MacNutt brought with him from North America into the Latin American context. They differed with what they perceived as the middle-class, otherworldly caste of the Charismatic Renewal in the United States. But they also struggled with their own disappointments over grassroots activities common to persons, such as themselves, who were inspired by the social teaching of the church and Liberation Theology. Something in the spiritual realm was missing. To remedy this, the participants believed, the Holy Spirit was "moving in power," showing them the way toward three objectives in Latin America. (Their language was becoming increasingly mystical). First they emphasized personal transformation as an element in social transformation. Second, they believed inner healing necessary to interior transformation. Lastly they saw renewal in Latin America as marked by concern for social justice and liberation.

Almost all the participants were working in *barrios*. Hence, they saw the movement as a renewal for the lower classes. For them, much more was involved than the healing of individuals which MacNutt emphasized. Thus when García and Jaramillo took to the airwaves every night for "Minuto de Dios," they stressed the building and repairing of communitarian ties within society. Colombians and other Latin Americans who have been socialized into a greater sense of community as part of their identity, heard and understood.

Ralph Rogawski believes that the charismatic movement in Latin America subtly changed not only the participants, but their vision of social change as well: "When God's power to enlighten and heal was brought to bear on the same situation we had been facing before the renewal, new priorities emerged after we had a greater spiritual vision" (Rogawski 1992).

The class basis of the Charismatic Renewal movement in Latin America in the 1990s is not uniform nor is the spiritualized liberation orientation Rogawski described perceived by all as its main thrust. Some decry the movement as one of the conservative forces that are destroying the progressive thrust of the Latin American church. Ralph Della Cava and others in Brazil have been tracking prominent Catholic charismatics and they see them as part of the right-wing of the Brazilian church. Della Cava focuses on the mass media efforts of Tom Forrest and others, including Lumen 2000 (television programming), and Evangelization 2000 (catechism programs). He depicts one widely viewed television show from Campinas as having a: "highly personal, pietistic, and individualistic spirituality -- the hallmark of charismatics everywhere and the polar antithesis of Liberation Theology with its primary emphasis on the social" (Cava 1992, 203).

Relations with National Churches

The middle-class, spiritualizing tendency of many charismatics fit well within the cultures of the North Atlantic countries. The velocity with which the movement gained a hearing, acceptance, and guidance in the United States was unusual. Historians date the movement in the U.S. church to February 1967. Two years later the Bishops Committee on Doctrine made a largely favorable report to the U.S. bishops conference; by 1973 an ad hoc committee of bishops had been formed to foster closer ties with leaders of the movement; by 1975 the committee had issued *Guidelines for the Catholic Charismatic Renewal*. Five years later Kilian McDonnell needed three volumes to collect statements from various countries, including some Latin American ones, by church authorities on the charismatic movement (McDonnell 1992).

In Latin America, the movement has had a more turbulent history and the bishops of various countries differed considerably in their reactions to the movement. In the countries where MacNutt helped initiate the movement, movement leaders rapidly sought and typically attained a working relationship with bishops, sometimes portraying their movement as an ideal expression of the spirit of Vatican II. National coordinators were named and some bishops, as the archbishop of Barquisimeto, become active in the movement. So successful were charismatic leaders in some areas that bishops interviewed by the author occasionally reported embarrassment at not being able to share in the enthusiasm of the movement.

However, the context of the times did not favor easy acceptance of the movement everywhere and some charismatics left the Catholic Church. Repressive military governments blanketed most of Latin America in the late 1960s and 1970s when the charismatic movement was being formed. Military governments brought about closed and confusing environments for churches which attempted to act as virtually the only public voices in society which had their own survival to protect, as well.

Catholic Charismatics Become Neo-Pentecostals

Troubles in Guatemala exemplify the obstacles some charismatic Catholics faced. Middle-class Catholics of Guatemala City, hearing of the charismatic movement from friends and family elsewhere, went to St. Louis, Missouri, where MacNutt, the Linn brothers, and other prominent CCR leaders had renewal centers. The Guatemalans returned home, filled with the enthusiasm for the movement. Dennis Smith of CELEP, reports in a 1991 interview that these Catholics were unable to find a priest or bishop who would guide them in "living in the Spirit." Smith says that Protestant middle-class friends (not Pentecostal) suggested a Protestant minister to help them. The charismatic neophytes, experiencing a strong desire for a deeper conversion and for the kind of satisfying worship they had experienced in St. Louis, agreed. Thus, Smith believes, was born neo-Pentecostalism in Guatemala.

Neo-Pentecostalism in Latin America expanded to include many other groups, some of Latin American origin, some directly from the United States, including the "health-and-wealth" varieties. From this group of talented and relatively privileged Guatemalans the first and the second neo-Pentecostal presidents of the country have been drawn, Efraín Ríos Montt and Jorge Serrano Elías.

The Guatemalan bishops' formal response to the Catholic charismatic movement came very late. The Guatemalan church was buffeted by the worst persecution in Latin America. Thousands of its more active members were savagely tortured and murdered. Thus, other concerns besides the charismatic movement occupied the Guatemalan church. Further, the first Catholic adherents were incomprehensible in their new language and unwelcomed by some priests who were troubled with the movement's upper middle-class character and (for Guatemala) its foreign origins.[5]

While the earliest adherents of the movement made a home for themselves outside the Catholic Church, more recent adherents effectively won over the bishops to the view that theirs is a movement with many positive qualities. In 1986, shortly after the military turned the presidential palace over to a civilian president, the Guatemalan bishops conference issued *Guidelines for Charismatic Renewal* (Cleary 1989, 67-71). In this document the bishops cited, "countless cases of witnesses from priests whose lives, once touched by this personal level of faith, have undergone a deep conversion of heart" (Cleary 1989, 67). The presence of priests greatly helped to make the movement acceptable.

The Guatemalan conference's statement also emphasized reservations, such as: "Experience shows that where there does not exist an almost extreme care over charismatic groups, they easily go off track, something that does not occur with other movements" (Cleary 1989, 69). Similar reservations were expressed by bishops in other countries but most of the bishops' concerns were taken care of informally through national coordinators of the Charismatic Renewal.[6]

[5] The foreign issue is accentuated by the presence of a vast predominance of foreign clergy and sisters, many with differing cultural and religious preferences.

[6] A survey of Latin American bishops conferences in the ten years following the Puebla conference (1979-1989) showed very few statements by episcopal conferences regarding the charismatic movement, beyond that of the Guatemalan bishops.

Confluence and Challenge

Pentecostals could be a great aid to Catholics in what has become the major effort of the Latin American Catholic Church: evangelization. Evangelization has come to mean a better instructed Catholic, one who has undergone a conversion, an adult commitment to live by the demands found in the Old and New Testaments. The mass shifting of the allegiances of native populations to the Catholic Church in the initial evangelization of the Spaniards and Portuguese sometimes meant a coercive change and often left an inadequately educated mass (Rivera 1992). Today, the lack of sufficient teachers, schools, and resources for radio or television have left the church with the challenge of "New Evangelization."

So vast is this challenge that in 1983 John Paul II announced nine years of preparation in order to gear up for the beginning of the New Evangelization and he indicated that the task will occupy the church for countless years thereafter. The content and method of the New Evangelization effort became a contested area as Catholic theologians and educators proposed and debated many different models in an ardent search for the best way to proceed.

Thus many crowded to hear Enrique Dussel when he took the platform of the alternative press conference at the Santo Domingo Conference in 1992. Dussel presides over CEHILA, an ambitious ecumenical effort to write and publish Latin American church history. Further, Dussel was the only major Liberation Theology figure available to the press at the Santo Domingo meeting. Dussel surveyed the history of Latin American evangelization in grand lecture style. Given the flaws of that evangelistic enterprise, Dussel searched for another model, but the only one he examined was evangelization by the Christians of the first centuries. He overlooked a model, closer at hand, which is winning millions in Latin America: Pentecostalism.

One of the great benefits to emerge from the Catholic-Pentecostal dialogue is that Catholics are learning to appreciate Pentecostal methods of evangelization at both a theological and a practical level. In a word, "Pentecostals are better at new evangelization -- ultimate challenge, decision, and conversion -- than we are," judges Kilian McDonnell (1992), the Catholic co-chair of the Vatican-sponsored dialogue with Pentecostals. "They have a great deal to teach us about the dynamics of what makes for a deep relationship with God and the church." It is this profound religious attachment, not the superficial ecclesiastical identification, that is the issue in the competition between Catholics and Pentecostals. In fact, developing a faith which will belong and stay with the church while withstanding the shifting loyalties aroused by a bazaar of religious options that are being presented in much of the world, including Latin America, has become a critical issue for both churches.

Catholic Attitudes

Pentecostalism is the second great model of evangelization in Latin America, great at least weighed on the scale of effectiveness. Enrique Dussel (1992) in his history of the Latin American church devoted only brief sections to Pentecostalism. Dussel, like so many Latin American Catholic intellectuals, never seems to enter into the world of the Latin American Pentecostal.

The ignorance which Latin American bishops and intellectuals display toward Pentecostalism is itself a phenomenon which needs explanation. When interviewed in Santo Domingo, Melinda Roper, former president of the Maryknoll sisters worldwide, explained: "In contrast to my growing up as the only Catholic among Protestants, the Latin American bishops grew up only with Catholics. To have non-Catholics around in abundant numbers is a new experience, with nothing in their background to help them deal with it. To them it [Pentecostal evangelization] does seem like violence and calls forth an instinctual need to defend."

Other reasons help to explain the myopia of the Catholic clergy as regards the Pentecostals. Pentecostals in Latin America tend to be poor and can be ignored, especially by the professional classes and bishops. Pentecostals tend to associate mostly with other Pentecostals. They tend not to publish in newspapers or journals read by the literate classes of Latin America; not until the last few years were there Pentecostals trained and capable of academic discourse. Finally, as mentioned earlier, Catholic bishops and pastoral workers can barely keep up with demands of newly committed Catholics for greater service: better preaching, more chaplaincy services for lay movements, and more attention to the poor. The Catholic Church buildings are filled with Sunday worshippers in a great many towns and villages.

Competition: Who Is Leaving?

From what religious background do the converts to Pentecostalism come? Not surprisingly, most are from Catholic backgrounds, but large numbers are former members of other Protestant churches. Whole congregations of historical Protestants joined Pentecostal churches in Guatemala and elsewhere (Burnett 1986, 190-191). Nor are all the former Catholics from the "cultural Catholic" group; what evidence we have thus far indicates that several other types contribute converts to Pentecostal churches: 1) Catholics from the Charismatic Renewal who found little sympathetic treatment in a local church, (Smith 1990) (although the vast majority of charismatic Catholics remain in the church and their numbers have grown at a fast clip); 2) former Catholics who continued to seek a form of religion, missing for them in post-Vatican-II Catholicism and attracting them to some form of Pentecostal religion;[7] 3) a significant group of upper and middle-class Catholics who resisted the pressure put on them for more equitable land distribution and other measures attributed to the social teaching of the church and who joined groups which until recently have been apolitical; 4) many Catholics in Central America who identified themselves as *evangélico* to avoid the blanket killing that fell upon active Catholics, such as catechists and Catholic Action members who taught the social implications of the Bible. This last group preferred for a time to be Evangelical and "safe," but some of these "converts" have been observed returning to Catholic worship and affiliation (Stoll 1992).

Competition: Who Is Winning?

Many Catholics allege disinterest in direct consideration of Pentecostals or theological dialogue with them because they believe that the best method of countering them is by improving pastoral care and intensifying current efforts. This is being done and has had an effect. Clifton Holland and PROCADES (the Proyecto Centroamericano de Estudios Socio-Religiosos) have provided data on the number of Evangelicals in Central America that is widely accepted among Protestant scholars including some of the writers included in this volume. In 1980-81 and in 1990-91 Holland and a large number of evangelical volunteers attempted to count the members of evangelical churches in the region. Interviewed in the process of completing the second decade's survey, Holland said: "The Catholic Church has stemmed the tide of Pentecostal growth."

In an attempt to check Holland's conclusion for myself, I used his survey for the early 1980s and walked all through Zona 19, a major metropolitan section of Guatemala City, counting churches and trying to estimate numbers of Sunday attendees. The evangelical churches which Holland's group identified were still there in 1990, with a few changes. But one Maryknoll pastor in the area, Carroll Quinn pointed me to the neighboring parish, also in Zona 19, of another Maryknoller, James Scanlon. Through knocking on doors and systematic programs of education, a group of 200 lay persons (all under 40) in Scanlon's parish had welcomed 1,800 persons into the Catholic parish in 1989.

[7] Timothy E. Evans, "Religious Conversion in Guatemala," Ph.D. dissertation, University of Pittsburgh, 1990. Everett Wilson, a Pentecostal scholar, disagrees with broad characterizations of Pentcostalism as "mystical," as Evans describes the attraction of Pentecostalism. (Interview, Grand Rapids, Michigan, 7 May 1993)

Timothy Evans conducted a religious survey in the Quezaltenango diocese of Guatemala, which includes the second largest city of the country and three rural provinces. He chose the region because he believed it typical of Guatemala for the social characteristics of the people and the types of evangelical and other non-Catholics groups present in the region. Evans concluded that Protestant growth rates peaked there during the 1986-90 period.

David Stoll tells similar stories. Stoll's book *Is Latin America Turning Protestant?* helped broaden interest in this question, previously of interest only to a few specialists, to thousands of readers and an increasing number of academics. Subsequent to the publication of his book, Stoll returned to the Ixcan region of Guatemala for further research. He reported in during an interview in September 1992 that the Catholic Church was attracting large numbers back to the Catholic parishes now that three young Catholic priests were allowed to work in a region which had previously been closed by the army to the Catholic Church.

Christianity Today, a major evangelical magazine, reports similar news (5 April 1993). Citing John Kessler and the study done for the International Institute for Indepth Evangelization, *Christianity Today* says: "There were far fewer Evangelicals than estimated [and] there are far more people leaving the evangelical church than suspected" ("When Evangelicals evangelise" 1993, 73). The magazine then quotes an economic development expert who says the "big evangelistic campaigns...have more of a positive effect on the Catholic Church than the Protestant church."

Christianity Today's attention to numbers and growth curves obscures basic processes taking place in religion in Latin America. Perhaps the Catholic Church has made some progress in retaining members, but the Pentecostal and Evangelical Protestant presence will not go away. The roots of Pentecostalism in Latin America are deep. The movement will continue to shape aspects of Latin American religion.

Theological Convergence

The situation is changing, too, for Pentecostals. They now have scholars in Latin America worth paying attention to. Norberto Sarroco in Argentina, Juan Sepúlveda in Chile, and a handful of others are doing the type of research and writing that can form the basis of theological dialogue which benefits Catholics and Pentecostals alike in Latin America. What common ground, what shared and deep theological sources are there? I suggest two.

The first is a new spirituality for Latin America. Dorado Gonźález speaks about this new spirituality in a fragmented world. (Ironically for a movement that comes from the plains of Kansas and the "hollers" of Tennessee, Dorado Gonźalez calls Pentecostalism "post modern"). Gustavo Gutiérrez, the father of Liberation Theology, has been searching for just such a new spirituality for the poor (Levine 1991, 32). Then, too, the Catholic Charismatic Renewal in Latin America was promoted as renewal for the poor.

These theological descriptions of the Pentecostal and Charismatic Renewal movements are bolstered by accounts from the social sciences which place both movements in the broader context of Latin America's popular culture. Daniel Levine views key groups in both traditions as creators and shapers of a new religious consciousness (Levine 1991, 33). In his view, Pentecostalism should not be described primarily as an expression of anomie or a retreat from the world, but as a creative religious response to changing social conditions, a response that reworks the religious message to fit the varying conditions of life. Innovation and reshaping have occurred in the Catholic Church also as in base Christian communities in which messages are read directly from the Bible and interpreted to fit the situation in the barrios or fincas. Religious messages are thus creatively received and reworked.

Conditions in Latin America are favorable for fostering great cultural changes, including religious ones. The turbulence of life in Latin America, unlike the situation in the United States, has furnished the conditions for the acceptance of religious innovations, among both Protestants and Catholics. As Levine has said: "Movements of religious revitalization find a readier hearing in transformative moments" (Levine 1991, 36). Thus, in my view, Catholics and Pentecostals in Latin America are unwitting partners in a similar enterprise, driven by the same impulse, to search for a new spirituality, a spiritual renewal, especially for the poor.

The second basis for theological convergence between Catholics and Protestants is articulated by Peter Hocken, a Catholic priest who is secretary of the Society for Pentecostal Studies. Hocken believes that the Catholic dialogue with the Pentecostal movement offers a model of ecumenism which differs from the dominant one which characterizes relations between the Reformation churches and the Catholic Churches. Pentecostals originated after the Reformation, and are part of the Holiness tradition. Hocken says that the dialogue between Catholics and Pentecostals springs especially from personal spiritual renewal and sharing in worship and ministry. This requires an interaction between theological sources and contemporary reality: a reflection on Scripture and tradition in light of the present situation and a reflection on the present situation in the light of Scripture and tradition. Hocken characterizes this as a "servant theology." Such theology resembles what the Latin American church does through its three-step methodology: description of reality, reflection on scripture and tradition, and pastoral conclusions. The main thrust of ecumenism in Latin America and its charisma (gift) for the larger church will probably not be Reformation-Catholic or Orthodox-Catholic but Spirit oriented meetings between Latin American Catholics and Pentecostals.

Convergence in Politics?

Three areas which Catholics and Pentecostals consistently mention as persistent barriers to fraternal relations are: proselytism, popular religion, and politics. The first two are treated above, politics will be treated here briefly since Pentecostal and evangelical politics is just beginning to evolve.

However much the Catholic Church contributed to the redemocratization of Latin America, the assessment of some observers is that the church in Latin America has been uncertain about its role in a democracy (Cleary and Stewart-Gambino 1992). During the 1990 presidential elections in Peru, some bishops reacted hastily and imprudently when a probably false report reached them of inflammatory remarks made about Catholics by Pentecostals. In Brazil and Argentina it took up limited moral issues and missed larger issues. In the initial transition to democracy, the church has been like a war hero: unsure of what to do in peace, but with great accomplishments remembered and hoped for. What is "the voice of the voiceless" to do after others recover their right to speak and appear in public debate?

The first obligation of a church which hopes to function effectively as a moral influence in a democratic Latin America may be its *ubicación* (placement) clearly on the side of the poor where it can speak effectively about how well or poorly the masses are able to participate in society. The millions of Latin America's poorest who receive almost none of society's resources or protections have no doubt that the voice of the voiceless is still needed for them. The Catholicism which existed before, say 1968, was a religion embedded in the status quo. This cultural Catholicism was unable to leaven the social structures of Latin America structures which the Medellín Conference characterized as in a situation of "social sin."[8] Reformed Catholicism, taking the side of the poor, has the opportunity of supporting structures which reduce class and racial barriers, of infusing considerations of justice and responsiveness to need in public debate, and of making governments accountable for their expenditures.

I see Pentecostalism as possessing a complementary relationship to the political culture. It is not the wholly otherworldly religion which some have portrayed, but a religion which centers itself, as well, in dealing with this world. Entry into politics means an assessment that here and now is a morally useful way of dealing with the political environment. Many of the concerns which Pentecostals have are shared by Catholics and one way to

[8] See: Puebla Conference final document, nos. 28, 435, 1300 and Juan Hernández Pico, "Martyrdom today in Latin America: Stumbling-block, folly, and power of God," in Johannes-Baptist Metz and Edward Schillebeeckx, eds., *Martyrdom Today* (New York: Seabury, 1983), p. 37.

show this is the support of Evangelicals for Alberto Fujimori (a Catholic) in Peru and of Catholics for Jorge Serrano Elías (a Protestant) in Guatemala.

Guatemala may offer a glimpse of Latin America as a whole. How to explain politics in Guatemala and the support of many Catholics for Ríos Montt or Serrano Elías? To presume a political culture like that of the United States helps not at all. If economically based stratification is the basis for politics, then Guatemala represents the case of a country where, unlike the U.S. or Europe, the processes of migration, urbanization, and other socioeconomic changes continue to outpace industrialization and thus fail to produce a working class conscious of its political interests. This situation creates competition and instability among all the sectors of the population.

The system of stratification emerging in Guatemala provides a basis for political control imposed from above. An apparent identity of interests, especially an interest in stability, exists between those of differing economic positions. As Bryan Roberts points out: "The poor [of Guatemala City] are quite prepared to cooperate with professionals and middle-class politicians in an attempt to improve their position" (Roberts 1973, 348). Had he not been disqualified, Ríos Montt would have likely been elected to the presidency. Serrano Elías, to a great extent his surrogate, won the presidential election in 1990 on the basis of a platform stressing social control, security, and a pulling together to save Guatemala from chaos and a downward economic spiral. Catholics and Protestants from very different social positions brought Serrano to power with much the same economic interests in mind. It is no wonder, then, that committed Catholics worked diligently in the Serrano campaign (Rottman 1990). He represented the safeguarding of perceived interests of both rich and poor.

I resist the commonly expressed view that Pentecostals are apolitical and not involved in this world. Pentecostals engage this world and attempt to shape it to spiritual and moral needs. They, like many Catholics, have a spirituality which engages the world in new ways. Hence, the possibility of a convergence deeper than verbal dialogue between Protestants and Catholics exists in Latin America.

Few persons in the Catholic Church in Latin America know anything of the history of Pentecostalism, the national character of its churches, or the dialogue taking place between Catholics and Pentecostals. If there is one place in the world where greater understanding between Catholics and Pentecostals would benefit the work of God, it is Latin America. The prospect dazzles.

Reference List

Barrett, D., ed. 1982. *World Christian encyclopedia.* Nairobi: Oxford University Press, 1982.

________. 1990. Interview with the author by phone on 30 October.

Bishops of Bolivia, Paraguay and Chile. 1988. On site interviews with the author during July and August.

Bittlinger, A. 1978. *Papst und Pfingstler: Der ömisch katholisch-pfingstlich Dialog undsein ökumenische Relevanz. Studies in the Intercultural History of Christianity*, Vol. 16. Frankfurt und Main: Verlag Peter Lang.

Bord, R. J. and J. E. Faulkner. 1983. *The Catholic charismatics: The anatomy of a modern religious movement.* University Park, PA: Pennsylvania State University Press.

Brown, R. McAfee. 1979. The significance of Puebla for the Protestant churches in North America. In *Puebla and beyond*, eds. J. Eagleson and P. Scharper, 330-346. Maryknoll, NY: Orbis.

Burgess, S. M., *et al.*, eds. 1988. *Dictionary of Pentecostal and charismatic movements.* Grand Rapids: Zondervan.

Burnett, V. G. 1986. A history of Protestantism in Guatemala. Ph.D. Diss., Tulane University.

Cleary, Edward, O.P. 1985. *Crisis and change: The church in Latin America today.* Maryknoll, NY: Orbis.

________. 1989. *Path from Puebla: Significant documents of the Latin American bishops since 1979.* Washington, D.C.: National Conference of Catholic Bishops.

________. 1992a. Evangelicals and competition in Guatemala. In *Conflict and competition: The Latin American church in a changing environment*, eds. E. Cleary and H. Stewart-Gambino, 167-195. Boulder: Lynne Rienner Publishers.

________. 1992b. Report from Santo Domingo. *Commonweal*, 20 November: 7-8.

Cleary, E. and H. Stewart-Gambino, eds. 1992. *Conflict and competition: The Latin American church in a changing environment*. Boulder: Lynne Rienner.

Davis, K. 1991. Caribbean. In *The Dictionary of the ecumenical movement*, eds. N. Lossky et al., 124-126. Geneva: WCC and Grand Rapids: Eerdmans.

Della Cava, R. 1992. The ten-year crusade toward the third Christian millennium: An account of Evangelization 200 and Lumen 2000. In *The Right and democracy in Latin America*, eds. D. Chalmers et al., 202-222. Westport, CN: Praeger.

Dussel, E., ed. 1992. *The church in Latin America 1492-1992*. Maryknoll, NY: Orbis.

Evans, T. E. 1990. Religious conversion in Guatemala. Ph.D. Diss., University of Pittsburgh.

González Dorado, A. 1992. La Iglesia ante el fenómeno social de las sectas. *Christus* 42: 650-651; (Nov-Dec): 50-54.

Hernández Pico, J. 1983. Martyrdom today in Latin America: Stumbling-block, folly, and power of God. In *Martyrdom Today*, eds. J. Metz and E. Schillebeeckx, 37-42. New York: Seabury.

Hocken, P. 1988. Dialogue extraordinary. *One in Christ* 24(3): 202-213.

Holland, C. 1990. Interview with the author by phone on 30 October.

Hortal, J. 1992. Panorama e estatísticas do fenómeno religioso no Brasil. *Perspéctiva Teológica* 24: 66-79.

John Paul II, Pope. 1992. Opening address to fourth general conference of Latin American Episcopate. *Origins* 22(19) (22 October): Section 12.

Knox, R. A. 1950. *Enthusiasm: A chapter in the history of religion*. Oxford: Clarendon Press.

Lara-Braud, J., trans. 1969. *Social justice and the Latin American churches*. Richmond: John Knox.

Levine, D. 1991. Protestants and Catholics in Latin America: A family portrait. Paper prepared for The Fundamentalism Project, Conference of "Fundamentalisms Compared," University of Chicago, November.

McDonnell, K. 1980. *Presence, power, praise: Document on the Charismatic Renewal*, 3 vols. Collegeville, MN: Liturgical Press.

________. 1992. Interview by phone, 19 October.

Mansfield, P. Gallagher. 1992. *As by a new Pentecost: The dramatic beginnings of the Catholic Charismatic Renewal.* Steubenville, OH: Franciscan University Press.

Míguez Bonino, J. 1967. *Concilio Abierto.* Bueno Aires: La Aurora.

Nuñez, E. 1982. Latin American Catholicism today. *CAM Bulletin* (Summer): 1-4.

Piepke, J. G. 1992. The religious heritage of Africa in Brazil. *Verbum SVD* 33(2): 165-184.

Pretiz, P. and R. Pretiz. 1993. Interview with the author, 8 March in New Haven, CT.

Puebla Conference final document. 1979. Nos. 28, 435, 1300. In *Puebla and beyond*, eds. J. Eagleson and P. Scharper, 122-285. Maryknoll, NY: Orbis.

Quinn, C., M.M. 1990. Interviews with the author, 19 July and 3 October, Guatemala City, Guatemala.

Rodano, J. A. 1992. Pentecostal-Roman Catholic international dialogue. *Mid-Stream* 31(1) (January): 26-31.

Richard, P. 1985. Central America. *Latinamerica Press* (9 May): 5-6, 8.

Rivera, L. N. 1992. *A violent evangelism: The political and religious conquest of the Americas*. Louisville: Westminister/Knox.

Roberts, B. R. 1973. *Organizing strangers*. Austin: University of Texas Press.

Robeck, C. 1992. Letter to Margaret O'Brien Steinfels, editor. Appeared in shortened form in *Commonweal*, 18 December, 30-31.

Rogawski, R. 1992. Interview with the author by phone on 25 March.

Roper, M. 1992. Interview with the author on the 12 October in Santo Domingo.

Rottman, E. 1990. Interview with the author on 16 July during a plane trip from Dallas to Guatemala City. (Rottman, a Catholic, was a leader in Serrano's party and an elected member of Congress.)

Sandidge, J. L. 1987. *Roman Catholic/Pentecostal dialogue (1977-82): A study in developing ecumenism*, 2 vols. Frankfurt und Main: Verlag Peter Lang.

Scanlon, J., M.M. 1991. Interview with the author on 22 November in Guatemala City, Guatemala.

Smith, D. 1990, 1991, and 1993. Interviews with the author on 14 August 1990, 14 August 1991, and 22 February 1993, in Guatemala City, Guatemala.

Stoll, D. 1992. Interview with the author at the Latin American Studies Association Congress on 24 September at Los Angeles, CA.

Strachan, R. K. and W. Dayton Roberts. 1981. *Harry and Susan*. Unpublished first draft, library. Seminario Bíblico Latinoamericano, San Jose, Costa Rica.

Synan, V. 1974. *Charismatic bridges*. Ann Arbor, MI: Word of Life.

When Latin Americans evangelize. 1993. *Christianity Today*, 5 April, 73.

Wilson, E. 1993. Interview with the author 7 May, in Grand Rapids, MI.

Wright, J. 1990. Medellín and Puebla: A Protestant view. In *Born of the poor: The Latin American church since Medellín*, ed., E. Cleary, 94-98. Notre Dame, IN: University of Notre Dame Press.

Contributors

SHELDON ANNIS is affiliated with the Department of Geography, the Center for Energy and Environmental Studies, and the Latin American Studies Program at Boston University. He has written and spoken widely on Third World development issues and is the author of *God and production in a Guatemalan town* (1988).

EDWARD L. CLEARY, O.P., is a professor of Latin American Studies at Providence College in Rhode Island. He has written and edited several books about the Catholic Church in Latin America, most recently *Conflict and competition: The Latin American church in a changing environment* (1992).

GUILLERMO COOK, a Methodist theologian, has taught in Protestant seminaries all over Latin America and is currently affiliated with Latin American Missions, Inc. His latest book, *New face of the church in Latin America: Between tradition and change*, is due out this year. He was a co-author of the CCCS sponsored book, *Let my people live: Faith and struggle in Latin America* (1988).

SAMUEL ESCOBAR, a Peruvian Baptist, is the Thornley B. Wood Professor of Missiology at Eastern Baptist Theological Seminary in Philadelphia. He has written extensively on the relationship of the Church to issues of justice. His two most recent books are *Liberation themes in reformational perspective* (1989) and *Paulo Freire: Otra pedagogía política* (1990).

ROGER S. GREENWAY is Professor of World Missiology at Calvin Theological Seminary and former Executive Director of Christian Reformed Church World Ministries in North America. He has authored and edited numerous works on urban missions including *Cities: Missions' New Frontier*

(1989) and most recently a second edition of *Discipling the city: A comprehensive approach to urban mission* (1992).

QUENTIN J. SCHULTZE is Professor of Communications Arts and Sciences at Calvin College. He has written extensively on the societal effects of the mass media. His numerous works include *Televangelism and American culture: The business of popular religion* (1991) and *Dancing in the dark: Youth, popular culture and the electronic media* (1991) a book he co-authored for the CCCS.

DAVID A. SMILDE is a Ph.D. candidate at the University of Chicago Department of Sociology. His research focuses on explanations for the growth of Protestantism in Latin America.

TIMOTHY STEIGENGA is a Ph.D. candidate at the University of North Carolina Department of Political Science. He is co-author of "Protestantism in El Salvador: Conventional wisdom versus survey evidence" in *Latin American Research Review* (1993).

EVERETT ALAN WILSON is director of the Centro de Investigaciones Culturales y Estudios Linguísticos in San Jose, Costa Rica, and Professor Emeritus of Bethany College, California. His research and writing focuses on Latin American Pentecostalism and includes "Passion and power: A profile of emergent Latin American Pentecostalism" in *Called and empowered: Global mission in Pentecostal perspective* (1991).